THE YALE ARCHITECTURAL JOURNAL

PERSPECTA 33

Mining Autonomy

Perspecta, The Yale Architectural Journal
is published in the United States of America
by the Yale School of Architecture
and distributed by The MIT Press.
Massachusetts Institute of Technology
Cambridge, Massachusetts 02142
http://mitpress.mit.edu

Printed in the United States by
Herlin Press, West Haven, Connecticut
Prepress by GIST, West Haven, Connecticut

ISBN 0–262–65061–4
ISSN 0079–0958

Send editorial correspondence to
Perspecta, Yale School of Architecture
180 York Street, New Haven, CT 06520

Design: Lesley Tucker, Mark Zurolo
Typeset in Eidetic Neo and Grotesque

THE YALE ARCHITECTURAL JOURNAL

PERSPECTA 33

Mining Autonomy

EDITORS

MICHAEL OSMAN

ADAM RUEDIG

MATTHEW SEIDEL

LISA TILNEY

THE MIT PRESS   CAMBRIDGE, MASSACHUSETTS   LONDON, ENGLAND

Embedded within each essay in *Mining Autonomy* is a series of stills taken from a digital "reading" of the texts by the installation-artist Ann Hamilton. In collaboration with the graphic designers and editors of *Perspecta* 33, Hamilton employed a thimble-sized video camera as a surrogate pencil to literally "read" the text on the page. In this way, technology helps to simultaneously approximate and question methods of cognating text: with the eyes and hand (or eyes in hand), reading, underlining and note-taking. In the context of this journal, the technique serves to lift the words from the page, emphasizing and refracting specific passages and preserving the act of reading itself.

Hamilton's existing body of work is strongly engaged in textual and architectural themes. The convergence of the two in the journal is a perfect medium for her participation. Further, the editorial emphasis on the topic of autonomy and the relationship of architecture to other disciplines, pushed us to seek another influence in our own work. It was our hope that Hamilton's work would begin to offer alternative readings of the journal.

Acknowledgements

The editors would like to thank Hans Baldauf '81, B.A., '88, M.Arch, Fred Koetter, Cesar Pelli, Robert A.M. Stern '65, M.Arch and F. Anthony Zunino '70, M.Arch, for their generous gifts to *Perspecta* 33. We are grateful to the Graham Foundation for Advanced Studies in the Fine Arts for its continued support of *Perspecta*. Special thanks to Jennifer Gross and Jock Reynolds of the Yale University Art Gallery for their support of Ann Hamilton's contribution to this issue.

Special thanks to Lauren Kogod, our faculty advisor. Without her sound counsel and accurate criticism, the issue would not have reached its fruition.

Thanks to Brendan Moran for his generous advice from the issue's start to finish. Peggy Deamer's insight at crucial points along the way provided valuable direction and focus.

Thanks to graphic designers Lesley Tucker and Mark Zurolo who brought their expertise, creativity and strong personal engagements to this project.

We would like to thank the members of the Board of Directors of *Perspecta*, *The Yale Architectural Journal*:

Peggy Deamer
Sheila Levrant de Bretteville
Michael Haverland
Gavin MacRae-Gibson
Cesar Pelli
Alan Plattus
Alexander Purves
Harold Roth
Robert A.M. Stern

Thanks to Carol Krinsky who provided generous and valuable help with copyediting.

We would like to thank Anthony Vidler for arranging translation and providing editorial assistance on Hubert Damisch's essay.

We are also grateful to Jennifer Castellon and Jean Sielaff of the Yale School of Architecture, Monica Robinson, Director of Graduate and Professional Schools Annual Giving and Development at Yale, and Sally Tremaine, Associate Director of Grants and Contracts at Yale. Thanks to Nina Rappaport for her indispensable assistance with publicity.

For help with images we would like to thank Laurel Bliss at Yale University Library, Teresa Johnson at UCLA Library and Kristin Murray at Art Resource.

Very special thanks to the many friends who have offered their support, advice and participation throughout the duration of this project: Catherine Aman, Daniel Arbalaez, Annmarie Brennan, Siobhan Burke, Jason Carlow, Alec Hathaway, Ed Mitchell, Todd Reisz, Alexandra Sova, Stephanie Tuerk and Jorge Zapata.

Editors' Statement

Perspecta 33: Mining Autonomy is a collection of essays that examines the evolving legacy of architectural autonomy and its relationship to architecture's potential to act as a critical agent. As its name implies, *Mining Autonomy* both draws from the richness of the intellectual project of autonomy and perhaps does some damage to its suppositions by forwarding the idea that the contemporary position of critical practice has shifted from the autonomous center to the periphery of the architectural discipline.

The argument for the autonomy of architecture – the belief that architecture is a self-contained project with its own legible, meaningful forms – is generally seen as an outgrowth of a larger understanding of the role of autonomy in the arts. But while the autonomy of the art object was considered an assertion against the perceived bankruptcy of mass-culture, architectural autonomy coincided not only with distinctions between external assimilation and resistance, but also with its own tradition of utility and functionalism. Ironically, the discipline's very emphasis upon its utilitarian nature had led to a perceived dissolution of its own professional boundaries by the late 1960s and early 1970s.

In the 1970s, the reemergence and redefinition of the notion of architectural autonomy at the Institute for Architecture and Urban Studies and in the pages of *Oppositions* became a way for architects to define their practice against technocracy while maintaining for architecture a 'critical' social role. Specifically, architects and architectural historians viewed autonomy as the only remaining position for architecture to gain sufficient distance from culture to resist the capitalist cycle of production and consumption and present new alternatives to the status quo. In contrast to this 'post-functionalist' position, other architects at the time reacted strongly against the perceived a-historicity of modern architecture and located the autonomy of architecture in its own formal history.

Although there can be no doubt that the situation of the current decade is radically different than that of the 1970s (economically as well as culturally), many of the same conditions of disciplinary uncertainty remain. New methods of architectural production (the realities of digital design, imaging and fabrication), growing environmental concerns and changing ideas about domesticity and urban space continually pose new questions to architects. How has the conceptual framework of architectural autonomy continued to influence the production of architecture? Have examples of contemporary critical work surpassed the usefulness of the autonomy model?

Far from abandoning the notion of autonomy, *Mining Autonomy* maintains a critical position that shifts its attention from the center of the discipline to its borders. Located at the interface between autonomous withdrawal and cultural determination, critical architecture occupies a position on the periphery where it acts as a mediator – translating knowledge from varied pursuits into the language and conventions of architecture as well as passing intelligence and speculation from the discipline to the world. Architecture is therefore capable of maintaining both its critical capacity while also engaging in its social and cultural context.

The Ledoux Effect: Quasi-Autonomy

Emil Kaufmann, Manfredo Tafuri
and the Claims

Urbanism and Intention
with Place

PERSPECTA 33
Mining Autonomy

HUBERT DAMISCH
Translation by ERIN WILLIAMS

Ledoux with Kant

This essay was originally published as the preface
to Emil Kaufmann's *De Ledoux et Le Corbusier:
Origine et développement de l'architecture autonome*, 1981[1]

Publishing delays sometimes have a beneficial effect in that they bring a semblance of justification to the exercise of writing a preface — by definition a risky undertaking. For if the publication, as well as the purchase of a book, always entails an element of risk (which cannot be measured in financial terms alone), a preface — whether it is the work of the author or of a third party — is supposed to offer publisher and reader a sort of guarantee, or insurance. The reverse is also true: to say that a text calls for a preface is implicitly to admit that it is not enough in itself, that it will only have its effect with appropriate clarification; that the reader will have no chance of recognizing its importance unless alerted to it in advance, not knowing how to read it without appropriate eyeglasses. This presents the distinct possibility of abuse, when the preface begins to take on the role of an advertisement or instruction manual.

It is different in the case of an historical text, and when dealing with a republication or a new translation. The French reader has discovered the work of Émil Kaufmann in reverse, so to speak: beginning with what appeared his crowning achievement, the great book *L'Architecture au siècle des Lumières* (1955) [*Architecture in the Age of Reason*], and only then becoming familiar with *Trois architects révolutionnaires: Boullée, Ledoux, Lequeu* (1952) [*Three Revolutionary Architects: Boullée, Ledoux, Lequeu*, finally arriving at the book published in Vienna in 1933, whose title alone signals Kaufmann's entire intellectual program: *De Ledoux à Le Corbusier: Origine et développement de l'architecture autonome*. This is a book that has neither the fullness of the two others, nor their weight of scholarship, but that contains the seed of an idea that Kaufmann was to take up tirelessly throughout his life as he deepened and developed all of its ramifications. It is a book with the appearance of a broadside or pamphlet, and one can see from both its title and date of publication that it was topical enough. At the moment when Nazism was triumphant in Munich and Berlin, strongly supported by a mass of academic rubbish, it was proof of great intellectual courage for a Viennese attempt to demonstrate the existence of a fundamental continuity between so-called neoclassi-

cal architecture and architecture already denounced by the totalitarian ideology as "international." All the more so in that Kaufmann pressed his insolence to the point of including under the banner of two French architects a certain number of German architects – beginning with Schinkel – that the new order claimed as an integral part of its heritage. (Not to mention the sang-froid with which Kaufmann demonstrated, in the face of this blackmail and even more in the face of the political hysteria of the avant-gardes, as he celebrated the aspiration to autonomy of a practice that was nonetheless potentially as profoundly socialized as that of architecture.

This book was then born of its time. Is this to say that it is only of retrospective interest, as a historical document? When everyone is proclaiming the failure of the Modern Movement and denouncing its "objective" connections with a technocratic order that ended up by adopting it as its own, what resonance can this thin volume and the thesis it articulates expect to find without being shored up by a large documentary apparatus? Nevertheless, if, as Jorge-Luis Borges would have it, a preface is no more than a form of lateral criticism, there is no reason to necessarily expect that the reader should be warned against the book that it introduces. To alert the reader to the resistances that this reading might elicit is, on the other hand, one of the rights generally granted to one who writes a preface. And since, in this case, there is a preface, why would this one not take advantage of the gap in time to invite the reader to find in it a way of seeing a little more clearly, since resistance always indicates conflict and it does no good to ignore it? It is then up to us to ensure that this translation too is born of its time, our own, caught as we are in the meandering ways of a discourse that has not yet broken with modernity – for reasons that the reading of this book should help us to unravel. For despite its brevity, it has lost none of its *edge*.

One could say that this is certainly the least to be expected of such a book: does not its central thesis suggest that a radical break interrupted the course of architectural production in the era of the French Revolution, a break which would form the distant origin of the Modern Movement? That the work of Ledoux could be presented as the paradigm of this break assumes that the old and the new are brought together within it in such a way that the rupture is only more evident. Yet it is to this that the most recent discourse on modernity is opposed: a discourse that, far from being one of a "break," works on the contrary to retie the threads, to reinscribe in the continuity of a history a practice from which for too long it had the pretention of freeing itself. The paradox that engages us in reading Kaufmann lies in the fact that he himself attempted to give this phenomenon an historical explanation, and that in a single stroke he restored to the Modern Movement both a past and a historical dimension. For to maintain that the break from which modern architecture in principal proceeds goes back to the end of the eighteenth century implies that this architecture does not begin with Le Corbusier, but rather that behind it lies an entire history, including – as we will see – its claim to the tabula rasa.

Kaufmann's thesis, that saw Le Corbusier as the true heir of Ledoux and Schinkel, was bound to scandalize the champions of a showy neo-classicism, à la Albert Speer, as well as those on the other side who felt that, after all, the proletariat also had a right to the "column." (Question: then does the proletariat have a right to the entasis? Can the proletarian column adapt itself to inflation?) Indeed, we often forget that the critique of functionalism did not originate yesterday. Among the Marxists, as well as in Frankfurt with Adorno, there were a few good minds who denounced what they regarded, as Brecht put it, "the last word of bourgeois architecture."[2] The last word but not the first; one can imagine that those who appealed to the revolutionary ideal might have judged as unsuitable the proposition according to which the program of the Sachlichkeit would have found its formulation in the period of the "Great Revolution" – French and bourgeois – of 1789. But Kaufmann's demonstration was no less shocking with respect to the habitual assumptions of art history. For this book, devoted as it seems to be to the investigation of the sources of the Modern Movement, does not obey the law of the genre. If one agrees with his thesis that Ledoux – as Kaufmann had declared from

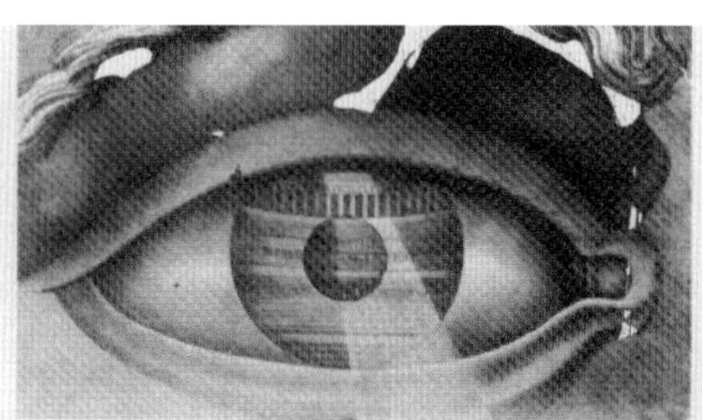

Emil Kaufmann

De Ledoux
à Le Corbusier

Origine et développement
de l'architecture autonome

Cover, *De Ledoux à Le Corbusier*,
by Emil Kaufmann, French edition 1981.

1928 on[3] — was a figure who signified a "personalizes break-point," in history, one has also to admit that he is also an end point for any historical tracing back in time of the Modern Movement. The question, then, would not be so much to search for *where he came from* (even if it is always permissible to support rather than oppose one's predecessors — as in the case of Ledoux in relation to Jacques-François Blondel, it is still a form of owing them something), but rather to know — in Kaufmann's terms — *where he went*, and to attempt to understand Ledoux not on the basis of his own antecedents but on that of the path that he opened up. It must be noted that Kaufmann only described the beginning of this path: as if, once he had demonstrated the direction in which Ledoux's work pointed, and how it became explicit in the teaching of Durand and Dubut, a route was would be traced that could no longer be mistaken.

Such language is, however, not that of Kaufmann but of Kant, in the preface to the second edition of *Critique of Pure Reason*. In this preface Kant makes reference to that other intellectual revolution traditionally associated with the name of Thalès, and concerning the beginnings of geometry, its "origin:" the demonstration of the isosceles triangle in as much as it derives from an a priori construction, the author of which was named Thalès "or any other name."[4] This is the Kant to which Kaufmann's text refers from the very first page. Does this mean that from the moment that architecture affirms its "autonomy" it accedes to a new and superior mode of historicity and that its development can be seen as parallel, from the point of view of logic, to that of science? That this fantasy (if it is one) constitutes one of the impulses behind an architectural ideology that purports to be "rationalist," evinced by its constant return in Kaufmann's work? Certainly Kaufmann affirms that if Ledoux's work has value as a symptom and demands to be interpreted as such, he did not for all that create modern architecture by himself: it would have been born anyway "even if he had never existed."[5] But such a proposition does not in the least undercut the paradigmatic reading that Kaufman proposed of Ledoux's work in 1933, for it was less important for him to write a "page of history" than to construct a *model* to show clearly, beyond all deceptive surface effects, the profound continuity of development that leads from Ledoux to Le Corbusier; a continuity which in effect only has meaning through assigning it a *revolution* as origin, pinning itself to the name of Ledoux "or any other name."

Indeed Ledoux, in his marked preference for the most simple and regular geometric configurations — the cube, the pyramid, the cylinder, the sphere — moves in this same direction: as if he had meant, in this moment of origin, to reconnect with the premier acquis, as Husserl would say, from which geometry was born. This premier acquis held that due to technical ability, the Greek succeeded in detaching certain "pure" forms from their bodily attachments. The Greeks pushed forms to their point of perfection, according to specifications suitable for the instruction of the geometric mind: surfaces ever more polished, whether flat or turned "in revolution;" edges ever more smooth, lines ever more straight or even, angles ever more sharp, points ever more precise, and so on.[6] The same process of autonomization of form is translated, with respect to the elements of architecture, by the rejection of all anthropomorphism, organic metaphors, and, in general, of *imitation*, beginning with that of the monuments of the past. In all things, one should *return to the principle*: if a column, considered according to its function (sachlich), is nothing more than a post put up to support a load (Viollet-le-Duc would say nothing less), there is no sense in trying to calculate its proportions according to those of the human body,

any more than to pretend to stretch it as one would a muscle: a simple cylinder will do the job.

If architecture is no more than the expression of a constructive logic, its reason for being should be sought in the act of building. In these terms, architecture, from the moment it obeyed an external determination, would be no longer autonomous but rather the object of empirical knowledge, technical and experimental, whatever the contributions of calculation. Nevertheless architectonic thought, even if it aspires to autonomy, does not operate in the register of speculative reason: its aim is not knowledge in itself; it has a task to accomplish, a work to realize, a world to construct. A matter of principles, it is only so inasmuch as pure practical reason is, in Kant's terms, immediately legislative: it is only autonomous to the extent that the will is conceived as independent of empirical conditions and, consequently, as pure will, determined by the sole form of the law called *moral law*. It is certain that Ledoux did not read Kant, but we know how much he owed to Rousseau, and how the reading of *Contrat social [The Social Contract]* informed his doctrine of autonomy. If the relationship between Ledoux and Kant is based on anything, it is from the point of view of this common derivation. "Return to the principle, consult nature: everywhere man is isolated": the formula of *L'Architecture* echoes the problem posed by Rousseau: to discover a form — that of the contract — through which "each is united to all, yet nevertheless obeying only himself and remaining as free as before."

For architecture then, the claim of autonomy has, in the first place, a moral connotation. One has only to read Loos (where ornament is associated with a form of crime) or Le Corbusier ("truth" is opposed to lies, as the purity of "whitewash" is to the false appearances of décor) to be persuaded of this: the rigor and the purity aspired to by the Modern Movement were those of the moral law. Indeed, the relationship of the Ledoux creator of the Salines de Chaux, to Le Corbusier, the apostle of the wall "lait de chaux" [whitewash], is salty enough — if I can say it — in the register of the signifier, especially if one recalls that Le Corbusier was himself born in La Chaux-de-Fonds. But if it is in fact necessary to think Ledoux *with* Rousseau, if not *with* Kant, it is to the extent that this other relationship allows one to understand how the rejection of rules handed down by tradition could for him be joined with the affirmation of another imperative: unconditional, legality. Baroque architecture was heteronomous inasmuch as it obeyed an external exterior determination — that of "suitability" [*convenance*] that called for the elements which composed a building to be combined, superimposed, and melded together in the unity of a single ensemble, following the rules of an *order* entirely of the façade, which was itself an image of social hierarchy. According to Kaufmann's explanation, the new principle of autonomy would, on the contrary, manifest itself in the egalitarian system of "pavilions" which assumes that the elements, for example the different "blocks" or "unités" (of habitation or otherwise) retain their independence, their freedom, their autonomy. The rationale determining the pavilions' placement and distribution, would only then appear in full clarity on the level of the plan. In this sense the rejection of the façade, which the twentieth century would recognize as one of the traits of architectural modernity, appeared from the beginning of the nineteenth century as the corollary of the affirmation of a universal and abstract legality. This legality was to be affirmed in the teachings of Durand, taking the form of a regular orthogonal grid inscribed within a square, which both regulated the mechanics of the composition and was informed every ensemble, as it would continue to do in the work of Mies van der Rohe: the grid as architectonic will and representation.

This double function reserved for the grid, both regulatory and generative, testify a posteriori to the universal pretensions of autonomous architecture. In the first place, the grid is presented in Durand as the mechanism for a change in scale. Kaufmann saw clearly that with Ledoux architecture had attained a new dimension, that of the masses [grand nombre]. The idea of autonomy is in fact meaningless if not brought back to the idea of equality, implying that all men have the right to architecture ("Taste, in its combinations with art, recognizes no difference between the poor or the rich"). In return architecture ought to be concerned with the needs of all ("Is there anything that the artist can disdain? The baths of Pluto, the warehouse of the merchant, the barn of the farmer must all carry his imprint.")[7] The project for an ideal city is thus no longer limited to a perspective view meant to produce an essentially picturesque effect but rather meant to respond in detail to all the functions of a town in the manufacturing era: "In [my town] I have placed every type of building required by the social order. One will see important factories […] give birth to peoples' assemblies. A town will rise up to encircle and crown them […]. For the first time one will see the magnificence of the palace and that of the alehouse on the same level."[8] Indeed, Ledoux treats the question of housing in terms that anticipate the solutions of the phalanstery, the garden city, or their modern equivalent "apartment block with communal kitchen."[9] Without going as this far, Kaufmann insists that one can see in Ledoux's concerns the beginning of a mechanization of the dwelling. In fact, it seems as though Kaufmann felt closer to Brecht than to Le Corbusier[10] in the sense that the idea of a "machine for living" seemed to contradict the very idea of autonomy. As Adorno would later say, "housing such as this is a slap in the face of the nostalgia for an independent existence, that anyway exists no more."[11]

But the adoption of the grid has still other repercussions, which one might call epistemological. Whereas the classical doctrine associated the idea of universal architecture with that of a characteristic (to the extent that Leibnitz recognized that the classical orders were a model of combination), of a repertoire of signs – signs that brought with them the rules of their combination and connection – the principle of autonomy places the accent less upon the elements of architecture than upon the rule that determines their distribution in a given space – a rule to which elements are subjected even in their layout. Not that Durand meant to break with the principle of combination: the *Précis d'Architecture* supplies the precise nomenclature of the pieces of the game to which architecture is reduced from this point on. But the game itself is no longer so much a question of syntax as it is of geometry, a geometry that is flat, elementary and above all *finite*. The Durand "system" retrospectively manifests the paradox of an architecture that wanted itself to be all the more "speaking" [parlant] even as it renounced the ordinary means of language. As if, in this case as well, autonomy had to be pushed to the point where architecture no longer borrowed its determination from articulated language. Autonomy would be pushed to the point where it would impose upon the symbolic – its articulations, its structures, its *frameworks* – a definition other than that calculated according to the procedures of discourse.

It was Louis-Ambrose Dubut who showed that the game is not affected in principle by the character of the elements at its disposal. when, In his *Architecture Civile*, he proposed to cover the same structure with either a "gothic" or "Italian" facade: proof, as Le Corbusier would say, following Viollet-le-Duc, that architecture – more than a question of style (in the singular) – is a question

of styles (in the plural). The architecture of the nineteenth century, marked as it was on the surface by the stamp of historicism and eclecticism, was able in its deepest structures to participate in the continuity of a development whose effects would not be revealed until the masks under which architecture had operated until that time were removed. From this point of view, the "regression" to neo-classicism was in fact no more than a symptom of the deterioration of traditional forms, as Kaufmann himself noted. In linguistic terms we could say that it would take a century to shift from an ornate and "baroque" manner of speaking, to a free and natural mode of expression. The shift was then from a mode of expression that took its models from tradition, to a mode of expression that some see as anti-historical, but which in fact is ordered around another notion of history than that imposed by a history of art understood as history of "styles": a notion that, arguable as it may be, demands to be taken into account in and of itself.

In this regard, it may seem that Kaufmann's work has the value of an historical symptom, if not a paradigm, in its own right, because of the way in which it ties the myth of origins to the myth of revolution. In his works on the French Revolution, François Furet has shown how its history has been conceived, with rare exceptions (primary amongst which one must cite Tocqueville) as a tale of origins, the dread of beginnings investing itself precisely in rupture, or the revolutionary "break."[12] If the revolution of 1789 became the originary figure of socialist historiography, it is because it appeared as the founding event – the inaugural moment of a history itself revolutionary – released from the determining factors that reduced history before the Revolution to a sort of "prehistory," as Marx termed it. From the moment that it is seen as the origin of a new epoch, as an absolute beginning, a new start from zero, from principle, the revolution becomes the matrix of a truly human and rational history. If it weren't for the fact that Le Corbusier had little sympathy for revolutions, Bolshevik or otherwise, and that he was more concerned with heading them off by means of architecture, one could understand how Kaufmann might have been tempted to rediscover in the myth of the "tabula rasa" something of the consciousness ready to shatter the continuity of history that is, according to Walter Benjamin, proper to revolutionary classes in the moment of their action. Did not the "Plan Voisin," which proposed the destruction of the greater part of "historic" Paris to make way for a few "autonomous" towers, depend upon the same lyrical illusion that prompted the revolutionaries of 1789 to introduce a new calendar and the insurgents of the July Revolution to shoot out the clocks?[13]

But Ledoux? Is there not a paradox in regarding him as a revolutionary architect and the paragon of the "break" when, by his own avowal, he only just escaped the "national axe" before welcoming the arrival of the Empire with understandable relief? Here the old debate over the consequences of political and social revolution for the domain of the arts reappears. If Trotsky could not repress the idea that the French language owed some of its "polish" to the sharp instrument named "guillotine,"[14] his contemporaries, ready as they were to recognize the initial range of the revolutionary event, were equally worried on the other hand that a similar rupture in the order of things and the continuity of time had remained for so long without effect on literature and art, to the point that it was necessary to await the explosion of Romanticism for taste to at last have its own Fourteenth of July (in the sense that for Victor Hugo Romanticism was "the French Revolution turned into literature"). As far as architecture is concerned, for Kaufmann to propose that with Boullée, Ledoux, and Lequeu it had its own "revolution" (the question remains as to the place that Soufflot should be assigned in this context), was simply yo make an analogy between this revolution and the political revolution. Indeed, he later recognized that he was incapable of explaining the change that architecture underwent around 1800, insofar as explanations and reasons of this kind can onlye sought in so-called "general" if not universal history.[15] For it is surely not an explanation to point to the process of the emancipation of the masses as related to the principal of autonomy. On the contrary, we know only too well that, as far as autonomy goes, the French Revolution worked to the contrary, in the direction of an ever more accentuated centralization, whose benefits Napoleon was to reap, to the great satisfaction – must it be repeated? – of Ledoux himself.

Why, then, speak of "revolutionary" architecture? The question, if it occupies us today, in the final analysis, bears upon the status that should be attributed to the very notion of *history* itself, in architecture as well as the other arts, and more generally to the work of thought – as with every practice through which man attempts to assure himself of the control of his destiny. The historian is free, according to his own point of view, to deny any and all descriptive and taxonomic relevance to the notions of heteronomy and autonomy.[16] In the present moment, when the history of architecture hesitates between a renewed form of the history of styles and a form of institutional analysis that ignores everything properly architectural, the idea of autonomy, in its philosophical sense, takes on the value of a regulative concept. To think of Ledoux *with* Kant is to recognize that in the matter of architecture, knowledge is not solely derived from history; or better said, in Kant's terms, a knowledge that *subjectively* presents itself as historical, according to the way it was acquired, can participate, *objectively*, in one form or another of rationality.[17] From this stems the problem of theory - of theory, not of doctrine – in its relationship to history: does not theory have to specify the object of this history, and what determinations belong to it alone.

To think of Ledoux *with* Kant leads one in fact to question what constitutes architecture as an object not only of history but also of thought – a thought that is itself bound by conditions, one will not fear to call formal, if not a priori. Architecture is constituted on this principle insofar as it is an object of desire, where the will – as Kant says – finds its determination. But architecture places in this category only empirical principles, in the same way that what constitutes architecture – insofar as it is a thing to construct – is subjected to constraints that attest, even in the constructive order, to the force of the symbolic. Architecture finds its determination both in what constitutes it as an object of desire – or of will as Kant would say – which in this context only concerns empirical principles, and in whatever constitutes it as a constructed object, an object itself subjected, as everything in the constructive order, to constraints that attest to the power of the symbolic order. Ledoux did not push the principal of autonomy to the point that Kant would have wished, to the point of viewing dependence on natural law as yet another form of heteronomy. "In all things, return to the principle:" this phrase of Ledoux's returns to support the idea that there are, in the field of architecture, principles that are not the product of history, just as in the area of law there are norms that derive from a law postulated as "natural." It takes no more than this – we have repeated it often enough – to stir up a revolution. But will the fact that revolutions necessarily fail, also be made a question of principle?

NOTES

1 Originally published as the preface to Emil Kaufmann, *De Ledoux & Le Corbusier: Origine et Développement de l'Architecture Autonome* (Paris: Editions l'Equerre, 1981). French edition of *Von Ledoux bis Le Corbusier: Ursprung und Entwicklung der Autonomen Architektur* (Vienna and Leipzig: Rolf Passer, 1931).

2 Bertolt Brecht, "Ce que nos architectes doivent savoir," *Les Arts et la révolution*, French trans. (Paris: 1970), p.143.

3 In the article "Ledoux" from the *Thieme und Becker Dictionary*.

4 Emmanuel Kant, *Critique de la Raison Pure*, trans. Jules Barni and Paul Archambaut (Paris: Aubier-Montaigne, 1973), vol. I, p.19.

5 Emil Kaufmann, *Trois architectes révolutionnaires* (Paris: Edition de la S.A.D.G., 1978), p.137.

6 Edmund Husserl, *L'origine de la géometrie*, intro. and trans. Jacques Derrida (Paris: PUF, 1962), p.210.

7 Claude-Nicolas Ledoux, *L'Architecture considérée sous le rapport de l'art, des moeurs et de la législation* (Paris: 1804); cited in Kaufmann, op. cit., p.162.

8 Ibid.

9 Ibid. p.42.

10 "The new ruling class should not begin its construction work with the construction of three million individual houses, nor slightly more comfortable housing barracks, but with that of large-scale residential buildings," Brecht, op. cit., p.144.

11 Theodor W. Adorno, *Minima Moralia. Réflexions sur la vie mutilée*, French trans. (Paris: Payot, 1983), p.85.

12 François Furet, *Penser la Révolution* française (Paris: 1978), first part.

13 Walter Benjamin, "Thèses sur la philosophie de l'histoire," in *Poésie et révolution* (Paris: 1971), p.285–286.

14 Léon Trotsky, *La Révolution permanente* (Paris: Rieder, 1932), p.7–8.

15 Emil Kaufmann, *L'architecture au siècle des Lumières*, preface, p.14.

16 Meyer Schapiro, "The New Viennese School," *Art Bulletin* XVIII (1936), p.258–266.

17 Emmanuel Kant, *Logique*, (Paris: 1979), p.22.

The Ledoux Effect: Emil Kaufmann and the Claims of Kantian Autonomy

I identify Modernism with the intensification, almost this exacerbation, of this self-critical tendency that began with the philosopher Kant. Because he was the first to criticize the means itself of criticism, I conceive of Kant as the first real Modernist.

CLEMENT GREENBERG 1960[1]

The idea of "architectural autonomy," the notion that architecture, together with the other arts, is bound to an internal exploration and transformation of its own specific language, has periodically surfaced in the modern period. Whether as a way of classifying the qualities of architectural "form" as opposed to "style," or as a way of defining the role of the architect in an increasingly specialized professional world, the assertion of autonomy has been a leitmotif of modernism, from the end of the nineteenth century, if not earlier. Art historians, beginning with Wöfflin and continuing with Riegl; architects beginning with Loos and continuing with Le Corbusier and Mies van der Rohe; critics beginning with Fry and Stokes, and continuing with Greenberg and Krauss, all in different ways and with differing agendas have established their grounds of debate on the relative autonomy of modernist aesthetic practices. More recently, in architecture, Rossi, Venturi, and Eisenman have, among many others, laid claim to the autonomy of the language.

Of all the writers and architects who have contributed over a century or more to the debate over autonomy, the Viennese historian, Emil Kaufmann, stands out as a consistent reference point for all subsequent discussions.[2] For while, in retrospect, Wöfflin's development of a formal method for characterizing architectural periods, and Riegl's proposition of a historical and cultural specificity to the interplay of vision and space could be seen as setting up the grounds for a modernist idea of autonomy in architecture and the other arts, it was Emil Kaufmann who was the first to join the analysis of historical architecture to Kant's philosophical position, derived from Kant, and who was the first to coin the phrase "autonomen architektur" drawing on Kant's own concept of "autonomy" of the will. And it was Kaufmann who served to introduce the twin ideas of autonomy and modernism to successive generations of architects and critics, beginning with Philip Johnson in the 1940s, but continuing with Colin Rowe in the 1950s and Aldo Rossi in the 1950s and 60s. More recently his work was at the center of a historical re-assessment of autonomy and the avant-garde in the United States in an essay by the historian Deltef Mertens presented at a symposium to honor Philip Johnson.[3]

ANTHONY VIDLER

VON LEDOUX BIS LE CORBUSIER

Yet Emil Kaufmann's thesis of the development of a modernism emerging in the work of Claude-Nicolas Ledoux in the 1770s and culminating in the work of Le Corbusier in the late 1920s, has had many detractors since the publication of his polemically titled *Von Ledoux bis Le Corbusier* in 1933.[4] Since then, the Viennese historian's view of architectural progress has been castigated as simplistic by critics like Eduardo Persico and Meyer Schapiro, used as a pathological symptom of the decadence of modernism by conservative historians like Hans Sedlmayr, and deemed a travesty of historical scholarship by researchers from Michel Gallet to Robin Middleton.[5] Castigated as having "suffered from an excess of generalization," blamed for his "obsessive search for underlying principles [. . .] pursued to an extreme degree," and "undermined" in David Watkin's words by a host of researchers following the lead of Wolfgang Herrmann's debunking of the traditional Ledoux chronology in 1960, Kaufmann is now largely forgotten.[6] Indeed, he is perhaps the only important historian associated with the so-called Vienna School of the 1920s whose work has not been comprehensively re-assessed for its scholarly and methodological qualities in the last decade. Hans Sedlmayr and Otto Pächt, even Guido Kaschnitz von Weinberg and Fritz Novotny, have been translated and their work analyzed in its historiographical and theoretical context. Yet, in Christopher Wood's recent and important introductory study to his *Vienna School Reader*, Kaufmann is relegated to a footnote.[7]

His work has not always been denigrated however. Publishing significant contributions to the history of French eighteenth century architecture throughout the 1920s, re-defining traditional "classicism" with the introduction of the idea of "neo-classicism," Kaufmann, in the second volume of Hans Sedlmayr and Otto Pächt's flagship journal of Viennese "strukturanalyse," published the first major assessment of the architecture of Claude-Nicolas Ledoux — one to which Meyer Schapiro, despite his measured social critique of its formal approach, dedicated a large portion of his 1936 review of the Vienna School's methods. In his notes for the unfinished *Passagen-Werk* Walter Benjamin cited liberally from Kaufmann's brief, but trenchant, treatment of Ledoux's life and work, *Von Ledoux bis Le Corbusier* — the first comprehensive monographical treatment of the French architect by any architectural historian.[8] Subsequently Kaufmann's discoveries have inspired generations of scholars to work in the architecture of the revolutionary period, whether or not they agree with Kaufmann that something "revolutionary" was to be detected in the pre-revolutionary and monarchical Ledoux. His work has posed questions to the historiographical treatment of the "origins" of modernism, and by implication to the entire construction of historicist history from Nikolaus Pevsner to Sigfried Giedion. It interrogated the nature of abstraction in relation to the geometrical forms employed by the Enlightenment and the modernist avant-gardes, and thereby challenged the premises of anachronism in history and criticism. It opened up the imbricated problems of form and politics, architecture and society, in a way that directly challenged the cultural ideology of National Socialism in the 1930s. His sobriquet "revolutionary architect," in his book *Three Revolutionary Architects*, published in 1952 as applied to the trio of architects Ledoux, Boullée, and Lequeu, a trio he had largely discovered and, so to speak, "invented," while much misunderstood, nevertheless succeeded in gaining them the attention of serious scholars.[9] His posthumous book *Architecture in the Age of Reason* was, on its publication, considered the last word on eighteenth century European architecture.[10] Finally, Kaufmann's work set all these questions within a philosophical framework that has not ceased to inform critical theory: that provided by Kant in his insistence on the "autonomy" of the will as a fundamental premise of bourgeois freedom. The link established by Kaufmann between Ledoux and Kant, as Hubert Damisch has noted in the essay translated in this volume, is one that, whether or not it is historically "verifiable," remains challenging to all interrogations of the nature of architectural language and of the place of the discipline in modern society.

Beyond this, Kaufmann's work, unlike that of many historians, has had a direct influence on architectural practice, and especially in the way that the modernism of the 1920s and 1930s was received, in the first instance, in the United States immediately after the War. Emigrating to the US in 1941,

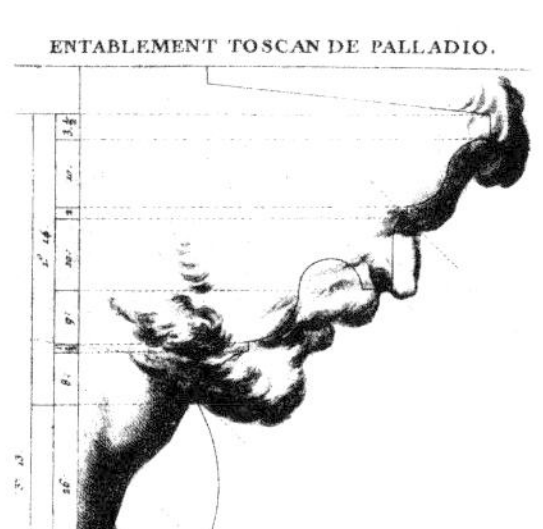

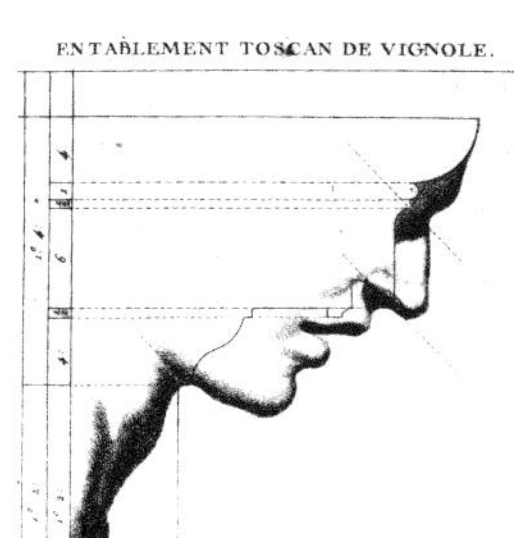

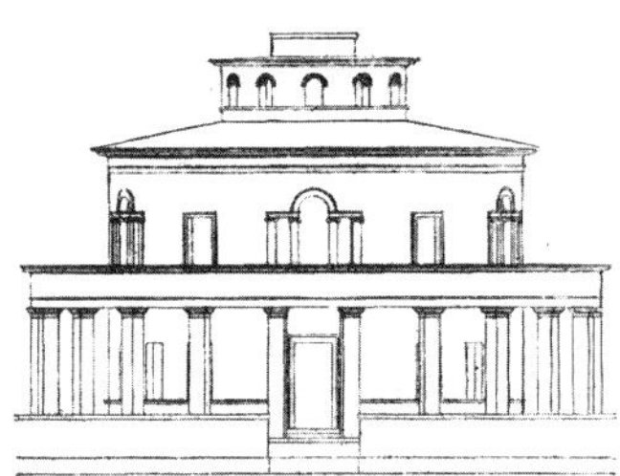

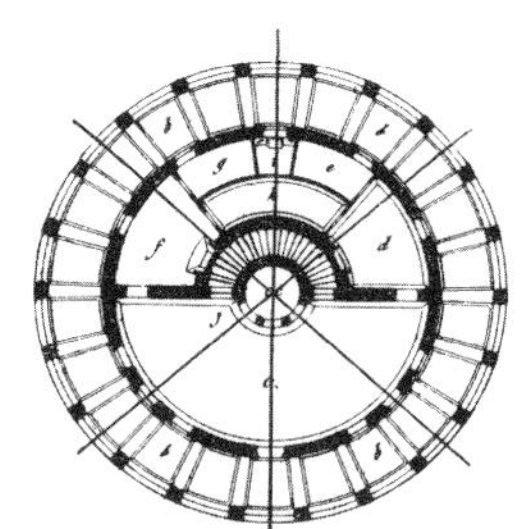

Left to right
Vergleich Architektonischer und Menschlicher Profile, J.F. Blondel, from *Cours d'Architecture*, 1771.

Haus "28", Louis Ambroise Dubut, from *Architecture Civile*, 1800.

Kaufmann was taken up by Philip Johnson, whose Glass House of 1949 was, according to the architect, deeply indebted to a reading of *Von Ledoux bis Le Corbusier*.[11] Later, Kaufmann's writings, and especially his *Architecture in the Age of Reason*, posthumously published in 1955, were, when translated, strong influences on the theories of architectural "autonomy" characteristic of the Neo-Rationalist school in Italy after 1971, and especially on the theory and design of Aldo Rossi, who reviewed his books in detail.[12] More recently, Kaufmann has been re-interpreted as a theorist of an architectural "autonomy" based on linguistic and disciplinary codes, as proposed by Peter Eisenman and others.[13]

Read today in the context of the detailed monographic research that was to have modified his once seemingly over-simplified conclusions, despite the unearthing of other architects to the fore to counterbalance the image of the "three revolutionaries," and the contextualization of their work in the light of new historical interpretations of "enlightenment" and "revolution," Kaufmann's analyses can be seen to regain much of their original force, as seeking to rise above stylistic differences and biographical details, to grasp the phenomenon of an "architectural enlightenment" in all its dimensions, intellectual and formal. At the very least, his theses bear re-examination as representing a critical stage in the development of the discipline of architectural history — as important in their own way as those of Riegl, Frankl, and Giedion — at the same time as they challenge questions to our contemporary conceptions of architectural form and our preconceptions of its political and social significance. In retrospect, as I shall argue, his analytical and historical approach, more subtle and resilient than critics have understood, acts as a fundamental critique of the very "school" with which he has been associated, the Vienna School, while it resonates with contemporary attempts to see "modernism" no longer as a brief (and failed) avant-garde experiment in the 1920s, but as a long process of political and aesthetic struggle, with intellectual roots in Enlightenment and Kantian philosophy.

FROM NEOCLASSICISM TO AUTONOMY

Emil Kaufmann was born on March 28, 1891 in Vienna; he studied first at Innsbruck and then Vienna with the Renaissance specialist Hans Semper, with the Byzantinist architectural historian Joseph Strzygowski, the classical archeologist Emanuel Loewy (1847-1938), and the historian Ludwig von Pastor (1854-1928). He was especially drawn to the teaching of Max Dvořak, however, with whom he formed a close friendship. He was awarded his doctorate in Vienna in 1920 and went on to forge an entire field by his "rediscovery" of three generations of French architectural theorists and designers from the 1750s to the 1820s, a field that he then expanded into the general examination of "architecture in the age of reason" in Europe. As Schapiro noted in his brief obituary in 1953, Kaufmann was unable to obtain a regular academic post (no doubt a result of rampant anti-semitism) and was obliged to work in a bank for much of his early career.

His first major article, written in 1920 and published in the *Repertorium für Kunstwissenschaft* in 1924, (interestingly enough, side by side with another ground-breaking architectural study by Paul Zucker, "Der Begriff der zeit in der architektur") outlined the bases for his study of late eighteenth-century architecture, by dividing a period generically known as "Classic," albeit in a late moment, into two. As explicated by Georges Teyssot, Kaufmann's essay, "The Architectural Theory of French Classicism and Neoclassicism," ["Die Architectkturtheorie der Französischen Klassik und der Kalssizismus"] established klassizismus as a period with a formal expression, or rather structure, of its own.[14] Here, Kaufmann was underlining what he saw as the distinct difference between French developments and those in other "Baroque" countries. Between Classicism in the mid-seventeenth century and Neoclassicism after 1750, there were, for Kaufmann, certain continuities of "clarity and truth" but sharp differences in composition, which seemed to him to move from a principle of "meaningful harmony" inherent in the work itself toward a principle of expression or communication provoking sensations beyond the work.[15] In an "historical" confirmation of Nietzche's 1878 assertion that "Stone is more stone than before," Kaufmann articulated tis shift, as one that finally relinquished the natural values of physical materials ("the demand that the material be granted its own physical properties and life") in order to privilege ideas alone.[16]

For it [Neoclassicism] the material is dead. Form has no other function than to be the bearer of ideas, the mediator of moods, to arouse emotions which are distinct from the sensuous material and which the material itself does not contain. The symbol of Neoclassicism is the non-sensual stone, the stone inhabited by genius.[17]

Kaufmann here established two clear points of reference for his analysis of the period 1750 to 1800: what he would call later "the universal animism of the baroque," where inanimate material took on organic forms, and its antithesis, post-Revolutionary form, where the material itself has its own laws: "For architecture after the Revolution," he wrote, "the stone is again stone." ["Baukunst ist der Stein weider Stein"][18]

In setting up in this way Classicism, on the one hand, and Neoclassicism, on the other, as the conceptual beginning and end points of his research, Kaufmann has identified the period 1750 to 1800 as a site of transition from one to the other; but more importantly as a site of struggle where the two tendencies and their compositional and philosophical corollaries are internally and often inconsistently manifested as architects press the classical language of architecture to its limits in the search for a means to express Enlightenment and Revolutionary ideas. The paradigmatic figure in this struggle, for Kaufmann, was Claude-Nicolas Ledoux whose architecture registered the shift from Classicism to Neoclassicism in an especially dramatic, and ultimately productive way. For Ledoux, argued Kaufmann, architecture was the very expression of the social ideals of the new bourgeoisie and the political ideas of the Enlightenment as developed in Rousseau's ideal of individual freedom and its Kantian counterpart, "autonomy."[19]

Kaufmann's first direct reference to "autonomen baukunst" was to occur in a short study of Ledoux's church architecture, centered on the project for the Church of Chaux, (probably designed in 1785, and published in Ledoux's *L'Architecture considérée sous le rapport de l'art, des moeurs et de la législation* in 1804).[20] Contrasting Ledoux's scheme with Soufflot's design for Sainte-Geneviève, to which it obviously was a response, Kaufmann identifies it with the qualities of the new "neoclassicism" he saw emerging with Ledoux's generation. The Neoclassical, as opposed to the Baroque, church was organized as a solid geometrical block, with reduced decoration and a distinct separation and identity of its functional parts — separate altars, for example, on different levels, for festivals and marriages, as opposed to funerals. As Kaufmann wrote,

Barrière de Chaillot,
Claude Nicholas Ledoux.

Barrière de la Chopinette
Claude Nicholas Ledoux.

Barrière de Reuilly
Claude Nicholas Ledoux.

Haus "3" from *Architecture
Civile*, Louis Ambroise
Dubut, 1800.

"In place of the conception of architectural form as living, organic nature, there enters the feeling for strict geometry."[21]

This theme is taken up again in the same year in the book-length article on "The City of the Architect Ledoux," ["Die Stadt des Architekten Ledoux"] contributed to the second volume of the Vienna art-historical school's flagship journal, the *Kunstwissenschaftliche Forschungen*.[22] In this first sketch of what was to become, three years later, his first book, Kaufmann gives the idea of autonomy a fundamental place, with the subtitle: "On the Realization of Autonomous Architecture" ["Zur Erkenntnis der autonomen Architektur"]. In this detailed study, Kaufmann, his critics notwithstanding, develops the argument for autonomy historically and with deliberate recognition of the complexity inherent in architectural practice. Ledoux, for him, is after all a transitional and pivotal figure in the shift from what he calls "Baroque" to what he has characterized as "Neoclassicism," and it is precisely the mixed nature of the work that allows him to comprehend the shift as an organic and slow process of internalization and cognition on the part of the architect as to the overall problem of architecture and its proper means of expression in an epoch itself undergoing radical shifts in its intellectual, social, and political forms. Thus Kaufmann's argument moves slowly towards the "erkenntnis" or "discovery" of autonomy, through a number of stages, represented by detailed analyses of Ledoux's designs in roughly chronological order culminating in a long section devoted to "The Autonomous Solution" ["Die autonome Lösung"].

First Kaufmann analyzes the dramatic change in plans for the Saltworks of Chaux between the initial project of 1771 and the final project of 1774, from a unified, square, courtyard plan, to a number of separate pavilions grouped around a semi-circle, as a sign of the move from "Baroque unity" [Barocken Verband] to the Pavilion-system of the nineteenth century [Pavillionsystem].[23] The break up of the project into functionally defined and formally expressed units was, for Kaufmann, an indication of the "principle of isolation," the emergence of an "architecture of isolation" [isolierneden Architektur] that paralleled the emergence of the modern "individual" consciousness [Individualbewusstseins].[24]

The example of the Church of Chaux affords Kaufmann an example of the transition from Baroque dynamic composition to Neoclassical "static" composition: the flattened, low dome andthe horizontal lines of the block reinforcing a sense of calm meditation, as opposed to the upward movement of Baroque churches. Further, the articulation of the different altars — one for festivals and marriages on the upper level, with a second for burials and memorial services below in the crypt, with its own entrances and exits towards the cemeteries, enunciates for Kaufmann a "principle of isolation" [Prinzip der Isolierung], one that corresponds to the sense of "distance" [Distanzierung] necessary for the communication of sublime effects.[25]

Kaufmann then advances his argument with the analysis of the two symbolic monuments, the "Panarétéon" and the "Pacifère," citing Ledoux's statements that "the form of a cube is the symbol of immutability" and "the form of a cube is the symbol of Justice" as a way of introducing the concept of "architecture parlante," or "speaking architecture."[26] Kaufmann had discovered this term, not itself of eighteenth century origin, in a mid-nineteenth century article satirizing Ledoux's attempts to communicate ideas through buildings and immediately saw it as both positive and apt in its characterization of the

aspirations of late eighteenth century architects to develop a truly social language of forms.[27] The "symbolic system" that Ledoux wished to deploy was, of course, itself dependent on the separation of individual buildings into identifiable masses, and their shaping as readable signs. Here, for Kaufmann, the pavilion system, the isolation of parts, and the articulation of the appropriate "character" of each structure, led naturally to what, in reference to Ledoux's design for the "Maison d'Education," he finally named "the new concept of the *autonomous* treatment of the materials."[28]

In this way, Kaufmann established the complex development of Ledoux's design practice as leading to the "autonomous solution" evinced in the series of nine-square plan houses deployed in the landscape of the Ideal City of Chaux, "all varied, all isolated," as Ledoux stated.[29] Such isolation, Kaufmann averred, marked the end of Baroque compositional practice, that of "concatenation" [Verband] and the beginning of the new building form [die neue Bauform], a form characterized by the Enlightenment pressure for "clarification" [Abklärung].[30] Kaufmann thus prepared the analytical ground for the syste-matic comparison of with the general method of the Enlightenment – that developed by Kant:

At the time when Kant rejects all the moral philosophies of the past and decrees the "autonomy of the will as the supreme principle of ethics," an analogous transformation takes place in architecture. In the sketches of Ledoux these new objectives appear for the first time in all their clarity. His work marks the birth of autonomous architecture.[31]

The theory of autonomy was given its fullest development in Kaufmann's second book, a slim treatise entitled, polemically enough, *Von Ledoux bis Le Corbusier*, published in 1933, and summarizing and developing the arguments put forward in "Die Stadt." In the Preface, dated "Vienna, May 1933," Kaufmann outlined his methodological premise. This was to be, he wrote, "something more than a monograph, and different to a mosaic of an artistic life." Rather it was to be seen as "a part of the history of architecture which, through the interpretation of the work of Ledoux, appears in a new light" at the same time as demonstrating "the importance of the great movement of ideas around 1800 for the domain of art."[32] This theoretical aim was expressed in the subtitle to the book, no longer "Zur Erkenntnis der Autonomen Architektur" but now the more dynamic "Ursprung und Entwicklung der Autonomen Architektur." The substitution of "Origin and Development" for "Discovery" represented both a firmer conviction in his own "discovery" and a sense of its historical implications for later developments.

From the outset, Kaufmann made it clear that he was seeing the French architecture of the Enlightenment and Revolution as equal or greater in importance to the already well-established tradition of German Neoclassicism as represented by Schinkel. His title, in fact, was a direct gloss on Paul Klopfer's *Von Palladio bis Schinkel*, an argument for the primacy of German architecture as it received the Renaissance tradition from Italy.[33] Kaufmann, by contrast, is concerned to emphasize the role of the French and Latin traditions in the continuation of Palladio's legacy to the present. His work in Paris had convinced him that it was the Latin countries that counted in the development of modernism. While philosophy, under the aegis of Kant, and poetry following Hölderlin, could be seen to have constructed the intellectual and literary foundations of Romantic modernism, it was in France and Italy that the work of the Enlightenment entered fundamentally into the visual arts, and

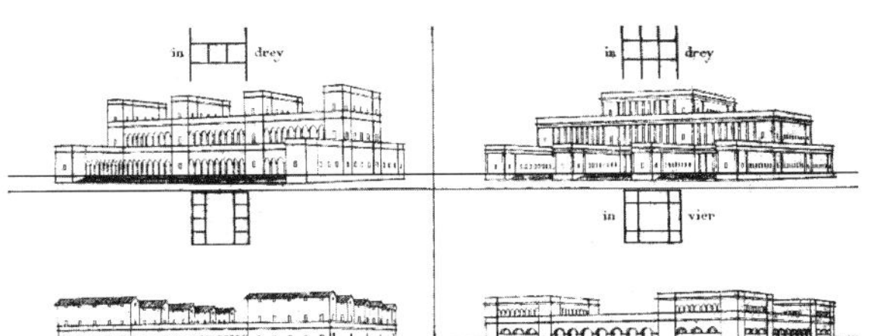

Lehrbeispiele ("Teaching Examples"), J.N.L. Durand, from *Abriss der Vorlesungen über Baukunst.*

especially architecture. This was accomplished, Kaufmann argued, by the final break with Baroque modes of composition ("heteronomous" as he called them) and the introduction in their place of modern forms of disposition ("autonomous" or "free-standing"). Once ratified by the Revolution, and despite attempts to veil the radical nature of the shift by means of historical styles, autonomy survived to establish the abstraction of modernism as the apotheosis of Enlightenment reason. He wrote:

If we are well-informed about the historic role of Italy as the initiatory land of modern times in the domains of art and society, we remain, by contrast, ignorant of the role of France as pioneer of a new art and creator of a new architecture. Towards 1800, as during the Gothic period, the decisive innovations come from the French architects. In the following work, I am first concerned to render justice to the artist who was the first, not with a vague intuition of distant goals but with a clear and full self-consciousness, to traverse the long route from the Baroque to modern architecture: Claude-Nicolas Ledoux. Placed at the frontier of two epochs, before and after the Revolution, his work is the first to announce the new artistic aims; it is the tangible witness to the appearance of a new world. But it is also my concern to show how his ideas and those of his epoch are transmitted to us, and how, in a way, the unity of the last hundred and fifty years is reflected in architectural activity. [VLLC, 5-6]

Kaufmann was immediately concerned to announce that it was the "revolutionary" period as a whole — 1770 to 1790 — with which he was concerned; precise dates, which for Ledoux were in any case hard to come by, were less important than a sense of the signification of the global shift in art and philosophy, as in the social and political realm. The years that saw the preparation of the "great revolution that was completely to transform the social system of the west" were "the same years in which the work of Kant matured." He writes: "Globally, there was a profound (we could say today, definitive) denial of the past; a clear and self-conscious rupture, a decisive step toward a new *autonomy*." For Kaufmann, the interconnection between these movements and the work of Ledoux was not accidental, but established by Kant and Ledoux's common respect for and indebtedness to Rousseau:

At the moment when, with the Declaration of the Rights of Man, the rights of the individual are affirmed, at the moment when, in place of the old heteronomous morality, Kant instituted the autonomous ethic, Ledoux laid the foundations of an autonomous architecture. [VLLC, 12]

The correspondence was direct: if for Kant the *Critique of Pure Reason* had accomplished "what numerous centuries had been unable to realize," for Ledoux "the moment in which we live has broken the chains that shackle architecture." [VLLC, 12; Ledoux, *L'Architecture*, 30] From a study of Ledoux, Kaufmann averred, would emerge the answer to three critical questions: the reasons for the "abandoning of the aesthetics of Baroque classicism," the "relations between the Revolution and architecture," and the "profound signification of neoclassicism and the architecture of the end of the nineteenth century." [VLLC, 12].[34]

The general concept of architectural autonomy, was, for Kaufmann, represented by a wide range of large and small-scale formal moves. The first, and most fundamental, because the most radical shift from Baroque modes of composition was the separation of buildings according to a quasi-functional identification, rather than their unified and hierarchical massing to include all functions. This step, taken by Ledoux at the beginning of his career as he jettisoned the courtyard preliminary scheme for the Saltworks in favor of a grouping of pavilions, was decisive:

The passage from the first to the second project reflects no less than one of the most important events in the history of architecture: the dismembering of Baroque concatenation [Zertrümmerung des Barocken Verbandes]. …In a remarkable parallelism with the general historic evolution, concatenation is replaced by the system of pavilionnate composition, which, after that moment, becomes predominant: this is the free association of autonomous entities.[Pavillonsystem…die freie Vereinigung selbständiger Existenzen] [VLLC, 16-17]

In this transformation of compositional techniques, the instrumental force, both for the production of the buildings and their historical analysis, was the rational plan: it is the plan which as Kaufmann noted "allows us to discover the fundamental reasons for the determination of forms," no doubt a first step that allowed for Kaufmann's historical connection of Ledoux with the Le Corbusier of the "plan as generator." And this plan, as with the three-dimensional form of the pavilions, is constructed not by any reference to a Baroque observer, but purely geometrically. Geometry operates as a calculated control of form for use; not only does the "rationality of the plan" [die Ratio des Planes] exercise "absolute sovereignty," but it offers a neutral system of order, entirely abstracted from the personal experience of a perspectival observer. Where "all baroque architecture was conceived as a function of the observer," now "the center of the new buildings is no longer the heart of the whole … It is no more than a geometrical point to which all the parts relate. The new buildings are assembled and not intimately linked [Zusammen-gesetz, nicht zusammengewachsen]. [VLLC, 19] In accordance with the spirit of autonomy, the new pavilions are entirely self-sufficient: as opposed to the Classical and Baroque system, inherited from Renaissance aesthetics, where "to detach a part is to destroy the whole," the pavilion rejects parts and becomes "an association of independent elements:"

If one wishes to characterize the architectural systems by formulae as reduced as possible one could define Baroque association in these terms: one part dominates all the others and nevertheless all the parts form a whole; the deep sense of the pavilion system can be translated thus: the part is independent within the frame of the totality. [Der Teil ist frei im Rahmen des Ganzen] Between the two systems lies a Revolution. [VLLC, 19]

Kaufmann was far from claiming that Ledoux ever threw off the Baroque sensibility entirely — in different ways, all of Ledoux's work exhibited its transitional character — indeed Kaufmann stresses in his analysis of buildings from the 1770s (the Hôtel Montmorency, the pavilion at Louveciennes for the Comtesse du Barry) and the 1780s (the Hôtel Thélusson) that "the opposed principles were living *at the same time* in the artist" — but he finds in Ledoux's "fanaticism" for geometry and rigorous planning an anticipation of the architect's later, more abstract projects. [VLLC, 20]

Here Kaufmann sees the influence of the desire of the Enlightenment for "clarification," or *Abklärung*, which when applied to architecture called for the use of "massive blocks" superimposed in compositions that, rather than relying on the effect of a central, principal, motif, gained effect through the simple strength of masses themselves. And while Ledoux is still free in his use of Baroque motifs to give his buildings character — the upturned urns and grotto in the Saltworks, for example — his preference was for the architecture to "speak" by means of its own stereometric forms, as in the designs for the House of the Surveyors (a vast elliptical tube), or the Coopers' Workshop (with its concentric rings and intersecting barrel-shaped form):

Experiments with forms themselves count among the most astonishing initiatives of this epoch. The preference for the simplest stereometric configurations is indicative of the gravity of the spirit of the age. Thus one finds in the proj-

Barrière de Pantin, Barrière de l'Ecole Militaire , Barrière St. Martin, C.N Ledoux.

ects of Ledoux, severe cubes (as one sees for example in the Country House of Jarnac or the House for a Man of Letters), the House of the Woodcutters in the form of a pyramid, the cylindrical Country House (also the Barrière of the Boulevard of La Villette, still standing, and the cylindrical House of M. De Witt) and finally Spherical House of the Agricultural Guards. [VLLC, 30]

Building up his argument for Ledoux as an originator of modernism, Kaufmann remarks on the fact that "our own epoch, linked to that of Ledoux, is open to experiments of the same kind which, even if they are without issue from an architectural point of view, are no less very significant of the indefatigable research for new forms [neuer Gestalt]." [VLLC, 32]

Bringing together all these compositional innovations, is, as Kaufmann had intimated in his earlier writings, the project for the Church of Chaux. Combining the demand for a single, free-standing mass, horizontal and static, with the separation of functional elements such as the altars, on different levels, it also construed a new kind of neoclassical "sublime." This was a sublime of "calm meditation in a solemn immobility," a sublime of individual self-absorption and contemplation as opposed to the Medieval "sanctuary of unworldliness" or Baroque "spiritual elevation." It was also a sublime of "distance," reflecting the idea common to neo-Kantians from Wölfflin to Warburg, Adorno to Karcauer and Benjamin, that objectivity and rationality requires a "keeping one's distance." [distanzhalten] [VLLC, 33] Finally, the entire effect of the Church, its own enlightened spirituality, is gained not by the introduction of painting, sculpture, images, or symbols, but by "the autonomous means of architecture." [die autonomen Mittel der Architektur] [VLLC, 34]

FROM KANT TO LE CORBUSIER

Autonomy of the will is the sole principle of all moral laws and of duties in keeping with them; heteronomy of choice, on the other hand, not only does not ground any obligation at all but is instead opposed to the principle of obligation and to the morality of the will.

Immanuel Kant, *Critique of Practical Reason*, 1788.

The connection that Kaufmann sought between architecture and philosophy, and ultimately between Ledoux and Kant was provided and historically grounded by Ledoux's reading of Rousseau. Rousseau was evoked explicitly and implicitly in many passages of *L'Architecture*. The obvious interpretation of "l'homme primitif" embodied in the plate illustrating the shelter of the poor; the enthusiasm for natural settings throughout the descriptions of the City of Chaux; the references to "le pacte social" and finally the overall adherence to a "return to origins," exhibited in Ledoux's theory and design. The key passage for Kaufmann, joining this "return" to "autonomy" is that in which Ledoux justifies the separation of each function in pavilions in the second project for the Saltworks: "Remontez au principe…Consultez la nature; partout l'homme est isolé."[VLLC, 43; LA 90] Kaufmann further draws parallels between Rousseau's social thought and the institutions designed by Ledoux for his ideal "natural" society. The strange phallic-planned brothel or "Oikma" masquerading as a "Fragment of a Greek Monument," resonated for Kaufmann with the sensibility of Schlegel's "Lucinde," a witness to the "autonomy of the pleasure of the senses" typical of the epoch.[35] Beyond this, Rousseau was behind Ledoux's emphasis on hygiene, physical exercise, education, communal living, and his more general preoccupation with the citizenry of his new ideal state as a whole – a "universal citizenry" or Weltbürgerlichkeit. If Ledoux was by no means an egalitarian along the lines of later revolutionaries such as Gracchus Babeuf, he certainly believed in a "pacte sociale" that endowed the poorest member of society with architecture – a characteristic that would later

appeal to the socialism of Hannes Meyer who, in 1942, lauded Ledoux for having given the pyramid (previously reserved for the elite) to the masses.[36]

But while the connection between Ledoux and Rousseau may be obvious, that between Ledoux and Kant remains uncertain. For, at first glance, the question of "autonomy," posited by Kant as the basis for moral principle, and taken up throughout the nineteenth and twentieth centuries as the watchword of bourgeois liberal politics, does not easily relate to architecture, either in theory or practice. First advanced in the *Critique of Pure Reason* as a "call to reason" to gain "self-knowledge" it presented the kind of paradox between law and self-will that has haunted political reasoning ever since. In Kant the "critique of pure reason" presupposes what he calls a "tribunal" that will ensure the claims of reason; a tribunal that operates "not by despotic decrees" but "in accordance with its own eternal and unalterable laws." As parsed by Adorno, this strange double imperative – the freedom to give oneself laws – represents the "supreme concept in Kant's moral philosophy," whereby "acting in accordance with laws appears as a function of freedom – or, conversely, freedom manifests itself as a function of the law." Such a principle might seem distant from any instrumental concept in architecture, save perhaps for a vague analogy between "freedom" and "order" in aesthetics.

For the generation of the 1920s however, Kant's principle of autonomy represented far more than a simple appeal to reason, or a century-old claim in the philosophy of knowledge. It was historically and conceptually the founding principle of bourgeois society, a product, as Adorno had it, of "the enthusiasm of the youthful bourgeoisie which had not yet started its never-ending complaints that reason cannot solve anything, but which still feels confident of its ability to achieve things by virtue of the powers of its own reason." Thus understood, the interrogation of autonomy was joined to the interrogation of bourgeois liberal democracy, under severe threat in the inter-war period. Inspired by the research of the Marburg school, under the leadership of Hermann Cohen, many philosophers in the early twentieth century, including Ernst Cassirer who studied at Marburg, were returning to Kant as the initiator of modern critical philosophy; Cassirer's two studies *Freiheit und Form* (1916) *Kants Leben und Lehre*, the first modern comprehensive philosophical biography, was published in 1918 and became the reference point for a new generation, including Kracauer, Adorno, and Benjamin who saw Kant, for better or for worse, as the beginning point of an investigation necessary for the development of a truly "critical" theory. Adorno, in particular, saw Kantian autonomy as a double-edged sword, much in the way that contemporary thinkers were characterizing Rousseau's social contract as implicitly totalitarian. For Adorno, questioning the implications of appeals to "reason" that had, under the impetus of science and technology already begun to exhibit their "dark side," autonomy in Kant, as the "kernel of his philosophy," articulated "a very dark secret of bourgeois society."

This secret is the reality that the formal freedom of juridical subjects is actually the foundation of the dependency of all upon all, that is to say, it is the foundation of the coercive character of society, its conformity with law. That is what lies behind the very strange theory that in Kant reason is a tribunal which has to sit in judgement over reason as the accused."[37]

It was, of course, the paradoxical nature of this dichotomy that led many humanists in the interwar period to interrogate their own objects of study, from philosophy to art history, at a moment when bourgeois autonomy, and its supposed links to reason and liberalism if not social democracy, was challenged by the movement from the "freedom" of law to totalitarian "coercion."

Kaufmann, in Vienna, was equally exposed to this neo-Kantian revival, but in taking up Kant as the founding father of modern bourgeois society, and

Title page, *Von Ledoux bis le Corbusier*, by C.N. Ledoux, edition 1985.

specifically in 1933, he was making a very different point to that of the Berlin theorists. Where the Frankfurt school sociologists were already looking at the paradoxes and problematics of Kantian idealism, and Cassirer himself was struggling with the difficulties of reconciling Rousseau and Kant in essays published in 1932, Kaufmann apparently blithely ignored such questions in favor of a generalized appeal to Rousseau/Kant as signifying an Enlightenment unified enough to provide an intellectual base, both for Ledoux, and for his interpretation. Such apparent simplification, however, is explicable on two grounds. Firstly, Kaufmann was concerned to sketch the intellectual framework for an architect who himself was anything but a systematic thinker, one who readily appealed to a wide range of authorities in his attempt to justify new forms. Kaufmann's seeming confusion, in these terms, was historically accurate in delineating the discursive breadth of Ledoux's sources, and its impact on design. Certainly Cassirer's study of *The Philosophy of the Enlightenment* published in 1932 had, together with his essay on Rousseau of the same year, the aim of constructing such a unity of thought.[38]

Secondly, and equally important, Kaufmann's own intellectual agenda reached beyond a purely historical interpretation. Embedded in the title of *Von Ledoux bis Le Corbusier*, and in its appeal to Kantian thought, was an implicit challenge to the emerging cultural politics of Austria and Germany, and a covert appeal to a "united" front based on the rule of law and reason as the basis for the restatement of the ideal of a liberal, social democratic, state.

Published in May 1933, two months after Hitler's takeover of power after the March 5 elections, was seemingly deliberately calculated to assert the social democratic values of Enlightenment, republicanism, and modernism, values under severe attack not only from Nazi ideologues who had denounced them, and the modernism that represented them as degenerate and Bolshevik, but also from conservative Viennese art historians like Strzygowski and Sedlmayr. The latter, who had joined the National Socialist party in 1932, then to become a loyal supporter throughout the occupation and War, was to wait until Kaufmann's flight to the U.S. before developing his own thesis of the "loss of center" using Kaufmann's own material to set out a despairing thesis of decline and fall where Kaufmann had seen only progress and justice. In 1933, however, as Damisch has pointed out, it was an act of real intellectual, if not physical, courage to set out the continuities between the French Revolution and Modernism, in a moment when Speer and his cohorts were finding monumental solace in the gigantesque revival of German neoclassicism.

Ledoux, in this context, was, more than a historical subject, a cover, or metaphor for the explication of liberal bourgeois society, if not a kind of utopian socialism in historical guise. The real subject of the treatise would then be the architecture of Loos, Walter Gropius, Richard Neutra, and Le Corbusier — the architecture of Modernism developed between 1900 and 1929. Kaufmann wrote:

The continuity of the development of post-revolutionary architecture can in a way be traced through to the beginning of our own period, which opens around 1900 with the Dutch Berlage and the Viennese Adolf Loos, a period one can usefully designate by naming its most self-conscious protagonist, the leader of the young French school: Le Corbusier [den Fuhrer des jungen Frankreich Le Corbusier]. [VLLC, 61]

The first mention of Le Corbusier in Kaufmann's writings is in a footnote to the article "Die Stadt," which points to the similarities between three statements by Ledoux, and the text of *Vers une architecture*.[39] The connection was understood as obvious as Ledoux spoke of "the appreciable feeling of a plan as stemming from the subject, the site, and the needs of the building, of the destructive effect of details on surfaces," and of the "forms described with a single stroke of the compass," the square and the circle as the "alphabetical letters used by authors in the text of their best works."[40]

Two years later, *Von Ledoux bis Le Corbusier* was to elaborate these analogies as systematically and historically grounded. Ledoux, Kaufmann argued in the last section of the book, was the progenitor of a modernism that was in no way formalist ("he did not confine his attention only to formal details, as did the Secession a hundred years later" [VLLC, 42]); rather "in his research he envisaged the totality of the reorganization of the body of the building itself and of the systems of large complexes of buildings." [VLLC, 42] Considering Ledoux's later works, and especially his group of town houses designed after the Revolution for Hosten, Kaufmann to introduced his first modernist comparison, not to Le Corbusier, but to Walter Gropius: referring to Ledoux's late works, he notes:

The principal artistic quality of these projects is the "play of masses" that Ledoux looked for above all. The formal principle on which these realizations were based corresponds to the leitmotif of our present architecture, as Walter Gropius has expressed it in the first volume of the Bauhaus books: "a variety starting with the same fundamental type obtained by the alternate juxtaposition and superimposition of repetitive spatial cells." [VLLC, 48]

It is clear that in tracing the development of autonomous architecture after Ledoux, and through the nineteenth century, Kaufmann is aware of the deterioration in aesthetic content, and of the deleterious effects of the incessant repetition of the "pavilion system." Thus he analyzes the teaching method and influence of Jean-Nicolas Louis Durand, who systematized Ledoux's own system for the École Polytechnique, repeating the fundamental elements of architecture as if they were so many geometrical points, lines, and planes on graph paper, and sees this method's effects on architects like Dubut. But it is equally obvious that Kaufmann is here only attempting to demonstrate that despite the overt historicist "clothing" of the pavilions in question, varied according to taste and stylistic revival through the century, the survival of the pavilion, and its fundamentally geometrical/functional foundation, allowed the principles of modernism to survive if not to prosper.

His assessment of the effects of autonomy on urbanism is, for example, bleak enough, and parallel to that of Camillo Sitte at the end of the nineteenth century: castigating the pavilion structures around the Place de l'Étoile, the Place Royale in Munich, or the Ringstrasse in Vienna, whose buildings

are set up, like isolated blocks. In their isolation, each one could, without hindering its attractiveness, be displaced to another site. It is of little importance that the parts have been realized and are of different appearance, as in Munich, or are contemporary and fit amongst themselves as in Vienna. The double aspect of the past century which, like Janus, looks at once forward and backward, appears even more clearly in that portion of the Ringstrasse with the monumental buildings of the Parliament, the City Hall, the University, and the Theater. Conceived according to an absolutely heteronomous inspiration, the buildings are destined for show. In this intention, each of them carries an old suit, passing for Greek, Gothic, or late Renaissance. But in this diversity there is also a new trait: the total indifference to the effect of the whole. Each building remains in a total isolation, none is linked in an ensemble. [VLLC, 61]

Yet, despite the moribund, half heteronomous, half autonomous aspect of the style-revival buildings of the Ringstrasse, the principle of autonomy survived to triumph in the younger generation of modernists following Berlage. Kaufmann is not inclined to enter into a detailed analysis of twentieth century modernism as a conclusion to his Ledoux monograph; for him, the simple "evidence" of Le Corbusier and his contemporaries is enough to make the point. Interestingly enough, it is Richard Neutra, the Viennese exile in California, whose *Wie baut Amerika* had been published in 1927, who is selected as the spokesman for modernism's continuity with the past, Roman, and Baroque: Neutra, quoted by Kaufmann, writes:

It is a long way from the plastic formalism of the Greek world to the twisted facades of the Baroque, but this route is not illogical, it always crosses so to speak the same region: that of a certain spiritual attitude towards architectural creation. The general principle the development of which we have wanted to demonstrate here in architecture is defined by Neutra in these terms: Dissociation, *juxtaposition, the strict delimitation of concepts, of the domains of thought and action, such seem to be the fundamental tendencies of this development.*[41]

It is, nonetheless, with Le Corbusier that Kaufmann concludes his little book, a Le Corbusier represented not only by *Vers une architecture*, but by the translated version of Urbanisme, Städtebau, and more recently still by the first volume of his *Oeuvres completes, 1910 to 1929*, published in 1930. Kaufmann was thus able to refer to the already commonplaces of the "fascination for the straight line," or the "return to the "fundamental realities of the sphere, the cube and the cylinder in great architecture" but also to extend his comparison with Ledoux to the layout and projected monuments of the Cité Mondiale, with its already contentious pyramidal scheme for a Mundaneum or world museum, reminiscent of the pyramids of Ledoux and Boullée. Kaufmann, as opposed to the trenchant critiques of the Marxist Karel Teige, lauds the "idealism" of this utopia as directly relating to, if not influenced by, that of Ledoux:

The resemblance between the epoch of Ledoux and our own is not limited (this will be one of our conclusions) to formal and thematic aspects. This resemblance does not only rest in the fact that in his epoch as our own one sees the new and important problem of the masses emerge as the powerful motive of solutions. Independently of the new demands of the real, one discerns now as at that epoch a new idealism. It appears in L'Architecture of Ledoux as in the writings of Le Corbusier, in the project for the Ideal City as in the Cité Modiale. It is in this idealism, founded on the new ideals of ethics and law, in which is, in the end, rooted, it seems to us, before 1800 even as today, the renewal of architecture.

Kaufmann concludes:

Because Le Corbusier has no less faith in these than Ledoux, because in the one and in the other the intimate link between art and life is as strong, one must cite, side by side, the master whose work crowns the triumph of the new principles and he whose activity has opened the way for these principles.

STRUCTURAL ANALYSIS

Kaufmann's methods of analysis, as well as those of the Vienna School with which he was to be loosely associated, have often been criticized for their incipient "formalism," and especially so from the left in the 1930s. Thus Meyer Schapiro, responding to the confused and contradictory "formalism" of the Viennese School, in an incisive review of the publications of the "New Viennese School" of art history, tried to redress the historical problem in terms of a less reductive political position. Assessing Emil Kaufmann's article "The City of the Architect Ledoux," and the later *Von Ledoux bis Le Corbusier*, Schapiro, while recognizing the merit of Kaufmann's rescue of Ledoux, pointed to the limitations of the formal approach in relating architecture to its social context. Kaufmann had attempted to join what he called Ledoux's principle of architectural "autonomy" – the derivation of an architectural aesthetic from internal requirements of construction and use rather than from any external, imposed artistic conception – to a similar characteristic of emerging bourgeois society, – "which thinks of itself as composed of isolated, equally free individuals." Schapiro argued that Kaufmann, in fact, had succeeded only in joining an architectural principle to a social principle, one found indeed in Ledoux's writings. "The correlation," Schapiro wrote, "is with bourgeois ideology, not with the actual class structure and conditions of bourgeois society, and depends more on quotations than on a study of social and economic history." In the light of our analysis of Kaufmann's theses of autonomy, we would have to conclude that Kaufmann might have readily agreed with Schapiro's critique: far from trying to develop a materialist history assuming the fundamental relations between base and superstructure, society and culture, Kaufmann's aims were surely more modest and confined to demonstrating the relations between thought about social form, and thought about architectural form.

But Kaufmann's method was not only attacked from the left. Like many social-democratic theses it was equally subject to criticism from the right.

Indeed, Kaufmann did not have to look so far for his enemies as the Berlin of Hitler's putsch: Hans Sedlmayr, another distinguished student of Wölfflin, and an editor of the Vienna school's flagship journal, the *Kunstwissenschaftliche Forschungen*, in which Kaufmann had published his breakthrough article, had, during these years taken sharp issue with Kaufmann's democratic and idealistic reading of the architecture of 1800, and precisely from a conservative, soon to become fascist, commitment. It is in comparison with Sedlmayr's approach that Kaufmann seems less and less the Vienna School historian, and more and more the student of Dvořak.

It was Hans Sedlmayr, of all the Vienna School historians, who took seriously the lessons of Riegl, in opposition to his dissertation advisor Julius Schlosser, in conceptualizing a method of art history that completely integrated architecture; developing Riegl's concept of Kunstwollen, as reinterpreted by his contemporary Panofsky, into what he termed a "Strukturanalyse" or analysis of structural principles. These were not, of course, the principles of structure, as an architectural historian might understand them. His well-known treatise on Borromini's church, San Carlo alle Quattro Fontane, found its structural principle not in the architectural structure, nor even in the "structural" organization of its intersecting spaces and volumes, but rather in the decorative treatment of the wall. As Christopher Wood notes, "In other words, structure may reveal itself in apparently marginal or meaningless features." [Wood, 25] Here Sedlmayr relies on Gestalt theory to introduce the notion of "shaped vision," that in his terms formed an objective and rational way of looking beneath appearances, of seeking out principles of form and organization not apparent in normal characterizations of function, style, and the like. Wood and Meyer Schapiro before him, have pointed out the entirely "specious" nature of this "rationalism," criticizing its intuitionist and implicitly racist undertones.

In Sedlmayr's terms, while Kaufmann had (the method after all was scientifically correct) analyzed the formal shifts he had entirely misdiagnosed the symptoms. Where Kaufmann saw renewal in revolutionary and modern architecture, Sedlmayr saw decay and decline; where Kaufmann saw increasing health in society and architecture, Sedlmayr saw decadence and death. Architecture was but a sign of the "huge inner catastrophe" set off by the Revolution, a "loss of center" and stability imaged by what for Sedlmayr was the most characteristic motif of 1800, the sphere, with all its implications of the destabilization – the literal deracination of traditional architecture. Kaufmann's heroes were Sedlmayr's devils: as the latter observed of Goya: "The more we study the art of Goya, the more intense grows our conviction that, like Kant in philosophy and Ledoux's architecture, he is one of the great pulverizing forces that bring a new age into being." [LC, 117] Sedlmayr, sensing an ally in his fight against the demon of modernism, cites Ernst Jünger approvingly in characterizing the *musealen trieb*, the "face turned towards the things of death," of the contemporary epoch.

More specifically, explaining his so-called "Method of Critical Forms," a method he claims is "capable of separating the true from the false," of "concentrating on that unconscious sphere of instinctive receptivity" and of "possession" in which "the soul of the age stands naked before us" – a method that is common to the pathologist and the psychologist – Sedlmayr finds in the image of Ledoux's architecture one such apparently bizarre but fundamentally symptomatic form that describes the folly of the modern age: the Sphere House of the Agricultural Guards that Kaufmann had seen as a brave innovation, a harbinger of modernist abstraction.

Such a radical new form, for instance, is inherent in the idea of using a sphere as the basic form of an entire house. Most people have treated this notion as nothing more than a bad joke or a very ordinary piece of lunacy, while the more charitable have looked upon it [and here he is referring to the conclusion of his sometime Viennese colleague Emil Kaufmann] as an "experiment with form." The thing is certainly insane enough, but if it were no more than that, we should hardly be justified in wasting much time over it.

A nonsensical idea, however, need by no means be wholly without significance . . . such abnormalities reveal very specific characteristics . . . Thus the sphere when used as the shape of a building is a critical form which . . . is a symptom of a profound crisis both in architecture and in the whole life of the human spirit. Here we are beginning to deal with the zone of the unconscious . . . [LC, 4]

Sedlmayr saw this non-architectural form as the fatal symptom of an abstraction that had, with Le Corbusier, reached its most nonsensical and anti-architectural end. Agreeing with Kaufmann that autonomy was the key (it "implies that architecture under Ledoux had as it were become conscious of its own true nature – it was the same idea that animated Loos and Le Corbusier"), Sedlmayr castigates the Maison Savoye at Poissy, the epitome of Corbusian modernism for Sigfried Giedion and perhaps for Kaufmann too, as it rested "upon its supports upon the lawn," nothing more than the image of "a spaceship that has just landed." [LC,107] Le Corbusier's pictures, wrote Sedlmayr in disgust," are full of floating transparent things." [LC,101]

Sedlmayr is here opposed to the "autonomous" nature of this geometrical architecture – its apparent repulsion for the earth, an architecture wishing to fly, transparent, floating in the air; and thereby no longer holding to its tectonic foundations, and dangerously open to the deleterious effects of what he calls "paper architecture." It is no coincidence that Sedlmayr uses Kaufmann as the scholarly source of every one of his critical description of the dreams, unhappy visions, and "shadow values" of Boullée's and Ledoux's architecture. Indeed, Kaufmann is acknowledged as the source of Sedlmayr's whole study, as, in his postface, he admits:

The very beginnings of this work were inspired by the research of Emil Kaufmann on Ledoux, which came to my notice in 1930. I saw at once that Kaufmann had succeeded in making a discovery of the utmost importance towards the understanding of our age, but that at the same time he had not wholly recognized the true significance of his own discovery, and that the phenomena so clearly perceived by him were not correctly evaluated. [LC]

Of course, this does not prevent Sedlmayr from claiming almost equal credit, as he recounts that he expounded the "thoughts . . . developed here" in *Verluste der Mitte* in a lecture given in 1934, and again in 1937 in a discourse that was not published," finally to set them down in 1941, and giving them "in university lectures in 1941 and 1944."[42]

This debate between Kaufmann and Sedlmayr has generally been seen, in art historical circles at least, as the starting point for the reevaluation of Revolutionary architecture, as well as the origin of many myths only recently dispelled by less formalistic and more historically dispassionate research. But, for the moment, I would want to hold such criticism, in order to follow up the fundamental distinction drawn by Hubert Damisch between what semiologists and their heirs over the last decades have spoken of as the "meaning of architecture," considering architecture as a system of communication, and the question, posed by Damisch of "what architecture means" in a specific moment. According to these distinctions, when Kaufmann wrote in 1924 of classicism as demanding a "harmony" that confined "signification . . . to the intrinsic qualities of the subject and their expression," and of neoclassicism as seeing form as having "no other function than to be the support for thought,

Left to right

Haus eines Holzfaellers ("House of the Woodcutters"),
C.N. Ledoux, from *Architecture*, 1847.

Kugelhaus fuer Flurwaechter ("House for the Meadow
Watcher"), C.N Ledoux, from *Architecture*, 1847.

Panarétéon (Haus der Tugenden) ("House of Virtue"),
C.N. Ledoux, from *Architecture*, 1847.

to transmit impressions, to provoke sensations," he was perhaps not so much seeing these two architectures as accomplishing this goal within their particular societies and cultures, as *aspiring* to that goal in their theories and ideals. Thus, similarly, when he speaks of Ledoux in the same breath as Kant and Rousseau, he was perhaps not so much claiming that there is an inner essence in Ledoux's architecture that is Kantian, nor certainly that Ledoux had read Kant or wished to be a Kantian architect, but more simply that there seemed to be a homology between, in their different realms, Ledoux's use of separate, independent, geometric forms, and say, Kant's desire for principles of independent critical judgement, and Rousseau's return to the principle of "natural man." I say "more simply," but in fact, such relations introduce a complexity in the interpretative structure that is belied by the crude juxtaposition, and that goes well beyond the equally crude "social/economic/formal" postulations of Marxist art historians of the period. Here, Kaufmann is less a follower of the psychological formalism of the Vienna School than an adherent of the principles of his mentor, Max Dvořak's, concept of "the history of art as the history of ideas."[43]

Admittedly, Kaufmann has been cast as a reductive systematizer in his attempt to construct an interpretative scheme derived from Riegl's kunstwollen that corresponded to architecture in particular. And yet his notion of an "architectural system" as developed in writings after his emigration to the United States offered a far more precise tool of analysis. As he defined it, "attention is focused not so much on problems of style, nor on descriptions of single features, nor even on the investigation into general form, but rather upon the interrelation of the several parts of the composition, and especially the relationship between the several components and the whole architectural composition itself."[44] But here we have moved beyond a generic "will to form," and even beyond Sedlmayr's static "structural analysis," to a flexible model that approximates not only similar types in music and literature, as well as painting, but also, in this case, the architect's own design procedures.

The architecture of the late eighteenth and nineteenth centuries has much in common with classical and Baroque art. But these common traits concern only the surface. The continued use of classical features creates a certain superficial resemblance between these periods preceding and following the Revolution. Only by an analysis based on the concept of an "architectural system," can we appreciate how fundamentally the mode of architectural composition was transformed. [JSAH, 13]

The comparison and matching of such a structure once identified with similar structures in thought and social life was entirely flexible and always shifting:

In the relationship between forms and system, each epoch establishes its own basic ideas of disposition and interrelation of parts. Either older forms are remodeled until they are perfectly adjusted to the new system of arrangement; or new forms proffered by new constructional methods are adopted if they accord with the new system; or natural forms are reinterpreted in keeping with the changed ideal of general disposition. The search for new forms is, therefore, a necessary consequence of the desire for a new system. Forms themselves are secondary factors; the system is the primary consideration. [JSAH, 18]

We might characterize this method, as opposed to the more psychological and teleological "structural analysis" of Sedlmayr, as not so much structural as "*structuralist*" paralleling similar contemporary attempts to identify systems of relationships in linguistics and symbols by, say, Cassirer and Panofsky in other domains.

But again Kaufmann's structuralism has a history that grounds it in temporality, and even though his history falls short of Schapiro's desired social and economic enquiries, it is rigorously enough based in intellectual develop-

ments. Indeed it is clear that Kaufmann intends us to see his "architectural system" as on the same plane as and commensurate with intellectual developments, as the manifestation, in other words, of the architect's thought processes. This is what he means when he speaks of "peering behind the facade of architectural development" to "discover the metaphysical background of building" in a particular era. [JSAH, 18] This notion of the particular era was fundamental to Kaufmann's view of the specificity of history. As he noted in a review of Nils's study of the work of Louis-Jean Desprez, "each epoch requires specific categories of treatment." New material should not be interpreted within the categories "derived, originally, from the production of another (as a rule prior) period," but rather according to "some new approach adequate to their novel ways." He concluded: "The idea of all-embracing categories is a chimaera. Still worse, of course, is the sterile application of categories formed on the accomplishments of a different period."[45]

Kaufmann elaborated on this in a review article of 1946:

We live in a time in which the gathering and recording of factual data are often considered the unique end of art history. No doubt such activity is indispensable. Yet one should not overlook the fact that it does not require much originality to transform a card file into a book, after having added just a few details to the findings of many predecessors in a field labored, perhaps, through centuries. One should rate higher the biographer who ventures out into unmapped territory, who discovers a forr proffers a new picture of a personality, and en era. Such a biographer is more likely to err in his evaluations and comments than the simple compiler, although the latter is by no menas infallible in his attributions. Art history should not care less about the epiphenomenon than the phenomenon. The biographer who struggles to grasp the meaning of artistic production will become a source of stimulus and progress for the discipline even when he errs. Needless to say, these remarks apply still better to those rare historians who, gifted with a keen vision, rediscover or reinterpret a whole epoch as, e.g., did the scholars who about 1900 inaugurated the study of the Baroque, or those who somewhat later brough Mannerism to light. Intepretative history alone is constructive history.[46]

In this quasi-autobiographical justification, we sense no only the pathos of the lonely explorer, the destitute scholar searching for his "California," but also the consciousness of the heroic role of scholarship itself as, building on its formative achievements, has the courage to invent its own future. More or less penniless after his flight from Europe, Kaufmann had eked out a living on grants from the Fulbright Committee and the American Philosophical Society, finding in the Avery Library and numerous other collections more general material for his expanding studies of enlightenment and renaissance architecture. He died forlornly on his second journey to Los Angeles in 1953 in Cheyenne, Wyoming. It was with characteristic humility that Kaufmann admitted in his posthumously published book: "I do not believe that I have solved the momentous problem of how the architectural transformation of about 1800 came to pass."[47]

VON KAUFMANN BIS JOHNSON UND ROSSI

The cubic, "absolute" form of my glass house and the separation of functional units into two absolute shapes rather than a major or minor massing of parts comes directly from Ledoux, the Eighteenth Century father of modern architecture (see Emil Kaufmann's excellent study Von Ledoux bis Le Corbusier). The cube and the sphere, the pure mathematical shapes, were dear to the hearts of those intellectual revolutionaries from the Baroque, and we are their descendants.

Philip Johnson, *Architectural Review*, 1950[48]

In retrospect, it was perhaps not entirely an accident, nor totally ironic, that Kaufmann's belief that architecture's "autonomy" was held to parallel the emerging "autonomy" of the bourgeois (modern) individual was to appeal so strongly to that paradigm of the high bourgeois architect Philip Johnson. Sometime between 1938 and 1940, with perhaps a brief stay in London on the way, Kaufmann fled to the United States; in 1942, he was asked to present his work to the newly constituted Society of Architectural Historians at the Cambridge house of Philip Johnson, whose visits to Germany with Henry-Russell Hitchcock had alerted him to the growing interest in eighteenth century neo-classicism. The text of this talk, Kaufmann's first English-language article, was published in the next year in the *Journal of the American Society of Art Historians*.

Based on Johnson's own encounter with German history and theory, it was Kaufmann who provided the convenient link between the neoclassicism of Schinkel, admired by both National Socialists and the then sympathetic Johnson, and the modernism of Le Corbusier and Mies, as he had described the trajectory of modern architecture beginning with the Enlightenment and culminating in Le Corbusier. Johnson had read Kaufmann's 1933 book *Von Ledoux bis Le Corbusier*, and was easily able to reconcile Kaufmann's formal linkage of Ledoux and Le Corbusier with his own predilection for Schinkel and Mies — *von Schinkel bis Mies* seemed a natural corollary to Kaufmann's *Von Ledoux bis Le Corbusier* as was the implied extension, "Von Schinkel, Ledoux, Le Corbusier, und Mies, bis Johnson." But of course, the entire architectural career of Johnson, racing to keep up with the stylistic zeitgeist, seemed to celebrate the aesthetic autonomy of the discipline.

Writing on his Glass House in New Canaan, Connecticut, in the *Architectural Review* of 1950, Johnson specifically cited Kaufmann's book in order to link the geometrical forms of Ledoux to his own cubic design. Architectural "autonomy," by which Johnson meant variously: the free play of architectural language as style, the independence of architecture from society, and the personal freedom to change style at whim, thence became a watchword of his practice. Indeed the entire article was a neat and entirely unabashed collage of Kaufmann, Le Corbusier, and Mies van der Rohe, in eight easy stages. First, Johnson illustrates Le Corbusier's 1933 plan for a village farm in order to describe the approach to his own house: "the footpath pattern between the two houses I copied from the spiderweb-like forms of Le Corbusier, who delicately runs his communications without regard for the axis of his buildings or seemingly any kind of pattern." Secondly, Mies's plan for IIT, 1939 is adduced for the formal layout of the two pavilions in New Canaan. This precedent is followed quickly by Theo van Doesburg's painting (the origin of Johnson's "asymmetric sliding rectangles"), August Choisy's plan and perspective of the Athenian Acropolis, one already commandeered by Le Corbusier to illustrate the dynamic force of non-rectilinear plans in *Vers une Architecture*, Schinkel's Casino in Glienecke, and, as a prelude to Mies's glass-house idea, Ledoux's spherical House of the Agricultural Guards, so much loved by Kaufmann and hated by Sedlmayr. But now, in 1949–50 Johnson has cast aside any residual affection for National Socialist culture, and prefers to follow the progressive path of modernism, from Ledoux to Le Corbusier; thence to Kasimir Malevitch and the Suprematist painting that afforded the plan of the Glass House with a circle in a rectangle, and finally to Mies, who concludes the eight points of Johnson's new architecture with the Farnsworth House, 1947–1950. Such a neat re-writing of history, a reversal in a sense of the progressive movement described by the historians of Kaufmann's generation, will be a leitmotif of "postmodernism" from the 1960s on.

The paradox, of course, is that Johnson, often criticized for "betraying Mies" in the obviously box-like and non-universal counter-horizontal space of the Glass House was there following Kaufmann's principles of autonomy almost to the letter. Revealing his deeper affinities with German neo-classicism and Schinkel, but disguising them by a side-trip to France and liberal, idealist classicist modernism, Johnson in fact produces a transparent "Ledoux" box, that "proves" Kaufmann's thesis even more powerfully than Le Corbusier (too wedded to the horizontally open Domimo diagram) could have ever accomplished. Perhaps this was the fate of "late modernisms," to authorize already written history rather than making it for themselves.[49]

RATIONALISM TO NEORATIONALISM

Thirty years after the completion of the Glass House, the architect Aldo Rossi, also working out of concepts he derived from Kaufmann's analysis of Enlightenment architecture, saw in the concept of "autonomy" a means of saving architecture from an increasingly disseminated field of aesthetic, social, and political authorizations, and understood the word to refer to the internal structure of architectural typologies and forms, as they formed part of the sedimented structure of the historical city.

For Rossi, however, as evinced by his reviews and critical writings from the late 1950s on, "autonomy" also represented the purest heritage of Enlightenment, and thence the modern movement, for an age that had lost its sense of roots in the eclecticism, and more to the point, in the adjustments required by the post-fascist political struggles of the immediate postwar period. In this context, Rossi's fascination with the geometrical forms of late Enlightenment architecture was more than a simple attempt to recuperate the sources of pre- and modernist minimalism, but was grounded in his reading of Kaufmann's writings, not only of *Von Ledoux bis Le Corbusier*, but also of his post-war books, *Three Revolutionary Architects: Boullée, Ledoux, Lequeu* (1953) and the more general, posthumously published, *Architecture in the Age of Reason, Baroque and Post-Baroque in England, Italy, and France.* (1955). It was these books that Rossi reviewed for *Casabella*, taking note of the earlier 1930s essays, and found in them a programmatic source for his "neo" rationalism, joining Ledoux, and Boullée (whose *Essai sur l'architecture* he translated and introduced in Italian) not only to Le Corbusier, but equally to his own modernist hero, Adolf Loos. The early critical writings of Rossi include ample evidence of his study of Enlightenment theory by way of Kaufmann, thence to be translated into research into specifically Italian examples (Milizia to Antonelli) and modernist parallels (Loos).

Thus for Rossi, the idea of an "autonomous architecture" was quite naturally joined to that of a "rational architecture." Thus, when in 1973 Aldo Rossi as curator of the international section of the Milan Triennale sought to identify those architects who, in Manfredo Tafuri's words espoused an "autonomy of language," he collected them together under the banner of "Rational Architecture." The premises of a "Neo- Rationalism" that became evident in the Biennale represented the beliefs of many Italian and French designers, from Aldo Rossi to Bernard Huet and Leon Krier, that architecture was in some sense a discipline of its own, that its "language" was derived from former architectures, and that its form and role in the city was as much a product of an historical urban structure, as it was of social or political concerns. Where, that is, in the politicized climate of the 1960s, society had been seen as the generator of space and shelter, in the 1970s, perhaps in reaction to the evident loss of architecture this implied, architecture asserted its own determinism. Fueled by Rossi's *Architecture of the City*, a kind of "structuralism" in urban analysis, and a semiotics of architectural analysis thus emerged as the equivalent of the revival of Russian Formalism, so-called "Cartesian" linguistics, and deconstruction in literary studies. "Autonomy" of the text and of the building were seen as

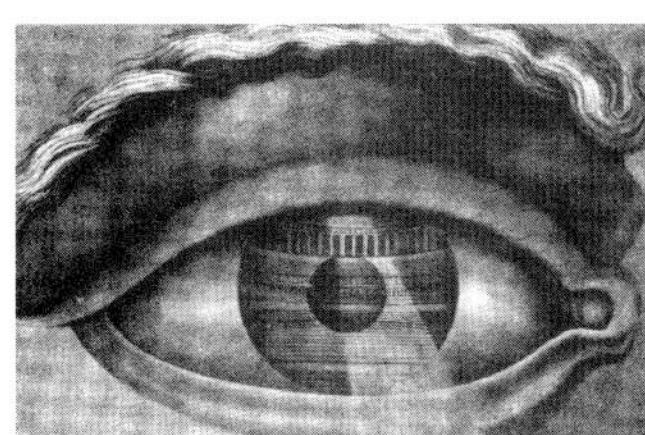

Blick in das Theater von Besancon, C.N. Ledoux, from *Architecture*, 1847.

parallel and complimentary facets of the refusal of socio-political narrative, the vagaries of urban development planning, and what Nikolaus Pevsner had already identified in 1960 as "the return of historicism."

Hubert Damisch, in his preface to the first (1981) French translation of *Von Ledoux bis le Corbusier* entitled "Ledoux avec Kant" with its echoes of Lacan's own aleatory preface to the Marquis de Sade's *La Philosophie dans le boudoir*, "Kant avec Sade," notes this peculiar fascination of the 1970s with the idea of autonomy, as directly linked to the continuity of Kantian thought, asking what it would be to couple Kant's analysis of the origins of geometry in the *Critique of Pure Reason*, with that autonomous geometry of Ledoux, in order to meditate on the special "autonomy" of architecture, from Ledoux to Le Corbusier to Loos and thence to the autonomies claimed by the new Neorationalism of the late 1970s:

At our present moment, when the history of architecture hesitates between a renewed form of the history of styles and a form of institutional analysis which ignores everything that comprises the proper material of architecture, the idea of autonomy, to take it in the philosophical sense, takes on the value of a regulating concept. To think Ledoux with Kant is to recognize that in architecture understanding does not proceed solely from history, or in other words, with Kant, that an understanding which subjectively presents itself as history with respect to the way in which it has been acquired, can participate, objectively, in one form or another of rationality.[49]

To think of Ledoux with Kant, Damisch concludes, is to ask what constitutes architecture as an object, not only of history, but also of thought, and thought that is constrained by conditions that are a priori formal, or in another sense, internal to the discipline of architecture.

CONCLUSION

This is not the first time that the idea of an historical language of architecture as a condition of its autonomy has been debated in architecture.
Peter D. Eisenman, "Autonomy and the Avant-Garde," 1996.[50]

In a conference honoring the career of Philip Johnson, and entitled "Autonomy and Ideology," the theme was resurrected, but now in a more distant, historical, sense, as one that neatly joined the trajectory of Johnson's work to a newly aroused interest in the various "modernisms" of the 1940s, 50s, and 60s, and this once more to a preoccupation with the discipline of architecture.[51] As presented at the 1998 conference, the Johnsonian saga was fundamentally reliant on "autonomy" as it made its first appearance in the Glass House projects and building of 1948–9. This desired "return to disciplinary roots," one that has naturally followed similar calls in the humanities and social sciences in the wake of the inter-disciplinary experiments and critical innovations of post-structuralism, seems to answer a number of concerns in a generation unconvinced by the pluralism of post-modernism. A return to the fundamentals of architecture, in the modern tradition generally represented by abstraction, minimalism, the pluralism of post-modernism, would counter architecture's always suspect relations to the "society of the spectacle" and its consumerist aftermath.

As evidenced by the papers given at the conference, historians, critics, and architects agreed generally that "modernism" in some form, whether classic "high" modernism or the less polemical but more socially present modernism of the immediate postwar period (corporate modernism, domestic modernism, suburban modernism), or even "counter-modernism" of the kind posed by Kiesler, was decidedly preferable to postmodernism, and more than this, to the "deconstructivism" that, in the Johnson itinerary, had supplanted it in the 1980s. Thus the conference proposed to satisfy a number of questions at once:

Johnson was endowed with an over-arching theme that superficially at least made historical and critical sense of his otherwise eclectic work; postmodernism was definitively abandoned, together with the relativizing theories that seemed to support it; and, in a nice turn of intellectual agenda, a new post-theory, pragmatic era implicitly opened up.

Beneath this often self-contradictory trajectory of the idea of "autonomy" in architecture, we can trace all the tensions evoked by the history of the concept of "Enlightenment," in the twentieth century. From the general assumption of "progress" and "reason" common to the Third Republic and its liberal interpretations of the Revolution, to the contested domain of social democracy after the First World War, to the defensive pro-modernist posture of the idealist avant-garde and its Popular Front allies in the 1930s, to the despairing and negative critique of Enlightenment developed by Adorno and Horkheimer in exile, to the reassertion of democratic values in the post-War Frankfurt School against the pessimism of a withdrawn and posthistorical conservatism, and thence to the renewal of "form" and "structure" as a renewal tactic for architecture in the 1970s, and finally to the quasi-nostalgic revival of the idea of autonomy itself in the 1990s; all this attests to the power of Kant's idea that, both formal and political, implies at once freedom and order, collective reason and expressed individuality.

NOTES

1   Clement Greenberg, "Modernist Painting," *The Collected Essays and Criticism* ed. John O'Brian. In 4 volumes, Volume 4 (Chicago: Chicago University Press, 1993), p.85.

2   The following article is an expansion of arguments made first in my *Claude-Nicholas Ledoux: Architecture and Social reform at the end of the Ancien Regime* (Cambridge, MA: MIT Press, 1989) and developed into two articles, "Researching Revolutionary Architecture," *Journal of Architectural Education*, August (1991), 206–211 and "From Ledoux to Le Corbusier, to Johnson, to . . ." *Progressive Architecture*, May (1991). Since then, the connections between Johnson and Kaufmann have been elaborated by Detlef Mertens in "System and Freedom: Sigfried Giedion, Emil Kaufmann and the Constitution of Architectural Modernity," in R.E. Somol, ed. *Autonomy and Ideology: Positioning an Avant-Garde in America* (New York: Monticelli Press, 1997), pp. 212–231.
My interest in Emil Kaufmann was initiated by Colin Rowe at Cambridge in the Fall of 1959, as, in my first week of architectural study, at my first and terrifying tutorial at his quasi-modernist apartment on Fen Causeway, and from the depths of his Eames Director's chair, abruptly swinging round to face me, he handed me a copy of the recently published *Architecture in the Age of Reason* with the question: "Well, and what do you make of concatenation?" Supported by this initiation I was able to make the relations between Kaufmann's modernism and his own subject matter of my first discussion with Philip Johnson in 1964. The longer term consequences of Rowe's first question are marked in my life-long interest in Ledoux and Le Corbusier. This particular essay grew out of three invitations:to present a paper at the conference "The Last Things Before the Last," organized by the PhD students in the School of Architecture at Columbia University; to respond to a paper by Barbara Johnson at a conference organized by T.J.Clark at Berkeley and the San Francisco MOMA under the title "What was Modernism and Why Won't it Go Away;" and to present a paper at the conference in Paris organized by ANY Magazine in 1999. A more developed version of this paper was read at a Getty conference on architectural history and art history in the Spring of 2000, and at a symposium on the "Culture of Disenchantment" hosted by the Center for Modern and Contemporary Studies UCLA, 2001. I have benefitted from the responses, conversations and debates at all these conferences.

3   The best contemporary summary of Kaufmann's contribution is by Detlef Mertens, "System and Freedom: Sigfried Giedeon, Emil Kaufmann and the Constitution of Architectural Modernity," in R.E. Somol, ed. *Autonomy and Ideology: Positioning an Avant-Garde in America* (New York: Monticelli Press, 1997), pp. 212–231. For a brief summary of Kaufmann's life, see Meyer Schapiro, "Obituary of Emil Kaufmann," *College of Art Journal*. Winter (1954), 144. For the contemporary assessment of Kaufmann, see Georges Teyssot "Neoclassic and 'Autonomous' Architecture: the Formalism of Emil Kaufmann 1891–1953," in Dimitri Porphyrios, ed., "On the Methodology of Architectural History," *Architectural Digest* 51 (1981), pp.24–29; Gilbert Erouart, "Situation d'Emil Kaufman," in Emil Kaufmann, *Trois architects revolutionaires: Boulee, Ledoux, Lequeu*, ed. Gilbert Erouart and Georges Teyssot (Paris, 1978), pp.5–11. See also, Monique Mosser, "Situation d'Emil K.," *De Ledoux a Le Corbusier: Origines de l'architecture moderne*, Introduction, J.L. Avril, Arc-et-Senans: Edition Foundation C.N. Ledoux, 1987, 84–89: Daniel Rabreau, "Critique d'Emil Kaufmann, 'Trois architectes revolutionaires,'" *Bulletin Monumental*, 1979, 78–81.

4   Emil Kaufmann, *Von Ledoux bis Le Corbusier: Ursprung und Entwicklung der Autonomen Architektur* (Vienna and Leipzig: Rolf Passer, 1933).

5   For responses to Kaufmann in the 1930s, see Meyer Schapiro, "The New Viennese School," *The Art Bulletin* XVII, 1936, 258–266; Eduardo Perisco, Scritti, critici e polemici, ed. Rossa and Ballo (Milan), p.210; Hans Sedlmayr, *Verlust der Mitte – Die bildende kunst des 19. Und 20. Jahrhunderts ald Symptom und Symbol der Ziet* (Otto Mueller Verlag: Salzburg, 1948), Translated by Brian Battershaw in *Art as Crisis: The Lost Centre* (London: Hollis and Carter, 1957).

6   Allan Braham, *The Architecture of the French Enlightenment* (Berkeley: University of California Press, 1980), p.7; David Watkin, *The Rise of Architectural History* (Chicago: University of Chicago Press, 1980), p.180.

7   Christopher S. Wood, ed. *The Vienna School Reader: Politics and Art Historical Method in the 1930s* (New York: ZONE Books, 2000), p.69.

8   Meyer Schapiro, op. Cit., and Walter Benjamin, *Das Passagen-Werk*, ed. Rolf Tiedemann, Gesammelte Schriften, Vol. 5 (1982). Translated Howard Eiland, Kevin McLaughlin as *The Arcades Project* (Cambridge, MA: Harvard University Press, 1999).

9   Kaufmann, *Three Revolutionary Architects, Boulee, Ledoux and Lequeu in Transactions of the American Philosophical Society* Volume 42, Part 3 (October, 1952) pp.431–564.

10   Kaufmann, *Architecture in the Age of Reason: Baroque and Post-Baroque in England, Italy and France* (Cambridge, MA: Harvard University Press, 1955).

11   See Franz Schulze, *Philip Johnson: Life and Work* (New York: Knopf, 1994) pp.157–8; 194–6; 216.

12   Aldo Rossi, *Scritti scelti sul'arcitettura e la citta*, 1956–1972, ed. Rosaldo Bonicalzi (Milan: CLUP, 1975), pp.62–71 ("Emil Kaufmann e l'architettura dell'Illuminismo," *Cassabella continuita*, 222 (1958)). Kaufmann's influence is seen also in Rossi's "Introduzione a Boulêe," [1967] The introduction to Rossi's translation of Boullee's *Architecture: Essai sur l'art* (Scritti scelti, pp.346–364) and the article "L'architettura dell'Illuminismo," [1973] (Scritti scelti, pp.454–478).

13   R.E. Somol, ed., *Autonomy and Ideology*.

14   Emil Kaufmann, "Die Architectkturtheorie der Franzosischen Klassik und der Klassizismus," *Repertorium für Kunstwissenschaft*, XLIV (1924), pp.197–237. This account of "neoclassicism" was elaborated in the review article "Klassizismus als tendenz und als epoche," *Kritische Berichte zur Kunstgeschichtlichen Literatur* (1933), pp. 201–214, which considered reviewed concepts of "klassizismus" from Riegl, Schmarsow, Paul Zucker, Frankl, Brinckmann, Giedion [*Spatbaroker und romantischer Klassizismus*, 1922], Wilhelm Pinder, and Wolfgang Herrmann [Deutschen Baukunst des 19. und 20. Jahrhunderts, 1932–330]. See George Teyssot, "Neoclassic and Autonomous Architecture," pp.25–26.

15   George Teyssot, "Neoclassic and Autonomous Architecture," pp.25–26. Teyssot has effectively analyzed the debates over this stylistic and periodic ascription, noting Sigfried Giedion's 1922 thesis entitled *Spätbarocker und romantischer Klassizismus* "Late Baroque Neoclassicism" and "Romantic Neoclassicism," which took off directly from Riegl's own attempt to revise the characterization of another neglected period, that of the Spätromische.

16   Friedrich Nietzsche, Human, *All Too Human A Book for Free Spirits*. Trans. R.J Hollingdale, Introduction by Richard Schacht (Cambridge: Cambridge University Press, 1996), p.101 [*Menschliches, Allzumenschliches*, 1878].

17   Kaufmann, "Die Architekturtheorie," p.226. Translation Georges Teyssot, "Neoclassic and 'Autonomous' Architecture," p. 24, slightly altered.

18   Emil Kaufmann, *Von Ledoux bis Le Corbusier*, p.45. See also "Die stadt des Architekten Ledoux," p.146: "Stein ist weider Stein."

19   After 1925, save for a slim book on the architecture of the city of Baden [*Die Kunst der Stadt Baden* (Vienna: Osterreichischer Bundesverlag, 1925)] Kaufmann concentrated his research on the architects of the late eighteenth century, especially Ledoux. He contributed the entry on Ledoux to the Thieme-Becker encyclopedia and an article on the German painter, Ferdinand Georg Walmueller. The concept of autonomous architecture, however, was present in none of these early studies, save perhaps by implication, as when, in 1929,
Kaufmann characterized Ledoux's architecture, with its geometrical play of masses, as "anti-Baroque." [Emil Kaufmann, "Architektonische Entwürfe aus der zeit der französichen Revolution," Zeitschrift für bildende Kunst, LXII, 1929–30, p.45.]

20   Emil Kaufmann, "C.N. Ledoux under der klassizistische Kirchenbau," *Kirchenkunst*, III (1931), p.62.

21   Ibid., p.62.

22   Emil Kaufmann, "Die stadt des Architekten Ledoux: Zur Erkenntnis der Autonomen Architektur," *Kunstwissenschaftliche Forschungen*, II, Berlin (1933). p.131–160.

23   Ibid., p.133.

24   Ibid., p.138.

25   Ibid., p.142.

26   Ledoux, *L'Architecture*, p.185, p.115.

27   Kaufmann does not provide a note to this source until the publication of his *Three Revolutionary Architects. Boullée, Ledoux, Lequeu*.

28   Ibid., p.146.

29   Ledoux, *L'Architecture*, p. 234.

30   Ibid., pp.152–3.

31   Kaufmann, "Die Stadt," p.153. Translation from Georges Teyssot, "Neoclassic and Autonomous Architecture," p.26.

32   Kaufmann, *Von Ledoux bis Le Corbusier*, p.3. All future references to this work will be in the text in the form [VLLC].

33   Kaufmann was direct in his criticism of historians who looked only to Schinkel and German Neoclassicism: "The 'Prussian Style' is no more than the German immitation of French Revolutionary architecture." Kaufmann, *Von Ledoux bis Le Corbusier*, p.50.

34   Central to Kaufmann's analysis of Ledoux was the treatise that Ledoux had published two years before his death, the magisterial first volume of a planned five volume work, *L'Architecture considérée sous le rapport de l'art, des moeurs et de la législation*. This work, with

its 416 folio pages of text and 125 engraved plates of Ledoux's built and ideal projects, constituted the main evidence for what was, in the 1920s known of Ledoux; indeed, despite subsequent discoveries of original drawings for specific projects, and archival verification of the dates of certain commissions, *L'Architecture*, with all its amphibolic excesses and architectural hubris still remains central to any interpretation of Ledoux. The two central post-Kaufmann studies of Ledoux remain, Michel Gallet, *Claude-Nicolas Ledoux, 1736–1806* (Paris: Picard, 1985) and Anthony Vidler, *Claude-Nicolas Ledoux, Architecture and Social Reform at the End of the Ancien Regime* (Cambridge, MA: MIT Press, 1989).

35 Kaufmann is here quoting F. Gundolf on Schlegel's "Lucinde," "an importance witness to a historical tendency: the first expression of the profound demand for an autonomy of sensual pleasures" in "the series of philosophical petitions in favor of the independence of the strengths and instincts of human nature, a series which is opened with Kant's affirmation of the autonomy of morals." [VLLC, 36].

36 Hannes Meyer, "La realidad Soviética: los arquitectos," *Arquitectura*, n.9 (1942); in English in *Task Magazine*, n.3 (1942). Reprinted in Hannes Meyer, Scritti 1921–1942. *Architettura o rivoluzione*, ed Francesco Dal Co, Padua: Marsilio (1969), pp. 214–215.

37 Theodor W. Adorno, Kant's "Critique of Pure Reason," ed Rolf Tiedemann. Trans Rodney Livingstone (Stanford: Stanford University Press, 2001), pp.54–55.

38 Ernst Cassirer, "Das Problem Jean-Jacques Rousseau," *Archiv für Geschichte der Philosophie*, XLI (1932), 177–213, 479–513. The intertwined histories of Kaufmann and Cassirer were again to intersect with the publication much later of the English edition of Cassirer's *Philosophy of the Enlightenment*, and Kaufmann's posthumously published *Architecture in the Age of Reason* (1955).

39 Kaufmann, "Die Stadt," p. 41.

40 Ledoux, *L'Architecture*, pp.65, 91,135: "Le sentiment apprécié d'un plan est à l'abri de toute domination. Il émane du sujet, il doit adapter à la nature des lieux et des besoins," (65) "Tout détail est inutile, je dis plus, nuisible, quand il devise les surfaces par des additions mesquines ou mensonges." (91) "Toutes les forms que l'on décrit d'un seul trait de compas sont avouées par le goét. Le cercle, le carré, voilà les lettres alphabétiques que les auteurs emploient dans la texture des meilleurs ouvrages." (135).

41 Richard J. Neutra, *Wie baut Amerika?* (1927), pp.62, 69.

42 Paranoia seems to have been the common disease of both Sedlmayr and Kaufmann. Sedlmayr concludes his study of the loss of center in sullen resentment that his formulation of Kaufmann's Ledoux had not been received as authoritative: "Whoever upholds the doctrine of "the lost center" can be certain from the outset to perceive the consequences of doing so personally. He will have against him not only those people who reject what is new because it is unaccustomed, but also those who only propagate what is new because it is "contemporary," "modern," and therefore interesting" "worshippers of the past and futurists united against him." Kaufmann's footnotes in *Architecture in the Age of Reason* are no less bitter: "Hans Sedlmayr, *Verlust der Mitte* (Salzburg, 1948), p. 98. Having myself pointed out the extraordinary significance of the revolutionary

designs and interpreted them as symptoms of their period (*Von Ledoux*, p. 11, 25, etc.), I certainly do not underrate what Sedlmayr terms *kritische Formen*. However, the large number of original and yet "normal" inventions reveals that the complex period with all its excitement was sound enough to bring about a true regeneration of architecture. In the Epilogue to his book, Sedlmayr points out that my rediscovery of Ledoux became the starting point of his investigation into the formative forces of our era. Though he does not fully agree with my interpretation, he nonetheless adopts most of my concepts and observations, especially those of the new decentralization in composition … the abolition of the old aesthetic canons … the increasing hostility to decoration … the new "mobility" of furniture … the altered relationship between structure and environment … the ideal of equality in architecture … the triumph of elementary geometry … the parallel phenomena in the graphic arts, particularly the fashion of the silhouette … the end of the Baroque anthropomorphisms and the new attitude towards matter … the coming up of new architectural tasks … the new sense of commodiousness … the presentation of new forms long before new materials fitting them were found … the continuity of the development after 1800 … the struggle of antagonistic tendencies in the nineteenth century … the appearance of a new structural order behind the masks of the various styles … and the typically nineteenth-century thought that perfect solutions of the past should be the standards for all the future." *Architecture in the Age of Reason*, Note 439, p.266. A few years earlier he was no less nervous in reviewing the book by Marcel Raval and J.-Ch. Moreux, *Claude-Nicolas Ledoux* (Paris: 1945), where he summarizes his "serious charge of plagiarism" in a long note. *Art Bulletin* XXX, no. 4, 1948, 288–291, note 3, p.289. Kaufmann was no less charitable to Helen Rosenau who had written on Lequeu and Boullée following up the leads provided by the Viennese scholar.

43 Max Dvořak, *The History of Art as the History of Ideas*, trans. John Hardy (London: Routledge and Kegan Paul, 1984). Dvořak's *Kunstgeschichte als Geistesgeschichte* had been published posthumously by his students (Munich: R. Piper and Co., 1924).

44 Kaufmann, "C.N. Ledoux," *Journal of the American Society of Architectural Historians*, July (1943), p.13. Future references in the text [JSAH].

45 Kaufmann, "Nils G. Wollin: 'Desprez en Suède,'" reviewed by E. Kaufmann, *Art Bulletin* XXVIII (1946), p.283.

46 Ibid., p.283.

47 Emil Kaufmann, *Architecture in the Age of Reason. Baroque and Post-Baroque in England, Italy, and France* (Cambridge: Harvard University Press, 1955). I would Like to think that Kaufmann on his first visit to Los Angeles had the satisfaction of finally seeing the work of Richard Neutra as it had emerged in the conclusion of *Von Ledoux bis Le Corbusier* as the ultimate destination for modernism: the utopia of a modernist social democratic California. I could even imagine the meeting of the two Viennese in Silver Lake. Certainly the copy of *Von Ledoux* in the UCLA library, bears Kaufmann's own careful signature as donated by the author.

48 Philip Johnson, "House at New Canaan, Connecticut," *Architectural Review*, CVIII, 645, (Sept. 1950), 152–159.

49 By contrast, as Mertens has noted, Kaufmann's "autonomy," already in the 1930s was adopted wholesale by

the architect Ludwig Hilberseimer, fellow exile with Mies van der Rohe in Chicago, as he asserted the language of the modernist avant-garde. In his book *Contemporary Architecture* of 1964, Hilberseimer joined together Russian Constructivism, Dutch Neoplasticism and Corbusian Purism under the heading "autonomous architecture," as if autonomy represented a kind of linguistic freedom.

50 Peter D. Eisenman, "Autonomy and the Avant-Garde: the Necessity of an Architectural Avant-Garde in America," in R.E. Somol, ed. *Autonomy and Ideology*, p.73.

51 R.E. Somol, ed. *Autonomy and Ideology*, p.73.

Quasi-Autonomy in Architecture: The Search for an 'In-between'

Recurrently, anxieties arise around such issues as these: can architecture be other than a mere servant to commercial/capitalist/ideological forces? Each society gets the architecture it deserves! Is not autonomous production the only way to avoid submersion in the material conditions of one's time? How can a formally driven enterprise like architecture address social issues responsibly (or at all)?

In the fall of 1991, I was invited to join what was dominantly a faculty colloquium at Harvard's Graduate School of Design. The event seemed to be an attempt to surface, and perhaps to resolve, competing positions within the pedagogy of the school. Did not an eminent international school of architecture need to conceive and represent itself as concerned with the most fundamental levels of its discipline? Should not the school represent to its students an ethical drive to address the social issues that confound the smaller and greater environments in which it finds itself?

At that point, it was easy to assert that social commitment in architecture could not be found through a vulgar Marxism that treats architecture as a mere epiphenomenon fully circumscribed by its infrastructural base. Nor could it be in any other form of social determinism that accounts for architecture wholly by forces external to it. Still more implausible was an architectural determinism in which the physical environment causes social behavior. How could one avoid determinism without finding oneself supporting a view of architecture as autonomous – without, that is, embracing architecture as a game, however beautiful or challenging the game might be? The morning ended inconclusively, with a general anxiety about choosing between social and disciplinary responsibility – the latter exemplified by concepts of autonomy in architecture.

The editors of this issue of *Perspecta* began from a position more congenial to me, seeking to examine "architecture's location between autonomous discipline and cultural product." The poles of autonomy and product are present in their formulation and invite the anxieties already noted, but the word "between" invites a discussion that does not remain polarized by those two positions.

STANFORD ANDERSON

Indeed, the editors anticipated the viability of an intermediate position when they referenced my article "Critical Conventionalism in Architecture" that opened the first issue of *Assemblage* in 1986.[1] One word from that essay, "quasi-autonomy," elicits the position to which I shall return here.[2]

In a polemical world, the exploration of positions away from the poles is often not welcome. Refusing to man the battlements at either pole appears, I suppose, wimpy. But our editors have risked entering such a discourse. In the portfolio section of this journal, K. Michael Hays recalls a time of polarization, around 1970, where he perceived a widespread concern with the instrumentalization of architecture, a concern that in turn elicited a significant reaction in the search for an autonomous architecture. In an aside, Hays noted that the editors, and even he, would not remember that time. With that prod, let me return to an unpublished essay that I presented at the Architectural Association in London and again at the ACSA Cranbrook meetings of 1966.

"Problem-Solving and Problem-Worrying" is a period piece to the extent that the problem-solving discussion illustrates the temper of the time and the instrumentalization to which Hays refers. That overt content of the essay sits recognizably in a more general sense of the malaise of architecture in the 1960s. The seeming triumph of architectural Modernism in the post-war years had by then degenerated to the rootless, decorative stylism of architects like Philip Johnson, Edward Durell Stone, and Minoru Yamasaki. Those architects and theoreticians who proposed problem-solving methods may or may not have troubled with criticism of this degenerative Modernism, but their search for a reliable, even scientific, method certainly gained attention through their ambition for an architecture that stemmed from a fundamental process based on empirical information.

My alternative of "problem-worrying" sought an alternative path, one that was in sympathy with the reciprocities of form and design exemplified in the only American architectural work of that moment that appeared to deserve critical acclaim – the work of Louis I. Kahn. Kahn was as strong in rhetorical persuasion as in architecture, but he was not one to polarize arguments or his

discipline. He remains a model for the value of inquiry between the poles.

So much for the setting of the 1966 essay.[3] In its critique of problem-solving, it already engaged the early developments in computation and design, at least some strains of which still seek to instrumentalize our discipline. In any case, the essay dwells on the "between" theme that has been a constant in my thought – and the reason for my participation in *Perspecta 33*. Since this historical piece is unpublished, and serves both as witness to a moment and grounds for a continuing position, we include the essay here in abbreviated form.

PROBLEM-SOLVING AND PROBLEM-WORRYING (1966)[4]

The notion of problem-solving, especially as architects have encountered it, is imbedded in a desire for justification. In stronger instances, there may be a belief that problem-solving routines will lead to justifiable results; in weaker instances there may be the belief that one's activity can be justified merely through using powerful, if misappropriated, techniques.

It is imperative that we do not warp human well being just for the sake of exploiting a technique – especially when the technique is a powerful one. As I shall argue in more detail, the concepts of problem-solving that interest architects involve either problems of achieving definite goals or problems of synthesizing from a body of established facts. Due to these characteristics of either definite goal orientation or inductivism, these notions of problem-solving are neither descriptive of the traditional behavior of the best architects nor applicable to the current problem situation of architecture. In contrast to "solving the problem," I will present another attitude toward problems –"problem-worrying." Let me attempt to characterize the notion of "problem-worrying" with words of a more positive connotation: architecture is concerned with structuring our environment to facilitate the achievement of human purposes where the purposes are incompletely known at the outset and cannot be extrapolated from known purposes. Indeed, human purpose is altered by the very environment that is created to facilitate it. The structuring of the environment must be accomplished, then, through the exercise of tentative foresight and critical examination of that foresight and the actions to which it leads. According to this description, neither the human purposes nor the architect's methods are determined in advance. Consequently, if this interpretation of the architectural problem situation is correct, any problem-solving technique that relies on explicit problem definition or distinct goal-orientation will distort the human purposes involved.

In architecture, the demand for systematic design arises from a situation that is quite generally recognized. Increasingly, it seems, the works of even our most renowned architects are open to serious criticism, and regardless of the severity of the criticism, architects are incapable of justifying what they do. Systems-oriented architects appear to interpret this situation in the following way: If our building were to fit its problem perfectly, then there could be no criticism and we could justify both method and product. Such a perfect fit, they continue, can only be achieved if we have a well-structured, detailed description of the problem and then generate the solution from the problem statement. It is fortunate, they suggest, that we have new sciences and tools that can aid the designer in this program of the complete definition of the problem and synthesis of the solution.

Certain recent developments in the United States that treat architecture as systematic problem-solving may be of interest. There are now signs that the exploratory studies in the adaptation of electronic communication and data processing, of systems analysis, and other new techniques are about to receive generalized, semi-official support from the architectural establishment. Recently, The American Institute of Architects and Princeton University entered into an agreement to study the key problems of the architectural profession and of the professional education of the architect. The principal intention is that the study will result in educational reform. Included in the first document from Princeton was "A List of Key Problems in Architecture." The list began with a problem stated as question and answer, as follows: 1) How can we improve competence in environmental programming? a) Develop more effective techniques of problem-stating and problem-solving. Top priority is given to the role of the program in architecture, to problem-stating, and this leads on to the satisfaction of the program, problem-solving.

I do not want to go too far in pre-judging the A.I.A./Princeton project, which is only getting underway.[5] However, I think their proposals do illustrate the second justificational approach to problem-solving that is more common among architects. Rather than seeking a clearly-defined goal (the first justificational approach), this approach is inductive, seeking to define the problem carefully in order to have a fixed standard against which to judge any proposed problem solution.

The desire to justify one's actions on the basis of their conformity with the original program statement denies consideration of the fact that any concerted set of design proposals and evaluations will alter the architect's understanding of the problem. There can also be no exploration of the fact that any proposal will entail unintended consequences. To whatever degree these can be foreseen, the problem should be reconsidered.

This approach can be criticized, then, in at least two serious ways: 1) the usual problem of inductivist methods is that they can never be sure of adequate data from which to synthesize, or even adequate data to check against; and 2) that the process of creative design is artificially simplified in order that it may be viewed systematically and its results justified by their consistency with an initial statement.

Systematic problem-solving design is not, of course, the only possible alternative to the current, easily criticizable situation of architectural design. If, then, systematic design is not the only alternative and is itself open to serious criticism, why should the adoption of these techniques seem to be imperative?

Our society certainly encourages an enthusiasm for new techniques, but such a compulsion is especially deeply rooted — explicitly and implicitly — in the thinking of architects. This compulsion stems from the acceptance of the nineteenth-century doctrine that architecture is the physical expression, and perhaps the fullest expression, of the spirit of the time. Once this notion is accepted for past times, and once it is realized that we live in a different time, the necessity arises to discover the spirit of our time and the forms that will express that spirit. Such a search for spirits and expressions can lead to various situations, but one compelling interpretation claims that the architect must express the spirit of the times through the use of the newest materials and techniques. The irony of the topic we are discussing is this: the search for a spirit of the times is a kind of historical phrenology that distracts one from actual problem situations. Yet in our instance the very spirit-expressing technique is one of problem-solving.

It appears that in the 1960s there is a double imperative for the use of problem-solving techniques; first, because we have what are perceived to be acute problems, and then because the very use of these techniques is taken to express our times. This combination of inductivist and historicist ideas, open to criticism in so many ways, encourages the use of problem-solving techniques as an end in itself. If the problem-solving routines should be inadequate to handle the complexity of the problem and therefore generate an environment that distorts human purpose, one can interpret the distortion as expressive of the times. This inadequacy must be embraced and solace found in knowing that another appropriate step of destiny was fulfilled. Under the historicist prejudice of modern architectural thought, what results from the use of a new technique is less important than the claim that use of these means is demanded historically. In such an inflation of means, there is the danger that a humanly important activity, providing physical environment that will facilitate the achievement of human purposes, will be artificially and detrimentally simplified in order that it fit the available techniques.

My argument may now be reformulated to say: There is no imperative that we must use any given technique. There is, however, an imperative that we attempt to better understand architectural activity, the problem situation within which it works, and the reasons for its often rather bad performance. At any rate, it is only through such an understanding of architecture's relation to its problems that we could come to know when and where to use which new techniques.

To achieve such an understanding of the architectural problem situation and of the response of the best architects to these problem situations will be anything but easy. I shall attempt to do this through an example and then deduce what appear to be some of its implications. What immediately concerns me is that an important human activity should not be artificially and detrimentally simplified in order to fit an extant mechanical routine. The danger of such an over-simplification stems both from the enthusiasm for mechanization and from the impoverished understanding of architecture fostered by modern architectural theory.

Architects see that any solution, any form, has implications beyond those that were intended, including implications for the reformulation of the original problem or need. Consequently, architects are as interested in the form as in the problem; they see a dynamic relation of form and problem as of the first importance. It is this reciprocity of form and problem that is not sufficiently recognized by the problem-solving designer.

This idea may be clarified by paraphrasing M.C. Beardsley's description of creativity: "…as the artist moves from stage to stage, it is not that he is looking to see whether he is saying what he already meant, but that he is looking to see whether he wants to mean what he is saying."[6] We can test the adequacy of architecture conceived as problem-solving and the universality of such conceptions as the frictionless fit of form and context by examining Le Corbusier's Carpenter Center for the Visual Arts at Harvard University. The Carpenter Center has been often criticized for being anything but effortless in its relations with people, with its adjoining neo-Georgian buildings, and with the Cambridge street pattern. However, it is important not to look for a well-oiled solution here, but rather for the way in which a problem was developed and left open to continuing development.

Harvard University had discovered that, in its own words, "colleges graduate visual illiterates."[7] Harvard then decided to conceive a teaching program that called for active participation in the visual arts. This program required a building; since the involvement was with the visual arts, the site chosen was near the Fogg Museum.

Teaching at the Visual Arts Center has the opportunity to be the most important factor in Harvard's program of education in the arts. As a complement to that didactic program, however, Le Corbusier and his building brilliantly reformulated the original problem. Any teaching program reaches only a small part of a university community, and very few people outside that community. If universities are to be concerned with general artistic illiteracy, they must instruct the entire community. The building itself must reach out and engage every person in such a way that even people who will never be formally enrolled at the Visual Arts Center have the opportunity to achieve new realizations about the potential of architectural form as a shaper of life. I had the memorable experience of observing such a realization. Without prior instruction, we brought some MIT freshmen to visit the Carpenter Center. A young woman completely untutored in architecture explored the Le Corbusier building. After she moved through the building for some time, she timidly explained that when she came to the top of the ramp, she felt herself to be all over the building at once. One could at least begin to analyze the objective qualities of the building that contributed to her reaction.

But for now, the important thing to note is that she had come to realize a potential in architecture that she had not even suspected. That she made her discovery by means of actual movement through the building is one of many indications that Le Corbusier reshaped the original problem in at least two ways. First, he made the building itself an active participant in the problem situation rather than a retiring, effortless framework. Secondly, the visitor and Harvard are forced to recognize that illiteracy about art is not a matter of vision alone. In this building art is not a spectator sport; all of one's senses and the whole of one's perception are engaged. One feels that the Carpenter Center is a world, a context, a problem, and we have the happy opportunity to form ourselves against it. That is, Le Corbusier's building may be seen as a complete inversion of the idea of frictionless, efficient design. It also stands in sharp contrast to any simple notion of problem-solving. Harvard still has not defined the original problem, nor solved it; but they have entered into the problem situation more fruitfully than anyone with a hard definition.[8]

Of course it could be argued that the buildings where we value such assertion from architectural form are unusual. As a matter of degree, this may be so; here I only want to demonstrate that we cannot accept problem-solving and effortless fit as universal concepts in architectural design. Elsewhere I suggest that a resistance to efficient design can be important in something as prosaic as housing for married students.[9]

In contrast to problem-solving design, I see the architect's approach as a sequence of activities encompassing at least the following stages: generalized understanding of the problem; various formal proposals; study of the implications of the proposals; successive reformulations of the problem and proposals; and the final selection of a form for its appropriateness to the reformulated problem. In this case, one must judge not only the fit, but also how the problem has changed. And one must judge the fit not in terms of frictionlessness, but in terms of whether the friction is suited to the new problem formulation. Does the whole — reformulated problem and form — resist criticism?[10]

But now it may be objected that I am describing architects as they exist rather than a potential figure with new capacities. Furthermore, in claiming that we have no clear statements of architectural problems, no axiomatic system for design, no specification of elements, no specifiable identification of a solution, and that the problem shifts with the form adopted, am I not forced to the awkward position that everything is relative, and to the admission that architects can justify nothing (and thus anything)? However, I think the understanding of architecture toward which my argument points not only conflicts with the notion of architecture as problem-solving, but also structures traditional architectural activities somewhat differently. The strongest and most flexible, rational system available should give the creative person free reign subject only to responsible, reasonable, and sensitive self-criticism, and the public tests of performance and criticism.

We return to a generally recognized situation that I mentioned earlier. Much of recent architecture is open to serious criticism, and architects have no way to justify their actions. Systems-oriented architects adopt new techniques and seek to analyze the problem into a rationally unassailable assembly of bits that can then be synthesized into an unas-

sailable solution. I contend that in most cases humans, their activities, and the environment itself change over time – the time of the day as well as a more epochal sense of time. Consequently the analysis of any problem involving more than artificially limited aspects of our being cannot be complete, nor can it be free of ambiguities and tensions. In analyzing the problem, we cannot know all of the bits, nor can we be sure of the unassailability of the bits or of our analytical structure. Neither can we be sure of our heuristics of synthesis. If we take the problem-solving approach, we certainly cannot do this haphazardly, but if we go through that process conscientiously we will never succeed in even stating the problem, let alone solving it. But since the environment will still have to be manipulated, certain aspects of the problem-solving system will be irrationally slurred over in the interest of achieving some result. Not only does this reintroduce irrationality, but the method is then built on a very curious assembly of some carefully researched data, loose assumptions, personal hypotheses, and particulars developed in relation to other hypotheses.

The reciprocal relation of problem and form I have advocated is indeed quite different from the concepts of problem-solving. In defense of the problem-solving approach, however, one should acknowledge that the continuing development of feedback systems appears to be providing models that more closely simulate the activity of architectural design. I only wish to express some reservation whether even a very refined feedback mechanism can compete with the human mind in such an improbable, controversial domain as that of environmental design for the facilitation of human purposes.

Thus, the call is not for artificially precise problems, rigorous systems, friction-less solutions, or justification of one's actions. Growth of architectural learning and practice rather calls for a relentless rational and sensible criticism that "worries" the problem, striving for a better problem – especially a better problem – and then also for a relation of problem and form that is resistant to criticism.

Along with our complex problems, we have complex techniques and many people with naive conjectures. We should be more systematic in recognizing these factors in setting up the conjectures, in criticizing them, and thereby learning and growing. But such an approach is not systematic in the sense of imposing a manageable structure; rather it seeks to discover the structure through an interesting situation of multiple conjectures and criticism.

Since we don't know what the situation is until we are involved in the process, it is no use later asking if we are saying what we meant. We learn through the process and therefore want to ask: "Do I mean what I am saying?"

In that paper of thirty-six years ago, I was clearly exercised about "instrumentalization." But resistance to instrumentalization, and even the form of my resistance is, I believe, still pertinent. In the paper I did not mention the other pole of Hays' concern, "autonomy," either as a response to the problem-solving position or as another position I sought to confront. Nonetheless, autonomy was present in the setting.

In 1964, Peter Eisenman, then a young professor at Princeton, invited a group of young architects (plus two modestly elder ones, Colin Rowe and Robert Venturi) to spend a weekend in Princeton discussing the state of architecture and how they might collectively intervene. Out of that meeting came an organization called Conference of Architects for the Study of the Environment (CASE). Among those who came to be involved (with their then affiliation) were Eisenman (Princeton, then New York), Kenneth Frampton (London, then Princeton), Michael Graves (Princeton), Donlyn Lyndon (University of Oregon), Richard Meier (in practice in New York), Henry Millon (MIT), Gio Pasanella, Jaquelin Robertson, and Richard Weinstein (all of Columbia and Mayor Lindsay's Lower Manhattan planning office), and myself (MIT).

The five years of the effective existence of CASE (there was no formally recognized termination), coincided with the turbulence known as "1968." That turbulence was recognizable in the results of another project initiated by Eisenman in 1966: the development of ideas for the urban transformation of Harlem culminating in the "New Cities" exhibition at the Museum of Modern Art at the beginning of 1967. Four university-based teams were involved: the architects just identified from Columbia; Rowe, Thomas Schumacher, Jerry Wells, and Fred Koetter from Cornell; Graves and Eisenman from Princeton; and Anderson, Millon, and Robert Goodman from MIT.[11]

The work of none of the "New City" teams would illustrate "instrumental-ization." On the other hand, at least the Cornell and Princeton projects could be characterized as explorations toward an autonomous architecture. Large portions of Harlem were eliminated in favor of abstract, often handsome exer-cises in form and/or figure/ground manipulation.[12] In contrast, the MIT proj-ect began with a series of developmental stages on the undeveloped islands in the East River and on filled land in the East River itself. Early stages also involved infill housing to transform the environmental character of the exist-ing large social housing projects. Only after years of the development of such new resources was the incremental upgrading of the Harlem fabric contem-plated. Within the membership of the CASE group (not so identified for the MoMA exhibit), a split appeared: a dominant position moving toward auton-omy versus one that saw architecture as an enterprise that did, indeed, have its own discipline, but had also to subject itself to material, social, and politi-cal criticism.[13] In 1969, together with MIT students, I organized an exhibition at MIT's Hayden Gallery (the predecessor to the List Gallery) titled "Form and Use in Architecture." The title is enough to say that the thesis of the exhibi-tion engaged the issues of the problem-worrying essay. The closing event of the exhibition in early 1969 was only the second public event of CASE.[14] It was also the demise of CASE, as most of the members saw the MIT exhibition as supporting both "instrumentalization" and (more from the MoMA experience) naïve social causes such as "advocacy planning." In contrast, one should think of these as also the years in which Peter Eisenman embraced the autonomy of "cardboard architecture" and designed his series of numbered house projects.[15]

I consider the MIT contribution, in both these exhibitions to have been exercises in "problem worrying." Within this approach, there was an effort to recognize the internal demands of the discipline of architecture as well as the "problem." The architectural example within the problem-worrying paper was, after all, of Le Corbusier's Carpenter Center. The "Form and Use" exhibition featured a section devoted to de Stijl architecture and design, including mate-rials on loan from Truus Schröder-Schräder whose famous house in Utrecht (1924), by Mrs. Schröder and Gerrit Rietveld, is often taken as the apotheosis of abstract form translated into architectural space. In the leaflet that accom-panied the exhibition, I discussed the house somewhat differently:

While Le Corbusier spoke of mass and the play of primary forms in light, the Dutch artists and architects of the de Stijl group undertook the exploration of form in a quite different manner. Rather than speaking of mass and Platonic forms, they attacked the problem of design armed with what they considered the fundamental elements of artistic construction: straight lines, planes, pri-mary colors, black and white. In furniture and architecture, sticks of unit cross-section and planar constructions simulated the fundamental elements. The formal system required the preservation of the integrity of the element — even when used in larger constructs; this was accomplished by having the elements pass by one another with only tangential connections. Such a formally derived relation of part-to-part is obviously the antithesis of the organic-functional analogy exemplified by the Richard Riemerschmid chair [in the exhibition; or one could think of furniture by Henry van de Velde].

In the Schröder House, spatial and utilitarian concerns are imbedded in the development of the de Stijl formal system. Direct experience of the Schröder House reveals the intellectual, formal principles that concerned the de Stijl group; it is the embodiment of a set of ideas in substantial form. How-ever, unlike buildings that embody a formal idea in whole, object-like volumes, the de Stijl forms of the Schröder House were generated additively. In this way the perceptual experience of the house and the demands of use contribute to the construction of the whole that is consistent with the formal intent but not wholly preconceived. Visiting the house, one becomes aware of the formal system behind the design, and simultaneously aware of the use-implications of the formal organization.

Even though the de Stijl group consciously suppressed the nature of materials, they do stand as one of the few exemplars of a solution to the form-use problem. De Stijl objects and environments attest to the possibility of con-ventions accommodating, even encouraging, patterns of use that are convinc-ing in both intellectual and utilitarian terms.[16]

Within the concept of quasi-autonomy there is a wide range of contribu-tive work, some approach autonomy while others are deeply engaged in the material and social conditions of the environment. I saw Eisenman's early work, notably the Toy Museum in Princeton, in the same light that I sought to cast on the Schröder House. The de Stijl and early Eisenman works are of fundamental importance to the discipline of architecture. They project new ways of conceiving material form, space, light, and, at least to my mind, impli-cations for use and meaning. Significantly, these "new ways" are deployed in such a manner as to give as much or more attention to their generalized poten-tials as to the specifics they initially served. It is in this that they approach autonomy and establish new references within the discipline.

One reason that works such as these by the de Stijl group and Eisenman remain within the domain of quasi-autonomy is their intimate scale. Also, a particular use is not defined. One is acutely aware of one's own body in, and in relation to, these environments — and with this, also the anticipation of one's occupation in various modes. Pure geometric forms, or even conventional architectural forms inflated to grandiose proportions — as one may see in the so-called Revolutionary architects of the late eighteenth century — cross another threshold in the question of the autonomy of architecture. We arrive at an autonomy that deserves its place in our conceptualization of architec-ture, but less assuredly belongs in our built environment.

I say only "less assuredly," for we might adopt Adolf Loos's position that architecture rarely enters the realm of art — perhaps only in confronting death.[17] So there may be a place for a gigantic cenotaph for Newton, but, despite its size, this is an infinitesimal part of what we want or need in our envi-ronment. De Stijl and Eisenman works, alone, also cannot comprise our envi-ronment. Even very clever architects do not conceive transformational formal

systems every time they pick up a pencil or mouse. Rather, it is also a high calling to comprehend the formal systems available within the discipline of architecture and then to bring these to bear fruitfully on our environmental needs and the materiality of building. Indeed, it is this broader task that could yield the larger architectural and urban environments in which we would choose to live.

When we broaden our focus in this way, less austere inventions also emerge as significant contributions to the discipline of architecture. In Le Corbusier's renowned Five Points, modern material and processes of construction are imbedded within the disciplinary proposition. Despite this complicity in material and time, the Five Points also opened significant general propositions about space, light, and environmental organization. The Five Points are as much or more a contribution to the discipline of architecture as are the concepts of de Stijl. But it is also the case that the Five Points could not have been conceived without the availability of reinforced concrete. There really is no technological invention in the Five Points; they are rather a significant architectural discovery within a recently available technology.[18] Stated thus, Le Corbusier's achievement invites the commentary: no invention is significant unless it is also a discovery. It is the element of discovery that saves an invention from being merely arbitrary.[19] The formalisms of the de Stijl and Eisenman examples may be more purely disciplinary inventions, but personal experience of the artifacts shows that they too are discoveries of space, light, and organization.

As in the example of the Five Points, the notion of quasi-autonomy is not limited to flights of high architecture and theory. Indeed, I have explored the concept in relation to city form (Savannah)[20] and workers' housing (Krupp at Essen and the Gutehofnunshütte at Eisenheim).[21]

As may be seen then, there is a significant range within the concept of quasi-autonomy. Some instances approach the austere; they provide those special, rare explorations within the discipline of architecture exemplified by de Stijl. Of course, the formation of the de Stijl group and its set of concerns can be convincingly explored within a particular historical setting. But its elemental propositions in matters of visual form do indeed have a high degree of autonomy. Whether in Mondrian's paintings, Rietveld's furniture, or the Schröder house, we recognize a physical tour de force to exemplify those elemental principles — and yet our minds can entertain the quite different levels at which we are addressed. The tactile qualities of Mondrian's paintings do not destroy their ideality. I think it is for the same reasons that, when we see a de Stijl work, we do think of Holland circa 1920, but can also grant these principles a generality that is not tied to that moment alone.

Even these special cases become instances within a universal notion of quasi-autonomy. Eventually they are tested and, if fortunate, given greater

House I (Toy Museum), Princeton, New Jersey. Peter Eisenman, interior.

effect by their performance. In speaking of a "universal notion," I claim that every environmental work (and other forms of human invention) participates in quasi-autonomous relationships. Nevertheless, this claim for generality does not give a meaningless whitewash to all works. We can make critical distinctions. Unlike the de Stijl example, Le Corbusier's Five Points participates quite directly in the material world. In contrast to the de Stijl case, there can be a relatively seamless relation between the disciplinary potentials espoused in the Five Points and a built work based on those principles. But for the same reason, the Five Points reveal a (valued) potential within certain material conditions: less general, more technically appropriate, than the De Stijl example; more technically and historically constrained than Le Corbusier acknowledged.

Even a banal work can be analyzed in term of quasi-autonomy but will be revealed as just that: banal. My own efforts at using the argument of quasi-autonomy to reveal a powerful example – and allow this to serve as a gauge of comparative works – is perhaps best demonstrated in my studies of the town plan of Savannah.[22] It is not special that one can analyze Savannah from the perspective of quasi-autonomy. It is the distinctive features and the historical performance of Savannah, revealed through an analysis of its quasi-autonomy, that make it special and indeed a comparative test for other city plans.

Finally, I want to recognize that the notion of quasi-autonomy is in no way limited to architecture or matters of the physical environment. Conventions, whether touching on social or environmental issues (and, after all, these can never be wholly separate), can be examined in terms of their quasi-autonomous relations. An illustrative example is the social category of "teenager." The concept is so imbedded in our society that at first it seems the years from thirteen to nineteen must have some unity that is in turn characterized by some inevitable traits. There are always and everywhere people of these teen years, and they surely have traits that are different from those who are either younger or older. What we make of this population, however, is at least as much or more a matter of the social construct we make for them, and they for themselves.

This is my simple advocacy: the fruitfulness of recognizing the strengths and the claims of, on one side, our theories and conventions, that should not be held dogmatically, and, on the other, the realities, that are in some ways obdurate but often remarkably and fascinatingly malleable. To seek to live only a life of the mind at one pole, or of materiality at the other, or of coercive power from either, is to impoverish one's self, one's discipline, and one's smaller or greater community.

NOTES

1 The essay had its initial form in a lecture for the conference "Conventions, Canons, and Criticism," organized by the author for MIT and held at the American Academy of Arts and Sciences in Cambridge, April 1982.

2 Actually I wrote "semi-autonomy." I now prefer "quasi-autonomy," so I use that form throughout this essay, even where it involves changing an earlier text.

3 On a different critical front, this was also the year of Robert Venturi's *Complexity and Contradiction in Architecture* (New York: Museum of Modern Art, 1966).

4 As noted, this is an unpublished essay first presented at the Architectural Association, London, in March 1966. It was repeated on 5 June 1966 at the annual teachers' conference of the Association of Collegiate Schools of Architecture, meeting at the Cranbrook Academy in Bloomfield Hills, Michigan. As produced here, the text is changed in minor matters of felicity, the elimination of such usage of the time as "the architect . . . he.," and abbreviation in accord with the current editors.

5 In fact I was happy to pre-judge the Princeton project and won the resources to stage an MIT conference "Inventing the Future Environment" (1966) that explored other views of the situation of architecture and planning. The resulting book was S. Anderson, ed., *Planning for Diversity and Choice: Possible Futures and their Relations to the Man-Controlled Environment* (Cambridge: The MIT Press, 1968); in German as *Die Zukunft der menschlichen Umwelt* (Freiburg i.B.: Verlag Rombach, 1971). The final report of the AIA/Princeton study was Robert L. Geddes and Bernard P. Spring, *A Study of Education for Environmental Design* (Princeton, NJ: Princeton University Press, 1967).

6 M.C. Beardsley, "On the Creation of Art," *Journal of Aesthetics and Art Criticism*, XXIII, 3 (Spring 1965), p.299.

7 A.D. Trottenberg, "College Graduates Visual Illiterates," *Saturday Review* (Feb. 19, 1966), pp. 73ff.

8 A similar argument for growth through "problem-worrying" could be made for the way in which Le Corbusier, at the VAC, continued to transform the architectural problem that he had set out in the Maison Domino in 1914. S. Anderson, "Architectural Research Programmes in the Work of Le Corbusier," *Design Studies* (London), V (July 1984), pp. 151–158. Reprinted (without illustrations) in K. Michael Hays, ed., *Architecture Theory since 1968* (Cambridge: The MIT Press, 1998), pp. 490–505.

9 "Sert's Concept of Living," *Architectural Design*, XXXI (August 1965), p. 376.

10 For reasons of time, the next two paragraphs were not read in London.

11 The exhibition was under the guidance of Arthur Drexler, Director of the Department of Architecture and Design of The Museum of Modern Art. See *The New City: Architecture and Urban Renewal* (New York: MoMA, 1967).

12 "An interesting outgrowth of the exhibition has been the establishment, in New York City, of the Institute for Architecture and Urban Studies, through the joint efforts of The Museum of Modern Art and Cornell University. The Institute will combine university, museum, and governmental resources as they may be brought to bear on what is now one of the most pressing questions of our time: what is to become of our cities?" Arthur Drexler was a motivating force in this foundation. Colin Rowe played a role in the affiliation of Cornell University, but the quoted paragraph gives no indication of the central role, once again, of Peter Eisenman first in the foundation of IAUS and then as its leader (with Rowe as a sidekick in the first years). A major project of the Institute was one on streets sponsored by the U.S. Department of Housing and Urban Development (1970–1972). It resulted in a housing project in Brooklyn and a book: S. Anderson, ed., *On Streets* (Cambridge: The MIT Press, 1978). In Spanish as *Calles. Problemas de estructura y diseño* (Barcelona: Gustavo Gili, 1981); and in Italian as *Strade* (Bari: Dedalo, 1982).

13 The MIT team worked without internal conflict, but there was a distinction within its members. Robert Goodman, who joined at my invitation, was a noted figure of the time in the political and social criticism of the architectural profession. Millon and I were more inclined to sustain disciplinary inquiry while sharing in Goodman's concerns. From the beginning of the project there was a bond to withdraw collectively if MoMA resisted the politicization of our project — a possibility that was always at hand and perhaps restrained only by the intense general politics of the time and notably in matters concerning Harlem. Perhaps it is of anecdotal interest that Michael Dukakis drew up the AGM partnership papers. On the politics of architecture and planning of that moment, see: Robert Goodman, *After the Planners* (New York: Simon & Schuster, 1971).

14 CASE meetings were private to the members and guests except for a public event at the University of Oregon and then this meeting at MIT.

15 In his 1976 editorial for *Oppositions 6*, Eisenman dismissed autonomy, at least as he perceived it to have been represented, as a continuing humanist enterprise, in the "Architettura Razionale" exhibition at the Milan Triennale of 1973. Eisenman anticipated an achievement in architecture, belatedly, of what the "modernist sensibility" had properly been, a new, non-humanist cultural attitude. I believe there can be important distinctions between vulgar Zeitgeist arguments and the invocation (offered by Eisenman) of an épistème as conceived by Foucault. What those distinctions would be, and how they relate to Eisenman's continuing work cannot be attempted here.

16 S. Anderson, "Form and Use in Architecture," photocopy leaflet for an exhibition of the same name, organized by Anderson at the Hayden Gallery, MIT (Jan. 28–March 2, 1969), pp. 8–10.

17 Adolf Loos, "Architektur," *Trotzdem* (Innsbruck: Brenner-Verlag), 1931; reprint (Vienna: Georg Prachner, 1982). Here and elsewhere Loos insists on differentiating the cultural roles of various artifacts, including buildings. Buildings typically do not fall in the realm of art, while an anonymous mound, of characteristic shape, may enter the realm of art. See Anderson, "Architecture in a Cultural Field," in Taisto H. Mäkelä and Wallis Miller, eds., *Wars of Classification: Architecture and Modernity* (New York: Princeton Architectural Press, 1991), pp. 9–35.

18 See note 8.

19 I was moved to this commentary by a brief argument of Christopher Ricks, but I do not wish to make him responsible for my appropriation. Ricks, "The Tragedies of Webster, Tourneur and Middleton: Symbols, Imagery and Conventions," in Ricks, ed., *English Drama to 1710* (London: Sphere Books, 1971), p. 307.

20 See *On Streets*, and "Urban Form and Society in the Great City: An Argument from the Quasi-Autonomy of Physical Form," in Luigi Mazza, ed., *World Cities and the Future of the Metropoles* (Milan: Electa, 1988), pp. 87–93; "Savannah and the Issue of Precedent: City Plan as Resource," in Ralph Bennett, ed., *Settlements in the Americas: Cross-Cultural Perspectives* (Newark, DL: University of Delaware Press, 1993), pp. 110–144.

21 "Critical Conventionalism: The History of Architecture," *Midgård 1* (University of Minnesota), I, 1 (1988), pp. 33–47.

22 See the previous note but one.

Manfredo Tafuri and Architectural Theory in the U.S., 1970–2000

DIANE Y. GHIRARDO

In the late 1960s, Italian architect and historian Manfredo Tafuri surveyed the situation of architecture and architectural practice with grim resignation. The concluding paragraphs of *Architecture and Utopia: Design and Capitalist Development*, express fairly well the monumental despair which suffused this and subsequent texts by Tafuri:

Modern architecture has marked out its own fate by making itself...the bearer of ideals of rationalization . . . it is useless to struggle for escape when completely enclosed and confined without an exit . . . No "salvation" is any longer to be found within it: neither wandering restlessly in labyrinths of images so multivalent they end in muteness, nor enclosed in the stubborn silence of geometry content with its own perfection . . . it is useless to propose purely architectural alternatives.[1]

For Tafuri, architecture since the Enlightenment had become the instrument par excellence of capitalist development, with the utopias proposed by its greatest avant-gardes nothing but vehicles of world domination and administration in the hands of rampant capitalist expansion. But in his dip into the history of Western European architecture, Tafuri conveniently failed to mention that architecture had also been an instrument of feudal exploitation, domination, and administration; an instrument of post-medieval colonial expansion, exploitation, domination, and administration; an instrument of colonization, exploitation, domination, and administration for Imperial Rome; and so on. Architecture's instrumental use by regimes of power is hardly new. What Tafuri averred, however, is that in the contemporary world, this instrumentalization had become inescapable, presumably because of the totalizing reach of the processes of capitalist rationalization. Buried in this formulation

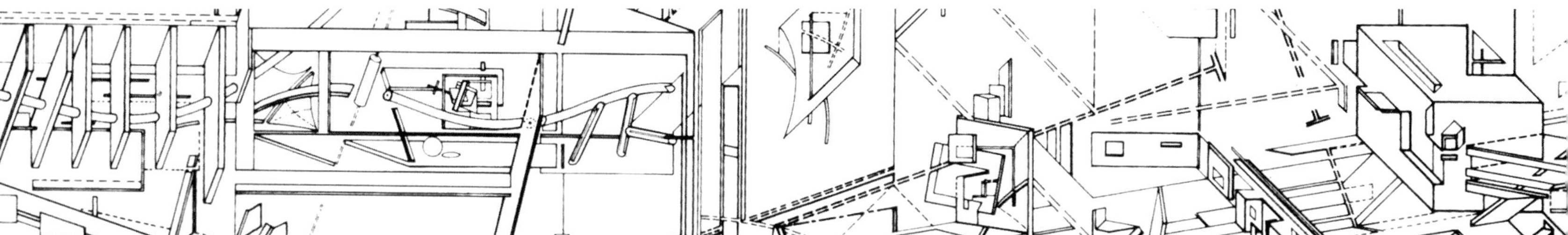

is the conviction that things had once been different, but that with the Enlightenment came a fall from grace with consequences as devastating for architecture as those confronted by Adam and Eve when banished from the Garden of Eden. The veracity, not to mention the logic, of this view is at best dubious; be that as it may, Tafuri was widely understood to be sounding the end of architecture, just as Arnold Schoenberg had announced the end of tonality, Theodor Adorno the end of art, and Francis Fukuyama later sounded the end of history. None of these millenarian predictions turned out to be true, as the Guggenheim in Bilbao, U2's *Joshua Tree*, and Vija Celmin's paintings demonstrate.

Like other European and American elites, Tafuri cast his stern gaze over consumerism, commercialism, the erosion of high culture by a sea of sentimentality and commodification, and a host of other ills associated with late capitalism, and, finding them at once depressingly pervasive and triumphant, conceded defeat. Even worse, the possible futures of architecture were as resolutely dreary as its unremittingly bleak present. With a future as bleak as Tafuri anticipated, why would one build at all? And if all actions are inevitably compromised by capitalism, how is it possible to do anything when every act can only repeat the initial capitulation? Contrary to what one might expect, in the United States the currency of Tafuri's theories (in some very particular formulations) and their offshoots survived the Nixon, Ford, Carter, Reagan, Bush, and even Clinton eras to enter the new millennium. In the space-time compression of the late capitalist order, nearly three decades is a long life span indeed for a theory, given that deconstruction in architecture went in and out in less than a decade. It does help that parts of the theories in Tafuri's various essays and books became the intellectual baubles of university faculty, graduate students, and journal editors, even if they barely penetrated the realm of practice.

While my aim here is not to recapitulate or even criticize Tafuri's theories, a few clarifications are in order, not least because Tafuri's position has so often been misrepresented.[2] Unfortunately, in most cases the translations of his admittedly complex and elusive prose are clunky and often wrong. But even the poor translations are clear enough about his key points, so that misrepresentation cannot be dismissed as misunderstanding.[3] In his 1976 review of the French edition of Tafuri's *Theories and History of Architecture*, Yves-Alain Bois accused Tafuri of "losing" the architectural object, and of opposing architecture as criticism because it rendered his own work as critic ineffectual.[4] Although Bois complained about the French translation, his critique could only be a willful misinterpretation, because Tafuri explicitly distinguished between a criticism within architectural language, and one external to it, a meta-language with the goal of exposing the underlying ideological system beyond the individual work.[5] More later about the misrepresentations; first, how did Tafuri position architecture?

What Tafuri viewed as the tragic fate of architecture in the capitalist economic system and within the relations of production certainly drove him to the limits of despair, for he viewed capitalism as a totalizing, all-encompassing system. But he began and ended his work from the perspective of the critic and the historian, as such undertaking a political critique of history and practice in which he insisted that architecture as pure form could never rupture capitalism's stranglehold. The essential other half of this observation, rarely quoted but absolutely bound to the first, was that for architecture, the only remaining choices were political ones. Tafuri offered no blueprints for action; that made it more difficult to tussle with him except on the level of theory. As he remarked in *Architecture and Utopia*, "Of course, once the work of ideological criticism has been completed, there remains the problem of deciding what instruments of knowledge might be immediately useful to the political struggle. It is precisely here that my discourse must end, but certainly not by choice."[6] The political foundations of his position are clear enough in the early 1970s from the litany of examples drawn from the architectural canon which he lined up in *Architecture and Utopia*. Tafuri described architects in each successive phase as launching utopian projects which then, one by one, revealed their inevitable imbrication in the system of capitalist rationalization. At several points in *Architecture and Utopia*, Tafuri specifically remarked that the challenge facing architecture was to bring together capitalist development and the reorganization and consolidation of the working class.[7] Thirty years later, the references to the proletariat and the working class have a quaint air about them, the musty smell of something long stored in a dusty attic, but had anyone paid attention to the political charge and the stance of the historian, upon which Tafuri's writings were predicated, we might have been spared a lot of the nonsense that has passed for theory in the subsequent three decades.

What is remarkable is that the architectural theory machine in the United States ecstatically embraced Tafuri's despair, deploying it as a trigger for a new architecture, while ignoring the political dimension fundamental to his critique. References to the social or political in most pronouncements remained little more than piously uncontroversial genuflections with about as much basis in actual social or political conditions – much less actions – as the decentered subjects featured during the 1980s and 1990s. How did this happen? Misreadings of Tafuri, and the cues for a new attitude toward architecture erroneously deduced from his critique, span the 1970s and 1980s and irradiated writers in many publications; in this essay, I refer only to a few of the most prominent, so-called theoretical texts written during three decades of iterations.

At the outset, it is worth noting that Tafuri insisted both on the separation of history/theory and practice, and on the necessity for the critic to establish a distance from the object of his inquiry. The single architectural object was never the subject of the historian or critic's analysis. In fact, the examples were interchangeable, because the task was to understand the broader intellectual and social environment into which buildings fit. He dismissed the theory and history produced by architects as interested and instrumental; architects should stick to practice, he believed, and historians/critics to critical history.[8] Striking as it did at the very heart of most architectural writing in the United States, this fundamental aspect of Tafuri's thought was simply ignored by architects who fancied themselves critics, historians, or theorists.

The journal *Oppositions*, which first published Tafuri's essays in this country and which led the charge to adopt bits of his theories selectively, is as good a starting point as any, because it is the fountainhead of multiple misrepresentations of Tafuri's thought. As has been the case with his pursuit of numerous other theorists, Peter Eisenman's fascination with Tafuri was entirely self-interested. Eisenman has always sought "critics" who would celebrate his own work and reinforce his own ideas about architecture. Amazingly, Eisenman continued to pursue Tafuri long after his death. In an article published in 2000, Eisenman twisted Tafuri's arguments, about the autonomy of history and criticism from practice, to favor a view of architecture as autonomous from everything else.[9] Despite Eisenman's assiduous efforts to entice him into his phalanx of theorists, Tafuri was one of the few who consistently

resisted – a fact reflected in his abrupt and total break from Eisenman in 1980. Nonetheless, *Oppositions* published Tafuri's essays, the work of his colleagues and students, and Eisenman's Institute for Architecture and Urban Studies (IAUS) invited Tafuri's colleagues to visit the Institute at various points.[10] Tafuri himself only visited the United States three or four times during the 1970s.

In 1974, Tafuri presented a lecture at Princeton University, later published as "L'Architecture dans le Boudoir: The language of criticism and the criticism of language," in *Oppositions 3*.[11] He outlined the objectives of the article on the first page, a passage systematically misunderstood as a manifesto for architects disenchanted with commodification to retreat to a neutral, autonomous realm for design. He wrote:

Today, he who is willing to make architecture speak is forced to rely on materials empty of any and all meaning: he is forced to reduce to degree zero all architectonic ideology, all dreams of social function and utopian residues. In his hands, the elements of the modern architectural tradition come suddenly to be reduced to enigmatic fragments, to mute signals of a language whose code has been lost…[The] purism [of architects from the late fifties] is that of someone driven to a desperate action that cannot be justified except from within itself. The words of their vocabulary … lie perilously on that sloping plane which separates the world of reality from the magic circle of language…[W]e wish to confront the language of criticism.[12]

In this essay, and most of the subsequent ones, Tafuri's concern was the role of criticism regarding four attitudes that he identified in contemporary architecture:

1. one in which language was seen as a purely technical neutrality
2. architecture as a manifestation of the dissolution of language
3. architecture understood as criticism and irony, as well as a position which denied architectonic communication in favor of "information"
4. an architecture which attempted to redistribute the capitalist division of labor.

Within the first three categories, Tafuri included designs by James Stirling, Aldo Rossi, Vittorio De Feo, the New York Five, and Venturi and Rauch, all of which he believed succumbed to one or another brand of empty formalism. In the fourth, he included the work of Raymond Unwin, Clarence Stein, Charles Harris Whitaker, Henry Wright, Fritz Schumacher, Ernst May, and Hannes Meyer.[13] By comparison with Le Corbusier, Ludwig Mies van der Rohe, and Walter Gropius, none of the latter group ranked in the pantheon of the great modern movement architects. Not surprisingly, commentators on Tafuri then and later conveniently ignored the only group whose work he advanced as offering an important contribution to architectural practice, although hardly a blueprint for action.

What did he find appealing about these architects? In the survey of twentieth century architecture, *Modern Architecture*, first published in 1976, Tafuri spelled out the ways in which Unwin, Whitaker, Schumacher, May, and Meyer offered alternatives to sterile exercises on language.[14] In the Frankfurt Siedlungen planned by May, for example, Tafuri held the signal feature to be the political decision to reject the speculative building practices characteristic

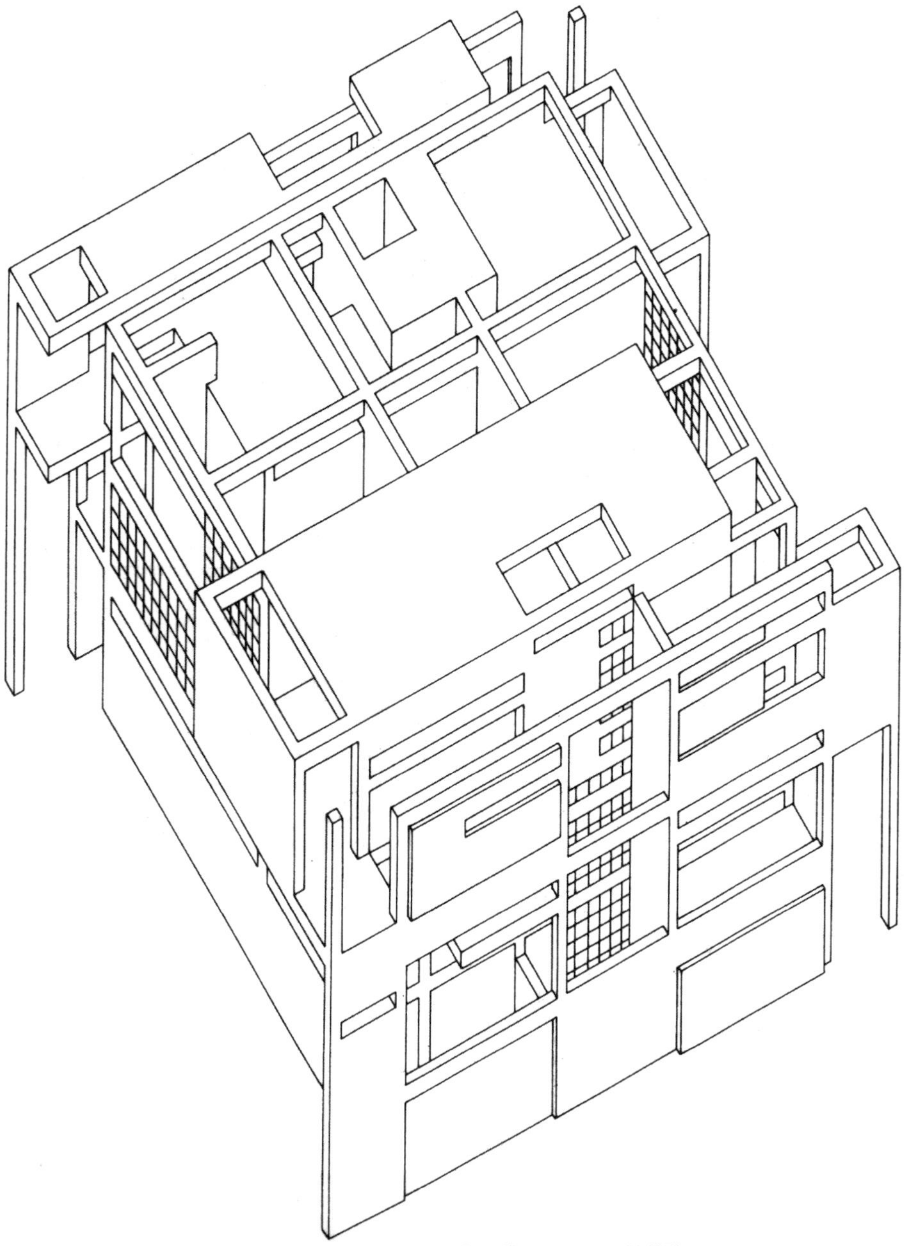

Peter Eisenman, House IV, 1971.

both of Haussman's transformation of Paris and the segregated cities of the United States in favor of low-cost housing situated conveniently near the workplace but integrated with nature.[15] Perhaps most important, these and the other projects Tafuri advanced, healed, he claimed, the breach between avant-garde aspirations for a new world and the "realistic possibilities of a democratic administration."[16] Tafuri considered drawbacks to work by these architects, such as those of Unwin at Letchworth, but he insisted that whatever its limitations, Unwin's scheme provided low density, high-quality architecture integrated into the natural setting.[17] What made projects such as Hampstead Garden Suburb praiseworthy was the architects' struggle to accomplish real projects for the middle and working classes rather than high-end, elitist designs for the wealthy, empty formal games, or aimless dreams of a better world in some vague future to be accomplished without effort, conflict, or failures along the way. At Frankfurt, for example, the Siedlungen expressed the housing policies of social democratic trade unions, even though ultimately they were "neutralized by the autonomous development of finance and monopoly capital."[18] The lesson to be learned was not the impossibility of doing anything, Tafuri argued, but rather that reforms needed to be extended with a coherent political strategy to the entire complex of institutions, and not only those involving architecture and building. Put another way, even though architecture became instrumental to late capitalism, this need not be its only result, nor did this mean that the architect should retreat into contemplative games.

Tafuri repeated this point numerous times. In a 1976 interview by Francoise Very, Tafuri spoke of "architecture without a capital A" as the most interesting because it does not wallow in its crises and problems; instead of talking, it acts.[19] Acting, or movement, Tafuri insisted, mattered more than results, and the movement that "tends toward something" constitutes the "rectitude of all political activity."[20] It is therefore puzzling that an astute critic such as Michael Hays could describe Tafuri's position as expressing the "ineffectuality of any resistance [to modernism]."[21] Even worse, Fredric Jameson excoriated Tafuri for his pessimism and for setting up a scandalous political impasse in his work.[22]

Given the choice between a responsible if not always entirely successful architectural practice and the heady avant-garde games of the New York Five and their progeny, between an architecture which Tafuri described as exploding out towards reality and an architecture of language games, it is not hard to figure out which has appealed more to theorists and designers since the 1970s. Never mind that Tafuri upbraided adherents of the latter approach for following "false paths laid out by the enemy that lead into the desert."[23] It is much easier to play games with cardboard, titanium, or computer graphics than it

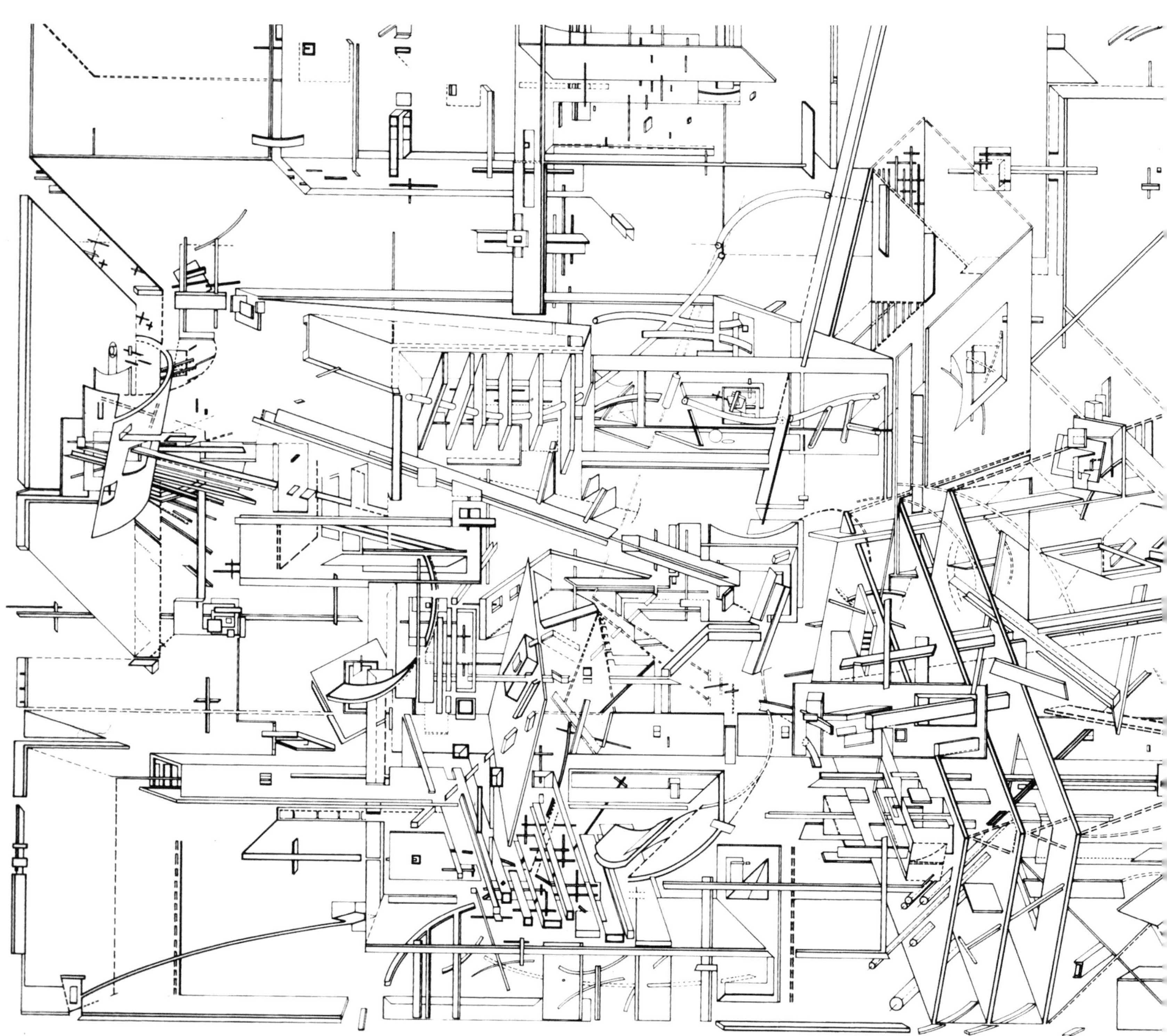

Daniel Libeskind, *Time Sections*, 1979.

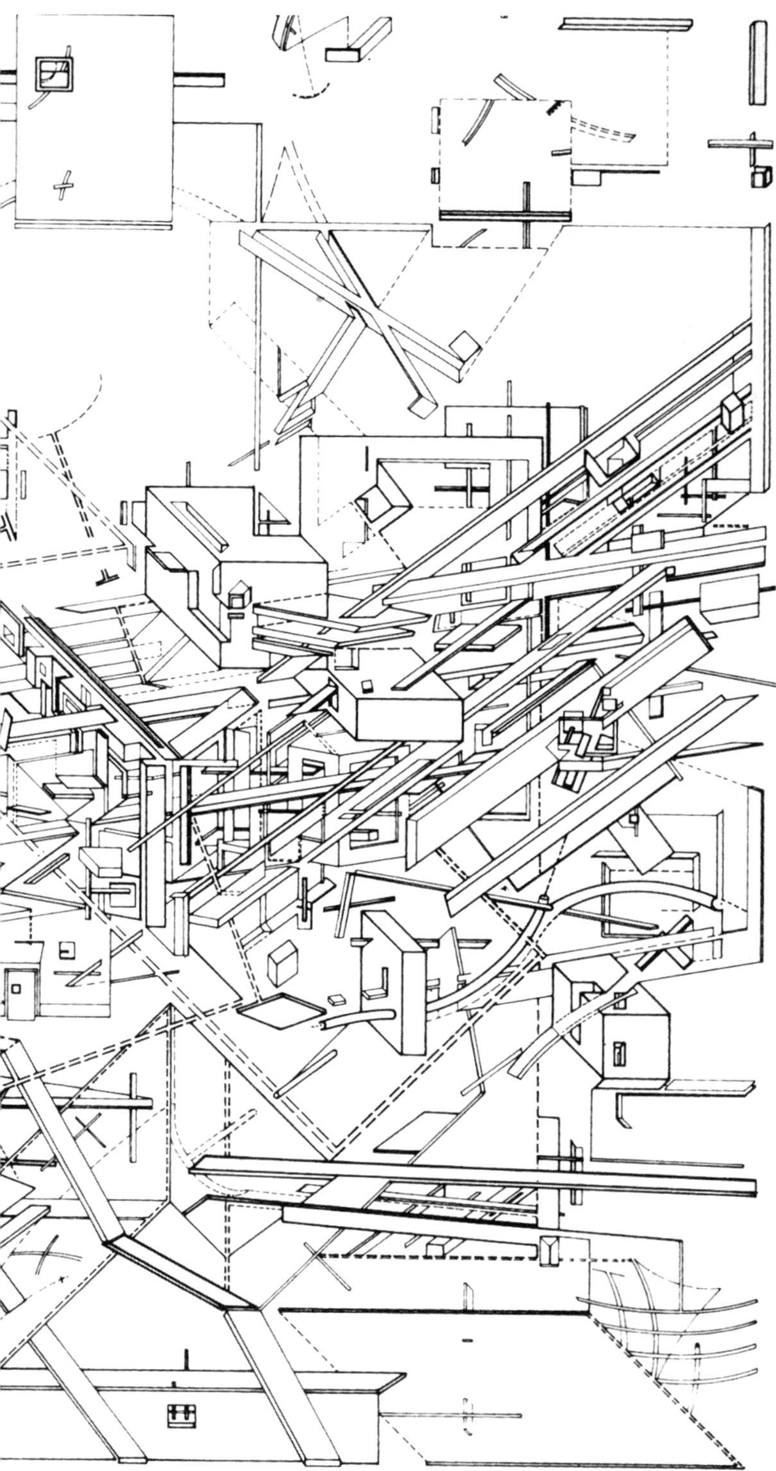

is to struggle with nearly intractable problems of affordable housing or urban sprawl, energy crises, or any one of a series of major problems which we confront today in the built environment. Those games are also less likely to offend the varied interests which comprise the purveyors of consumerism, commercialization, and capitalist rationalization (who also end up patronizing architects in one way or another) than might more direct confrontations.[24]

When Peter Eisenman announced the arrival of Post-Functionalism in 1976, he wrote of an architectural form different from what he referred to as form as a relic of old, humanist theory, a new form which exists in an atemporal, decompositional mode, as something simplified from some pre-existent set of non-specific spatial entities. Here, form is understood as a series of fragments – signs without meaning.[25]

Together, these two formal "tendencies...constitute the essence of this new, modern dialectic. They begin to define the inherent nature of the object in and of itself and its capacity to be represented."[26] This position has affinities with Tafuri's observations about the "fragmentation of the order of discourse," the "silence of form," "empty signs."[27] Even at the time, Tafuri specifically referred to Eisenman's designs as emblematic of a tendency to "repossess ...the unique character of the object by removing it from its economic and functional contexts... placing it in parentheses with the flux of objects generated by the production system."[28] In 1976, Tafuri described the "exasperated formalism" of Eisenman as producing "sadistic" spaces precisely because "only by ruling out all reasons and demands having nothing directly to do with architecture can Eisenman keep his architectural language intact."[29] Eisenman later echoed Tafuri's writing when he proposed an architecture for the late twentieth century "as an independent discourse, free of external values – classical or any other; that is, the intersection of the meaning-free, the arbitrary, and the timeless in the artificial," an architecture which consisted only of self-referential language.[30] This echo was just that – a displaced and disembodied version of Tafuri's position.

Although it would be convenient to argue that figures such as Eisenman and later Libeskind fully believed that the act of building was so compromised that autonomy was the only defensible position, and that the only way of advancing a critical position was to stand aloof from the world of practice, it just wasn't so. Eisenman's indifference to political, economic, and functional considerations is legendary and longstanding, and expresses nothing more than an unwillingness to be troubled by such nasty inconveniences. The remaining members of the New York Five did not adopt such drastically polemical positions as Eisenman did, and cheerfully built for any multinational which issued invitations. The litany of clients for whom the apostles of autonomy later built (or wanted to build) alone ought to put to rest any notion that autonomous architecture represented anything other than a convenient public relations device at a time when clients were scarce, such as during the late 1970s. Even so, Tafuri was initially more tolerant of the retreat into purity and empty formalism, for he discerned it to be, at least in some cases, an expression of anguish in the face of the totalizing power of capitalism.[31] But it did not take long for this tolerance to evaporate with regard to Eisenman and the so-called American avant-garde, ending up only a few years later in an attitude of wry amusement.[32] Although he penned critiques of purism and of postmodernism, Tafuri also reminded his readers that the struggle over postmodernism was but "a war of words in confrontation with other words, a struggle

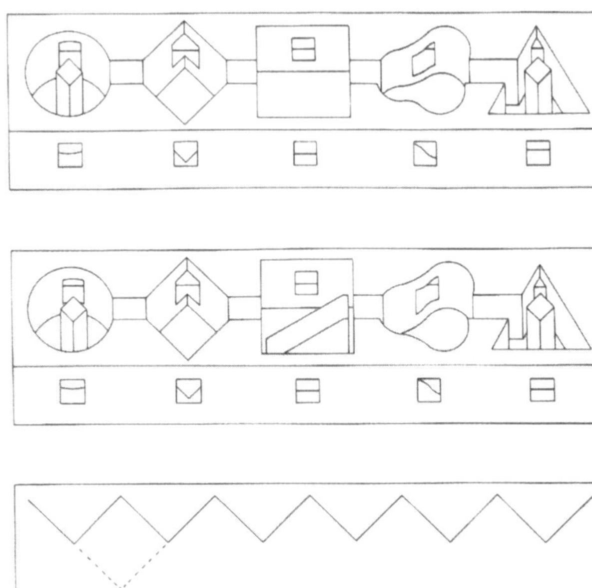

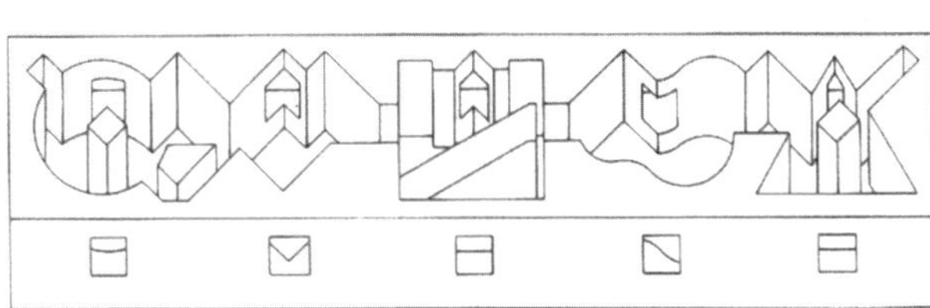

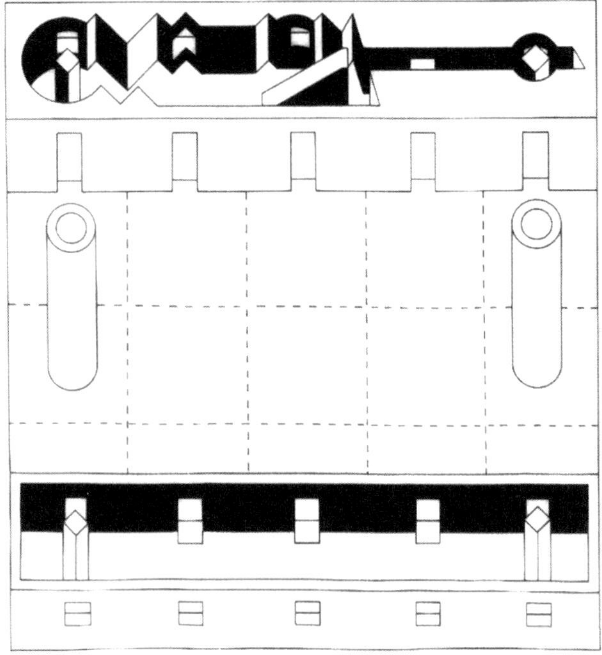

Bernard Tschumi, image from *Manhattan Transcripts*, 1982.

of restricted languages for an impossible rule over that which possesses other languages."[33] Even if both Aldo Rossi and Eisenman conducted research in architectural purity, the gulf between them was enormous, Tafuri held. He considered Eisenman's "will to abstraction" as only superficially similar to that of Rossi, as a quick look at the products of their respective followers illustrates.[34] Tafuri wrote that Rossi "dismisses the importance of form in favor of a decorous reserve, almost as if to signify that only thus can communication be re-established between the 'little world' where architecture rises and the 'big world' where it is obliged to reside."[35]

Of course, Tafuri considered the mournful diagnosis of the state of architecture in an era of late capitalist hegemony an indictment, neither cause for celebration nor a blueprint for a new methodology, but this did not appear to trouble Eisenman, Bernard Tschumi, or Hal Foster unduly.[36] They triumphantly announced the erosion (or end) of history, the appearance of the decentered subject, the end of representation, and the arrival of a thoroughly autonomous, independent architecture, architecture as an end in itself.[37]

Although Tafuri certainly spoke of ends, for Eisenman, Tschumi, and Foster and other theorists floating aloft in ecstatic indeterminacy, architecture now joined an extremely select group of entities which were their own – and only – justifications, but with which all of these theorists would have been loath to be affiliated: God and evil come readily to mind. So while architecture was an end in itself, paradoxically elsewhere there could be no ends, or teleology, and no history. Whatever else one can say about *Architecture and Utopia*, it did propose an interpretation of history roughly from the Enlightenment to the Modern Movement, a history understood as a sequence of events, contradictions, dialectics, ideas, and actions in the eighteenth century which followed one another and led to ideas and undertakings in the next two centuries – in particular, the absorption of architecture into the processes of capitalist rationalization, with all of the consequences we have mentioned. Because Tafuri used criticism to expose a view of that history at variance with standard ones, and because he asserted the possibility of interventions only on the political level, he was not troubled by the prospect of having served up something that could pass for a meta-narrative. Subsequent theorists, however, in the thrall of decentered, ahistorical and autonomous subjects, and architecture for the sake of architecture, chose to seize the results of that analysis untethered from the historically grounded interpretive framework from which it emerged. To do otherwise might even mean having to admit meaning into the scheme of things, which would of course lead to dismantling the whole postmodernist scheme of decentered subjects and indeterminacy, from which ends, origins, or foundations were absent.

Although by the 1980s the attention of the architectural-theoretical establishment had shifted to new sources (Derrida and Lacan especially), the groundwork for connections with the newest trends in continental European thought had already been shaped by the contacts with Tafuri, himself an omnivorous reader who was familiar with the works of Michel Foucault, Derrida, Lacan, and others by the time he wrote *Architecture and Utopia*. Here and in other essays of the early 1970s, he had introduced most of the French writers who subsequently dominated theory in the United States.

With the advent of poststructuralism and deconstruction, architectural theorists embraced the new doctrines about language and its indeterminacy. Dogmas such as truth, reality, and certainty were precisely what poststructur-

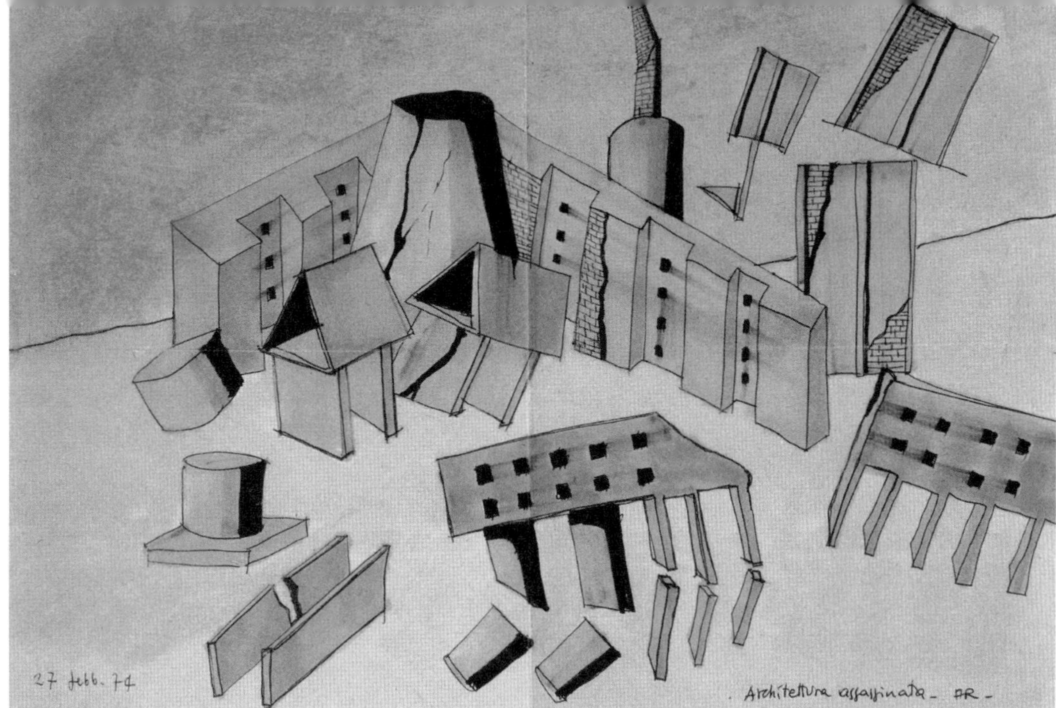

Aldo Rossi, *Architettura Assassinata*, 1974.

alist and deconstructivist architectural theorists aimed to banish. That they did so by proposing their own dogmas of indeterminacy, decenteredness, and the fetish of discourse is an embarrassment no one was eager to admit. One of the thrills of reading the writings of postmodernist (or poststructuralist, or deconstructivist) architectural theorists is the blithe indifference with which they treat such logical inconsistencies, as we shall see: the free play of signifiers can have no roots in history or meaning – and might disappear if any were found necessary. The inspiration for this came directly from Derrida, who wrote of architecture in the following terms:

The "Tower of Babel" does not merely figure the irreducible multiplicity of tongues; it exhibits an incompletion, the impossibility of finishing, of totalizing, of saturating, of completing something on the order of edification, architectural construction, system and architectonics.[38]

Following up on this, in 1988, Mark Wigley rejected the notion of "ground-as-support" and followed Derrida's notion that the structure (of architecture) stands not on the ground but on an abyss:

Deconstruction leads to a complete rethinking of the supplemental relationship organized by the architectural motif of ground/structure/ornament … The edifice is erected by concealing the abyss on which it stands. This repression produces the appearance of solid ground.[39]

And later, in speaking of ornament as a "violation of structure," and architecture as the possibility of building, Wigley celebrated the indeterminacy which deconstruction made possible in architecture:

Such a gesture does not constitute a method, a critique, an analysis, or a source of legitimization. It is not strategic. It has no prescribed aim. Which is not to say that it is aimless. It moves very precisely, but not to some end. It is not a project.[40]

Or, as Jeffrey Kipnis put it, deconstruction offered what he called "motifs" for architectural design:

Do not destroy; maintain, renew, and reinscribe. Do battle with the very meaning of architectural meaning without proposing a new order … [to] destabilize meaning. To destabilize meaning does not imply progression toward any new and stable end, and thus can neither mean to end meaning nor to change meaning.[41]

Many of the deconstruction texts of the late 1980s and early 1990s were enshrined in tomes on architectural theory. Abandoned by practitioners like Libeskind and Eisenman once they started to obtain commissions, and by theorists because it soon became thoroughly unfashionable, deconstruction and the texts that celebrated it still gather dust. After all, none of these theorists

– globe-trotting travelers all – wants to travel with a decentered subject who is a pilot and for whom reality is only a discourse and a crash nothing but an array of free-floating signifiers. Did many of the architectural theorists fully grasp the dimensions of the poststructuralist and deconstructivist theories they wholeheartedly embraced? Bernard Tschumi unwittingly revealed a certain haziness about some fundamentals of deconstruction in 1988, when somebody evidently forgot to tell him that in the deconstructivist era, systems were out: "disjunction becomes a systematic and theoretical tool for the making of architecture." [42]

Despite the embrace of the end of the classical, the end of meaning, the end of history, the dissolution of representation, and so forth, the 1980s-era theorists resorted to didactic pronouncements as rigid and totalizing as the meta-narratives that they supposedly were besieging, and they often trumped the adversary when it came to grandiosity of scope. One good example of this – what we might call an "a-formal formalism"– is that of Daniel Libeskind, from his suite of drawings, *Chamber Works*:

Architecture is neither on the inside nor the outside. It is not a given nor a physical fact. It has no History and it does not follow Fate. What emerges in differentiated experience is Architecture as an index of the relationship between what was and what will be. Architecture as non-existent reality is a symbol which in the process of consciousness leaves a trail of hieroglyphs in space and time that touch equivalent depths of Unoriginality.[43]

What dynamics triggered three decades of theoretical delirium in which poeticizing reflection passed for theory, and what does it all have to do with Tafuri? Certainly with the economic expansion of the 1980s notions that building was impossible and that the only option was political action became progressively less attractive to architects, especially academic ones, who eventually found commissions in the economic climate of the 1990s. But it was also precisely this group that hankered for intellectual fortification, so a bracing dose of suitably enigmatic European theory was just the ticket. The problem was, which one? Addressing this query set the stage for the spectacle of thirty years of trying on and discarding borrowed theories with the rapidity of a commodified consumer at an outlet sale. Much of Tafuri's body of theory ended up in the pile of discarded garments, especially when he called for architecture to be politically engaged. What remained were Tafuri's references to "no salvation possible," an architecture "empty of any and all meaning," and the claim that Tafuri had sounded the death of architecture – but these hung on as handy excuses for engaging only in work on the language of architecture, empty formalism. An otherwise assured historian, Joan Ockman stumbled over Tafuri's views on architectural labor by reading him through the rosy spectacles of Eisenman.[44] Refracted through Eisenman's distorted lens, in

Ockman's account, Tafuri ends by preferring the purism of the New York Five to engaged work. Yet as early as 1976, Tafuri dismissed architecture as miserable when it preens with maximum pomp; he professed much more interest in architecture with a small "a," and as examples offered the cooperative building programs of communist-governed Italian cities which gathered workers together with builders but harbored no illusions about "resolving" the housing problem.[45] Her description of Tafuri's view of "history as tragedy" is worth countering with Massimo Cacciari's observation in his eulogy that Tafuri taught the most difficult lesson: the art of disenchantment together with hope and faith.[46]

Tafuri was not outlining an agenda for a new architectural production disengaged from political reality. On the contrary, it was to the critic and the historian that he addressed his remarks as an approach to the criticism and history of architecture. Of the work of the New York Five, for example, Tafuri tellingly commented: "In the face of such products, the task of criticism is to begin from within the work only to escape from it as soon as possible so as not to be caught in the vicious circle of a language that speaks only of itself."

The task of the critic and that of the historian are different ones:

Thus we abandon the object itself and move into the system which, in itself, gives meaning. And criticism thereby explicitly moves its inquest from a specific task to the structure that conditions the total meaning of the object ... The role of criticism is the violation of the object in question.[47]

But if architecture demands engagement with political, social, and economic systems and institutions, criticism requires distance, Tafuri insisted, something in short supply today. The closeness of theorists and architects who mutually celebrate one another, cite one another, invite one another to conferences, write books and publish articles about one another, and hire one another, is almost incestuous, and certainly leaves no space for debate, let alone the distance that Tafuri deemed essential for the practice of both history and of criticism. Indeed, in 1986, Tafuri argued that there is no criticism, only history, a history not of objects, but of men, in which the challenge is to understand how a work of architecture fits into its own time. The historian examining current work, he held, must create an artificial distance.[48] Instead, what we have today in architectural theory is a more robustly-structured version of the very system Tafuri challenged, a system that gives meaning to and fetishisizes architectural objects, and which endows its practitioners with the status and rewards typical of a well-oiled component of capitalist rationality. In short, we have a system of theory production and architectural production by theorist/practitioners that is complicit with the commodification of capitalist hegemony Tafuri explicitly criticized — and against which most of these theorists and practitioners have repeatedly railed. Although presented as autonomous, independent of politics and economics, this work was directly instrumental, and that was the problem: the denial of instrumentality by veiling the work as autonomous as much as the fact of instrumentality. That is, to assert that architecture is autonomous and therefore not instrumental to political ends covers the fact that architecture is deeply imbricated in politics, and that is just as much a problem as specific cases of instrumenality. As Tafuri astutely observed in 1980, these experiments in private languages reveal above all the desire to "remain on the stage ever more grotesquely miming in an effort to entertain."[49]

Mark Wigley observed that despite the power and significance of Tafuri's bombshells on history, theory and practice, there has been little sustained dialogue generated by his work. In the United States, his views were subdivided "into little tasteless pieces for consumption by the Anglo Saxons. Little has been added to his master's voice beyond a series of useful footnotes."[50] Instead, Wigley claims that Tafuri's impact registers elsewhere: ". . . research not directly influenced by Tafuri and which makes only occasional references to his writing might actually be the most disruptive legacy of his work."[51]

Even though Tafuri called for a separation of history and criticism from practice, Wigley claims that "new forms of research" have one foot on each side of the gap, "testing its limits without ever simply bridging it, scrutinizing its contours closely – "[52] What Wigley calls a "non-prescriptive Architectural Theory" challenges "the discourse" in new ways. "Tafuri," he says, "won't go away. His threat lives on in writing that he would no doubt have hated." Wigley is probably correct on that count, but not for the reasons he imagines. Tafuri would have loathed the slick repetition of the celebratory texts, the absence of rigorous scholarship, and the construction of a theory-criticism establishment; he would have dismissed most of it as empty language games on a par with much of architectural practice.

Having replaced an older regime, this system of theory/practice itself now needs to be dismantled, or, to reframe an observation from *Modern Architecture*, what possibilities are open to a discipline such as architecture that is as yet incapable of posing to itself the problem of its own place in the political arena?[53]

NOTES

1 Manfredo Tafuri, *Architecture and Utopia. Design and Capitalist Development* (Cambridge MA: MIT Press 1976, translation of *Progetto e Utopia* (Bari: Laterza, 1973), p.181.

2 See, for example, the introductions to Tafuri's essays published in *Oppositions* 3 (May 1974); *Oppositions* 5 (Summer 1976), *Oppositions* 11 (Winter 1977), *Oppositions* 17 (Summer 1979); Peter Eisenman, "The Wicked Critic," *ANY* 25–26, (2000), 66–70, and indeed, many of the articles in that publication.

3 In this essay I use the existing English translations of Tafuri's work because this is how most Americans were introduced to it; I only offer my own translations where it is less significant for the history of the misrepresentations.

4 Yve-Alain Bois, review of *Theories and History of Architecture*, in *Oppositions* 11 (Winter 1977), p.118–123. Bois berated Tafuri for not having "paid more attention to architectural form" (p.119) and for being "incap[able of] render[ing] account of a building," a task Tafuri acquitted perfectly well in a very different type of book, *Modern Architecture*, but which was certainly not called for in *Theories and Histories*.

5 Manfredo Tafuri, *Teorie e storia dell' architettura* (Bari: Laterza, 1968), p.129–130.

6 Tafuri, *Architecture and Utopia*, p. x.

7 Ibid., p.xi, 181, 182.

8 Richard Ingersoll, interview with Manfredo Tafuri, "There is no criticism, only history," *Design Book Review* (Spring 1986), p.8–11.

9 Peter Eisenman, "The Wicked Critic," *ANY* 25–26 (2000), p.70. Eisenman projected his own need for surrogates onto Tafuri, holding that Piranesi became a surrogate for Tafuri. Eisenman also wrote: "The dissolution of form and the void of the signifiers become the negative in itself. The construction of a utopia of dissolved form becomes the recuperation of the negative. In Piranesi's 'discovery' of Tafuri, architecture is nothing more than a sign and an arbitrary construction." In this Eisenman completely ignores Tafuri's own ideas about his critical enterprise, including being an analyst of the events of history rather than a seeker of surrogates or puppets into whose mouths words could be placed.

10 Among the colleagues invited to and published by the IAUS were Giorgio Ciucci, Francesco Dal Co, Franco Rella, Georges Teyssot, and Massimo Cacciari.

11 Manfredo Tafuri, "L'Architecture dans le Boudoir: The language of criticism and the criticism of language," *Oppositions* 3 (May 1974), now in M. Hays, ed. *Oppositions Reader* (New York: Princeton Architectural Press, 1998), p.291–316. Although the number was dated 1974, *Oppositions* was famously one to two years behind the publication date. In 1987, Tafuri massively transformed this essay for publication in an edited volume of his essays, *The Sphere and the Labyrinth: Avant-Gardes and Architecture from Piranesi to the 1970s*, trans. Pellegrino d'Acierno and Robert Connolly (Cambridge MA: MIT Press, 1987), p. 267–290. I quote from the text as it was when it influenced theorists during the 1970s and most of the 1980s.

12 Ibid., p. 292.

13 Ibid., p. 310.

14 Manfredo Tafuri and Francesco Dal Co, *Modern Architecture*, trans. Robert Erich Wolf (New York: Harry N. Abrams, Inc., 1979), originally published by Electa in Milan in 1976 under the title *Architettura Contemporanea*. Because the authors singled out the chapters which each wrote independently, it is possible to single out Tafuri's views; here I refer only to chapters Tafuri claimed as his own.

15 Ibid., p.181.

16 Ibid.

17 Ibid., p.38.

18 Ibid., p.183.

19 Francoise Very, "Entretien avec Manfredo Tafuri," *AMC, Architecture, Mouvement Continuitè* 39 (June 1976), p.64–68.

20 Ibid., p.67, translations mine.

21 K. Michael Hays, "Tafuri's Ghost," *ANY* 25–26 (2000), p. 38.

22 Fredric Jameson, "Architecture and the Critique of Ideology," in J. Ockman et al., *Architecture/Criticism/Ideology* (Princeton: Princeton Architectural Press, 1985); Jameson, "The Politics of Theory: Ideological Positions in the Post-modern Debate," *New German Critique* 33 (Fall 1984), p.53–65.

23 Ibid., p.312.

24 For a fuller discussion of this point, see my article, "The Architecture of Deceit," *Perspecta* 21 (1984), p.110–115

25 Peter Eisenman, "Post-Functionalism," *Oppositions* 6 (Fall 1976), now in *Oppositions Reader*, p.12.

26 Ibid., p.12.

27 Tafuri, "L'Architecture dans le Boudoir," p.296, 299, 300.

28 Ibid., p.307.

29 Tafuri and Dal Co, *Modern Architecture*, p.409.

30 Peter Eisenman, "The End of the Classical: The End of the Beginning, the End of the End," *Perspecta* 21 (1984), p.154–172, now in M. Hays, ed. *Architecture Theory Since 1968* (Cambridge MA: MIT Press, 1998), p.522–538; the text cited is on p. 530.

31 Tafuri, *Architecture and Utopia*, p.ix; see also "The Ashes of Jefferson," p.302.

32 "Entretien," p.65.

33 Tafuri, "The Ashes of Jefferson," p.301.

34 Ibid., p.300.

35 Tafuri and Dal Co, *Modern Architecture*, p.410.

36 Hal Foster, "(Post)Modern Polemics," *Perspecta* 21 (1984), p.145–153; Bernard Tschumi, "The Architectural Paradox," *Studio International* (September–October 1975), now in Hays, ed. *Architecture Theory Since 1968*, p.218–228. Tschumi writes of a labyrinth from which it is impossible to escape, and of an "architecture [that] can never be."

37 In his text "The Historical Project,'" *Oppositions* 17 (Summer 1979), Tafuri had already introduced the theories of Jacques Derrida, Jacques Lacan, Gilles Deleuze and Felix Guattari to English readers, and his critique of the language games of the New York Five were articulated again in "The Ashes of Jefferson," in Italian in *La sfera e il labirinto: Avanguardia e architettura da Piranesi agli anni '70* (Turin: Einaudi 1980) and translated into English in *The Sphere and the Labyrinth*, p.291–303.

38 Jacques Derrida, "Des Tours de Babel," trans. Joseph F. Graham, ed. J. Graham, *Difference in Translation* (Ithaca: Cornell University Press, 1985), p.165, cited by Wigley, p.672.

39 Mark Wigley, "The Translation of Architecture, the Production of Babel," in Hays, *Architecture Theory since 1968*, p.661–675; the quote is from p.670.

40 Ibid., p.671.

41 Jeffrey Kipnis, "Twisting the Separatrix," *Assemblage* 14 (April 1991), now in Hays, *Architecture Theory since 1968*, p.710–742.

42 Bernard Tschumi, "Notes Towards a Theory of Architectural Disjunction," *Architecture and Urbanism* 216 (September 1988), p.13–15, now in Kate Nesbitt, ed. *Theorizing a New Agenda for Architecture: An Anthology of Architectural Theory 1965–1995* (New York: Princeton Architectural Press, 1996), p.170–172.

43 Daniel Libeskind, *Chamber Works: Architectural Meditations on Themes from Heraclitus* (London: Architectural Association, 1983).

44 Joan Ockman, "Venice and New York," *Casabella* 619–620 (January–February 1995), p.57–71.

45 "Entretien," p.67. As evidence for Tafuri's preference for the work of the New York Five, Ockman cites Tafuri's comment from *Architecture and Utopia*, an essay written before he had any contact with or knowledge about this group.

46 Ockman's comment is in "Venice and New York," p.64; Cacciari's is from the eulogy "Quid tum" delivered in Venice on 25 February 1994, exerpted in *Casabella* 619–620, p.168.

47 Tafuri, "L'Architecture dans le Boudoir," p.307.

48 Ingersoll, "There is no criticism, only history," p.8–11.

49 Tafuri, *La sfera e il labirinto* (Turin: Einaudi, 1980), 368–9, translation mine.

50 Mark Wigley, "Post-Operative History," *ANY* 25–16 (2000), p.47–53; the quotation is from p.53.

51 Ibid.

52 Ibid.

53 Tafuri and Dal Co, *Modern Architecture*, p. 40.

CHRISTOPHER WOOD

Why Autonomy?

Autonomy, which is a synonym for freedom, is a privilege that artists tend to enjoy only in modern societies. Free or sovereign artifice is a powerful force. In traditional societies that rely heavily on poetic language, carved and painted figures, and buildings to generate the mysteries of state or cult, art is granted relatively little autonomy.

In the West over the last five hundred years, art gradually lost its traditional connections to state and cult, and the idea that the fine arts might be liberal arts, and therefore permitted to run free, emerged as a compensation. At first the autonomy of art was guaranteed by local potentates who hoped that by protecting art they might harness it to their parochial political ends. The first haven of the modern artist was thus the princely court of the Renaissance.[1] The princely patron extracted a talented artist from the coils of urban guild restrictions and from the levelling mechanisms of a craft whose interest it was to run art as if it were a business. Eventually, by the nineteenth century, European society as a whole came to share the prince's belief that artists were properly exempt from the old customs. From then on, artists were permitted to do what they liked, more or less, without having to answer for it.

Autonomy in a different sense was also an internal goal of art, again one that could only be realized after the fundamental disengagement of art from religion and statecraft carried out in the early modern period. This is the sense that the artwork itself, and not just art-making and the art-maker, might be self-motivated and self-sufficient. Since artworks are not living, sentient things, this can only be a metaphorical goal — unless the artwork is literally, magically, meant to come to life. Animation of the artifact was in fact a central, if unrealistic, goal of much of ancient art-making. The ancient craftsman, disciple of the engineer Daedalus, dreamed of fashioning an automaton that would speak and move of its own accord.[2] This conception of artistic "realism" actually survived deep into modern European times. As late as the eighteenth century, artistic time and talent were still being invested in the project of constructing an artificial vitality.[3] An automaton would be a work of art without meaning, for a work such as that would naturally be capable of deciding for itself what it wanted to say.

Nineteenth and early twentieth-century artists and thinkers, dissatisfied

with the meager technologies of artistic realism at their disposal, resigned themselves to a merely metaphorical vitalism and automatism: the ideal of a work of art closed in upon itself, infinitely dense, irreducible in much the same way that a human soul is irreducible, and signifying nothing. Some described this new ideal of closure and independence as monadic, invoking a term central to the metaphysical philosophy of Leibniz. The early twentieth-century aesthetician Benedetto Croce, pointing to the distinction between artworks and symbolic representations, said that the artwork had no doppio fondo, no "double" or "false bottom" like a magician's suitcase.[4] Representations, when explored, yield hidden meanings; artworks, by contrast, simply are what they are. Artworks do not issue any invitations. Many modernist theorists have held this view of the artwork, and yet at the same time felt it necessary to justify the artwork to modernity. Theodore W. Adorno, for instance, in order to rescue the monadic work from complete irrelevancy, argued that the very existence of a self-sufficient, self-contained artifact is an implicit critique or negation of the practical world.

With such arguments, the modernist artist has been licensed to make things that are no longer used in ordinary ways. These pointless but strangely potent artifacts are cordoned off from the rest of the material world by various framing and labelling devices. Some makers of these privileged things win great fame and material rewards, but it is arguable that they do so only by betraying their commitment to autonomy — by performing as glorified interior decorators, for instance, or by penetrating the spheres of glamour and celebrity. Most art-makers are not at all famous. Negation is meant to be its own reward. Art-making, according to the logic of autonomy, successfully finds its target in direct proportion to its disengagement from the business of the world. Autonomy is just another word for nothing left to lose.

Architecture, by contrast, is always answerable and never disengaged from the business of the world; and it would have plenty to lose if it were to disengage itself. Unlike painting, architecture historically never gave up its close connection to authority. Architects still represent society's understanding of itself, still shelter and shape the central symbolic activities of social life, and still mediate between man and nature in ways that painters or sculptors can

only envy. Architecture does not need to simulate vitality through a posture of monadicity. And there is clearly no need for society to compensate architecture with the gift of autonomy. It is amazing that architects would try to claim this ambiguous privilege, unless they were announcing their own withdrawal from the world.

There are places of privacy, leisure, and luxury imbedded within the architectural field where quasi-autonomous experiments can be carried out: villas, pavilions, gardens, caprices. Here, and in its virtual projects, architecture does win for itself some of the freedom and eloquence enjoyed by painting or poetry. Architecture's situation resembles that of fashion. The inescapable tasks of clothing and sheltering prevent either fashion or architecture from attaining autonomy. But clothes and buildings are symbolic machines and those who operate these machines naturally crave discursive freedom. Fashion and architecture are thus always striving towards autonomy, but only achieving it ephemerally and spectacularly in the experimental modes of their respective industries: on the one hand, haute couture, and on the other, the architectural caprice and the utopian project.

Once beyond the caprice and the project, the ideal of autonomy in architecture is not much more than a mystification. It is true that individual buildings can eventually, by the mysterious workings of reception, achieve something like autonomy. It is not completely meaningless to say that the Parthenon or the cathedral of Reims are monads. But it is hard to set out to build an autonomous building. In the modern world, where people tend to disagree wildly about the ultimate grounds of meaning and value, it is impossible to do so. The vision of an autonomous architecture descends from the early Romantic idea that life itself may be thought of as a work of art and shaped according to aesthetic principles. This idea encouraged the inflated and heroic image of an artist who would teach non-artists how to live. Trying to reshape the world by making poems or paintings is one thing; trying to do it by making buildings is like operating heavy machinery under the influence of a potent drug. Architectural self-rule would be misrule.

Of course, architects do blunder into the lives of cities and perpetrate quasi-criminal affronts to human dignity and freedom, again and again. Soci-

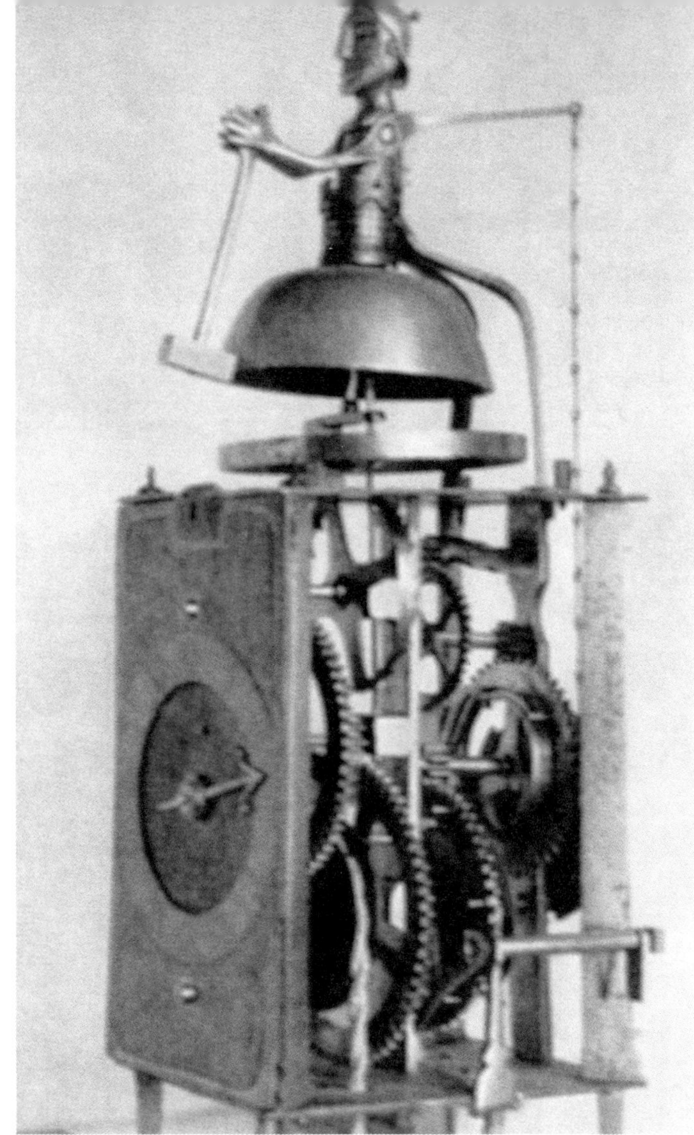

Clock with automaton,
16th century.

eties seem to forgive them this. It is ironic that the much feebler fine arts, with their philosophically well-established claims to autonomy, are from time to time made to answer for their crimes in petty ways, with injunctions and obscenity charges and the like, whereas architecture goes completely unpunished. The reason for this is that painters and poets are almost universally conceded their sovereignty, even if their exemption from responsibility is sometimes absurdly contested. Architects, by contrast, whatever they themselves might imagine, are not at all held by society to be sovereign; rather, buildings are rightly understood to be the products of complex collective forces, conjunctions of circumstances, and the exigencies of technology and materials. There seems to be no other way of explaining why architects are not held responsible for the crimes of architecture.

To be fair, architects who ask for autonomy today usually are not asking for carte blanche or a heroic license to shape life for the rest of us. They are asking for a recognition of the systematicity of architecture. Architecture is autonomous or free, in this view, because it is capable of generating meaning out of its own internal symbolic resources without having to rely on auxiliary iconographical devices and without having to wait for its cue from the commission, the function, or the materials. Architecture is seen to be capable, for instance, of exercising an Adornian, oppositional critique by manipulating differential relationships conventionally established within the history and the system of architecture. This model of a closed system of art is the ideal cultivated in art academies since the Italian Renaissance: the ideal of an art about other art, and not about the world, an art that manages yet to say something about the world through its transfigurations of prior art. More recently, the doctrine has been updated with structuralist and hyperstructuralist linguistic theory. This body of theory has become the model for any theory of systematically generated meaning. One can see why a theory of autonomous architectural meaning would turn to structuralist linguistics for support. Structuralism provides a model for the non-motivation, or freedom from external directives, of the architectural sign. Signs themselves, in structuralist theory, are meaningless marks that take on meaning only when differentiated from other similar-looking or sounding marks. According to a structuralist theory of architecture, signs are linked to signified contents only by the internally established customs or conventions of architecture itself. Architects generate meaning by manipulating those conventions – by making choices and combinations among intrinsically meaningless conventions. Here one sees how the old ideal of the work of art as automaton might survive in a modern context.

A deconstructive approach, meanwhile – which is not an overturning but an extension of structuralism, a neo- or hyperstructuralism – maintains that the link between sign and signified is inherently unstable by virtue of the material conditions of signing. Traditional structuralism, according to this view of things, had naively treated signs as if they were ideal, abstract entities. But real signs in time and space are constantly drifting away from the historical and local convention-systems that alone endow them with meaning. According to hyperstructuralism, any linguistic statement will always be revealed to be a statement of the impossibility of stating anything. Once you accept the linguistic model of architectural meaning, you can easily see how the deconstructive project, with all its explosive potential, could be translated to architecture.

But the linguistic model of architectural meaning is a spurious contrivance. It is a weak metaphor that has been allowed to survive as the foundation for entire edifices of architectural theory. To understand how this could have happened, one has to look back to a more general theory of artistic autonomy: the "formalist" and "aestheticist" thinking of the late nineteenth and early twentieth centuries, itself a kind of moderate, domesticated version of the enthusiastic "absolute" idealism of the early nineteenth-century German philosophers. The art critic and aesthetician Konrad Fiedler, for example, dismayed by crassly materialist theories of artistic creativity and by the "realist" project in painting, argued in 1881 that art had no need to emulate the world

and no reason to be constrained by it. For Fiedler, the world itself was the creature of the mind. "The truly artistically gifted nature," he maintained, "brings forth in itself so to speak that process, now arrived at a new freedom, in which reality is generated for man." Art for Fiedler was real enough without having to look like reality.[5] The Viennese art historian Alois Riegl, following Fiedler, argued at the end of the nineteenth century that the historical mutations of artistic form obeyed an internal logic that unfolded independently of practical function or material conditions. Riegl demonstrated this with relative ease in his 1893 history of the development of ornamental motifs in the ancient world. More provocative was his later attempt to see through the superficial mimetic or symbolic content of early medieval and eventually Renaissance and Baroque sculptures and paintings, and instead perceive their deep structural formal principles – one might say their ornamental principles. By seeing through content, Riegl prepared these works for insertion into an immanent, independent history of form.[6]

Riegl was less interested than some of his contemporaries were in the notion of the closed or monadic work of art. In his writings, it was the spirit of art-making itself that was autonomous: self-sufficient, self-propelling, a mysteriously vital force. For Riegl, the work of art generated by the spirit, once it had been broken down by the critical eye into its formal elements, turned out to be wonderfully open to the world. In principle, the work's deepest meaning – its bearing on politics and society, on fundamental ethical questions – was legible in its manipulations of line and color in the picture plane and in pictorial space.

Riegl's schema provided the framework for a sophisticated cultural history of art. But it seems that his vision of the homology between art and life does not support a critical aesthetics, a doctrine of art's autonomy that would underwrite art's exceptionalism and justify its fictional, hypothetical moment. Consequently, there have been a number of attempts to assimilate Riegl's vitalist "will to art" to theoretically more complex models of systematic autonomy.

It has been tempting, for example, to compare Riegl's reduction of pictorial meaning to a matter of simple formal choices to the structuralist linguistics of Ferdinand de Saussure.[7] Riegl was an exact contemporary of Saussure. The rediscovery and theoretically-informed rereading of Riegl in art history since the 1970s followed closely upon the post-war discovery of Saussure. Since then there has been a tendency to project the insights of language-based structuralist thought back onto late nineteenth-century German aesthetics and art history. Francesco Dal Co, for instance, credits Fiedler and Riegl with recognizing that artistic products, no less than linguistic statements, must be understood as representations, that is, as negations of any "simple reflection between subject and object, as 'artificial' constructions" cut off from any foundation of meaning, and as "autonomous events" yielding up truths only about themselves.[8]

But this attempt to justify the aestheticist project by linking it to modernist insights into the groundlessness of linguistic representation, an attempt launched by Fiedler himself, is impossible to sustain. Painted pictures and buildings can bear meaning, but it is seldom their principal function to do so. And even when they do represent something, paintings and buildings do so in ways that have little to do with linguistic representation. Any later extensions of Riegl's ambitious formalism that imagine they are underwritten by linguistic theory must be evaluated with care. Certainly there are special cases when artists and architects seem to be choosing among an array of formal possibilities whose links to various concepts are agreed upon by a given community of beholders, an array functioning therefore something like a code. Through these choices, the artist or architect seems to be generating textual meaning. But such quasi-codes are never really agreed upon within a community, nor do its members agree which elements of pictorial or architectural form are coded and which are not. Architects may argue that the code is established by the history of architecture. But the history of architecture has to be learned from travel and books, and every individual learns it differently. Every student of the history of architecture has his or her own constantly shifting idea of the code. Real language cannot afford this pluralism. Language functions only because grammar is embedded in the brain at birth and because the local linguistic code is learned in early childhood and only incrementally expanded later. Beholders of painting or architecture who are not at all familiar with the alleged code can derive pleasure and meaning, not to mention use-value, from the picture or building, whereas language is nearly useless to someone unfamiliar with the code.

Language, finally, derives all its flexibility and its economy from two principles: the arbitrariness and the double-articulation of its material signifiers. The form of the signifier is arbitrary in that it is unconstrained by any external considerations; any signifier will do as long as everyone agrees to recognize it. The signifier is doubly articulated in the sense that words, which can be multiplied infinitely, are built from combinations of a tiny number of phonetic modules.[9] Pictorial or architectural signifiers are neither doubly articulated nor arbitrary. Ornamental motifs seem to be the closest to arbitrary formal signifiers, and it is in this domain that writers on art have been most tempted to turn to the model of language. But here, too, the analogy is weak. A truly arbitrary signifier gets attached to its concept not because any feature of the signifier makes it especially appropriate to that concept, but entirely because of custom. In art and architecture, there is always some reason why one signifier is formally preferable to another for representing a given content. Horizontal elements in a building cannot simply be used to signify anything at all; it would be difficult to have them signify "verticality," for instance.

Structuralist systematicity may appear at first to hold out the hope of an articulate, possibly critical representationality – a discursive autonomy – for buildings and pictures alike. Yet without true arbitrariness, conventionality, and double-articulation, pictorial and architectural representation can only attain that weaker, more general sort of autonomy described by late Romantic aestheticism: the fine, pure vision of the formal imagination as a perpetuum mobile.

A stronger version of the analogy between architecture and language is even harder to sustain: the idea that art or architecture's autonomy might be guaranteed not by the arbitrariness of its signifiers, but by their very non-arbitrariness. If horizontal elements mean what they do for deep and ineluctable reasons, the argument goes, then perhaps architecture has a kind of grammar which can be manipulated to generate meanings. Riegl himself introduced the analogy in planning a "historical grammar" of the visual arts.[10] But this analogy underrates the power of grammar and unfairly borrows the prestige of grammar to justify ultimately non-grammatical operations. Grammar is innate and cannot be manipulated. The system of pronominal designation of the first and second persons, in particular, is indispensable to the construction of a sense of self – literally, not figuratively, indispensable. Since grammar is inseparable from human subject-formation, it is not easily manipulated to poetic or representational ends. When architects generate meaning by deliberately confusing our expectations about inside and outside or wall and support, they are operating with a freedom that language-users do not enjoy. The architects here are provisionally liberating architectural elements from their customary functions and meanings in order to introduce them into a systematicity in which they will carry new meaning. To argue that architecture thus does what language does is to mix two levels of language, and to imagine that the elements of grammatical deep structure can be loosened and pushed around as if they were signifiers. The better analogy is not with language itself but with poetry: the building liberates and redeploys the elements of building as if they were words. The difference from poetry is that words have no other purpose than to carry meaning, and no one mistakes a poem for a non-poetic use of language, whereas an architect who builds a poem cannot be certain that all the future users of the building will recognize it as a poem. What architects are asking for when they ask for autonomy, and what societies will want to think about twice before granting, is poetic license.

In assessing claims that architecture might make to discursive autonomy, one has to be alert to hidden and restrictive idealisms. The art historian Riegl understood the supposedly free generation of meaning as a manipulation of a finite supply of markers within a severely regulated system. Riegl's sense of the limits of human freedom was characteristic of his epoch. By the late nineteenth century, the achievements of inductive scientific research and empirical historical scholarship weighed heavily on the imagination. Laws of nature had been discovered and confirmed by repeated experiments. The mind and the spirit, too, it was feared, would soon be submitted to definitive explanation. If a Romantic philosopher around 1800 could still conceive of freedom as the invention of entirely new laws – new societies, new forms of the spirit – the disillusioned thinker of 1900 could only conceive of freedom as, at best, a capacity to operate within a framework of pre-existing laws. History itself seemed a monumental burden that threatened to stifle all creativity and all reflection. Oscar Wilde and Walter Pater agreed that the human will would never again enjoy that "naïve, rough sense of freedom" that it had enjoyed in pre-historicist times.[11] In *Problems of Style*, Riegl chided the contemporary Arts and Crafts movement for encouraging modern artists to choose their motifs freely from the natural world, contrasting these meaningless options with the self-generating, "essentially more artistic," and lawful unfolding of ornamental form in the classical Mediterranean.[12] Riegl conceived of freedom as a surrender to the laws of history.

It seems that Saussure's structuralism derives from a similar impression of the limits on the symbolizing faculty. Riegl and Saussure, as noted, were contemporaries. But again the analogy between art and language is flawed and cannot be used to vindicate the idealist aesthetics entailed by Riegl's schema. Language's laws are real, and they are the basis for language's efficacy. The limiting conditions of language did not develop historically and cannot easily be dismantled. Saussure was describing an ahistorical system; languages may have their histories, but language does not. Art, by contrast, has few laws, and it certainly has a history. What Riegl presents as a permanent "grammar" of artistic form is in fact not much more than a taxonomy of form derived from a descriptive history of Western art. Laws of formal morphology of the sort Riegl divined in art history are fictional and dangerously easy to exaggerate. Art in Riegl's system is thus not at all free, but rather always hurtling towards a projected future where art will converge with spirit and embody the highest aspirations of humanity. Riegl's notion that art is disengaged from matter and pursues its own abstract ends independently of any practical or symbolizing tasks imposed on it – that art is an autonomous activity – is an idealist and potentially an illiberal notion.

The restrictive idealism hiding within the ideal of autonomy, and the consequent threat to practical, everyday freedoms, takes various forms. The eighteenth-century German writer and art historian Johann Joachim Winckelmann, for example, saw social and political freedom literally embodied in the ideal Greek nude. As Alex Potts has explained, freedom for Winckelmann is "not just the condition that makes possible the imaginative creation of an ideal beauty. It is also the subjective state of being figured by that beauty, through its apparent embodiment of a state of unconstrained narcissitic plenitude, which he identifies most immediately with the self-absorbed, free-standing, naked male figure."[13] For the neo-classicist Winckelmann, freedom was not an opening outward but an arrival at a fixed aesthetic resting point. For others, freedom was a mystical aspiration, perhaps the aspiration to escape from the humiliating conditions of earthly and temporal life: the ideal of Weltflucht, or flight from the world. An echo of that yearning is heard in the architectural theorist's dream of a "language of architecture, which in a sense exists outside of and thus autonomously of any style," an architecture no longer doomed to register its own historical time.[14]

One further proof of the inappropriateness of the linguistic model of meaning to architecture is art historical formalism's inability to deal with architecture. Early twentieth-century art historians like Heinrich Wölfflin submitted both painting and buildings to formalist analysis; the levelling use of photograph or slide comparisons made this easier. But in the long run formalism could not keep architecture in play. Most important formalist art history and criticism of the twentieth century, from Lionello Venturi and Clement Greenberg to Michael Fried and Rosalind Krauss, simply leaves architecture aside. This omission is surely an acknowledgement that architecture is about empathy, appetite, movement, absolute dimensions, and the passage of real time and the occupation of real space. It cannot easily reduce all these to metaphor as painting and sculpture manage to do if they want. The vectors of need and desire and the calculus of absolute dimensions disturb the premise of systematic autonomy upon which formalist analysis depends.

Architecture is so patently involved with the problem of somatic experience that a formalist treatment of architecture, in order to make sense at all, must subscribe to a dualist, even, idealist conception of the mind-body relationship – that is, a conception of mind's superiority to body. The Renaissance artist and art historian Giorgio Vasari, for instance, was able to bring painting, sculpture, and architecture under the idealist common denominator of disegno, or the mental idea underlying a work of art. In his *Lives of the Most Eminent Painters, Sculptors, and Architects* (1550), a biographical history of Renaissance art that was at the same time a theory of disegno, Vasari gave painting, sculpture, and architecture equal status and attention. Vasari had no reason to isolate architecture because for him all three arts were self-evidently "semi-autonomous:" capable of generating meaning through disegno, but only within the confines of their practical functioning in the world. Not until the modern doctrine of the autonomy of painting and sculpture emerged in the nineteenth century did architectural history begin to be cut off from the rest of art history. In the twentieth century, architectural history and criticism has followed its own paths, in many ways independent of the development of art history and art criticism. Any formalist art history is a contrivance, but a rigorously formalist architectural history would be an outright fantasy.

Much twentieth-century architecture asserted its own representational freedom, even claiming that architecture could articulate critical or opposi-

tional views by manipulating the "language" of architecture. Given what we know about the political opportunism of the makers of some of the most formally eloquent buildings of the century – Ludwig Mies van der Rohe or Philip Johnson, for instance – it seems that formalist freedom amounted to little more than the intellectual freedom to change sides when it was convenient. Even more pernicious is the use of the doctrine of autonomy as a mask for a vulgar-Nietzschean conception of the "strong architect's" arbitrariness and superiority to constraint. Only the strong architect, the theory goes, can resist the pressures of the world and deliver an authentic critique. It is astonishing that architectual theorists loyally rush to the defense of this self-image of the architect by invoking autonomy, arguing, for instance, that a "critical signature" allows the architect to resist the "massive centralization and standardization of the postwar building establishment."[15] How gratifying it must be to architects to be compared to the auteurs of the cinematic nouvelle vague! But all this carping is perhaps unfair, given that political opportunism is part of the job description of the architect, who must treat constantly with corporate and state power. The intellectual community seems to realize this; how else can one explain the consistently charitable critical treatment of celebrated architects, sharply contrasted to the constant ideological vigilance and moralism that canonical modern poets and philosophers face.

Some conservative thinkers have seen aesthetic autonomy as one of the keys to the larger catastrophe of Modernism, with no more striking emblems of that catastrophe than the utopian projects of high modernist architecture. Hans Sedlmayr, for instance, a reactionary Austrian art historian and critic, derided the "cosmopolitan" and supposedly "pure" architecture of Le Corbusier. Sedlmayr, here drawing on the research of Emil Kaufmann, traced the rootlessness and despiritualization of modernist architecture back to the visions of the French Revolutionary architects Ledoux, Boullée, and Lequeu.[16] Autonomous architecture as envisioned by Ledoux and realized by Adolf Loos and Le Corbusier was architecture that had "become conscious of its own true nature." But architecture achieved this, according to Sedlmayr, by abandoning its representational responsibilities and instead pursuing absolute geometrical ideals. Quoting a contemporary reviewer of Kaufmann's book, Sedlmayr declared that "autonomy was slavery," anticipating, by a single year, the famous mantra from George Orwell's novel 1984: "Freedom is Slavery," one of the three slogans inscribed on the façade of the Ministry of Truth, a building, incidentally, that might have been built by Ledoux, pyramidal in form, in white concrete, three hundred meters high.[17]

Sedlmayr was a follower of Riegl and a radical formalist, and in his own art history not only preserved Riegl's model of an autonomously unfolding "life of forms," but also developed a concept of the density and irreducibility of the individual artwork more explicit than anything found in Riegl. This is paradoxical, for Sedlmayr was at the same time identifying the idea of autonomous art as the source of all Modernism's troubles. He deplored modernity's loss of a stable and ideal image of man and modern art's abandonment of the project of representing that image. He deplored the self-reflexivity and solipsism of the modern work of art. I find that this apparent contradiction persists in writing on modern art to the present: it is often the conservatives lamenting modernity's chaotic dynamism who most fiercely defend the two kinds of autonomy, both the independence of the artmaking process and the irreducibility of the artwork. The reason for this seems to be that these two ideals of autonomy still imply humanism: an integral image of man, confidence in the range and capacities of the will, hope for betterment. Autonomous art, however, even if it has its historical roots in that image of man, was never required by its constitution to contribute to that image, as Sedlmayr would have pointed out regretfully.

So the anti-modernist Sedlmayr supported the ideal of autonomy against what the avant-garde had done with it, while the avant-garde itself embraced the critique of autonomy. Indeed, the avant-garde was in many ways framed as a critique of autonomy. This paradox persisted into the 1960s and 1970s, when the so-called neo-avant-garde was able to draw on new theoretical weapons and mount an apparently final, devastating challenge to the idea of aesthetic autonomy. The neo-avant-garde espoused an outright anti-humanism, involving a critique of authorship that followed from the hyperstructuralist and psychoanalytic critique of integrated subjecthood, and a critique of the aesthetic that followed from the philosophical deconstruction of the work and the frame. We are in a strange situation now, in the wake of that challenge. The critique of artistic autonomy carried out in the 1960s and 1970s has to be said to have failed, repeating the failure of the "historical," early twentieth-century avant-garde. The sharp critiques of the ideology of artistic "freedom" levelled by the neo-avant-garde have been instantly and eagerly absorbed by its own institutional targets, the museums, commercial galleries, and art history textbooks. Those institutions were designed to protect the freedom of the visual arts and are not easily rattled when painters and sculptors exercise that freedom, no matter how unpredictably. Artistic autonomy in our society is as safe as it ever was. The critique of architectural autonomy, by contrast, carried out concurrently in these same years, was quite successful. Those who carry on defending architectural autonomy seem to be animated by the same spirit of futility as those who carry on critiquing artistic autonomy.

The two fields, art and architecture, are thus intellectual mirror images of one another. Adornian neo- or post-avant-garde art criticism, exemplified by the influential writings of Benjamin Buchloh, is intellectually paralyzed because it feels itself bound to identify and endorse art that purports to dismantle the ideal of autonomy, even as it must recognize that art is inseparable from the ideal of autonomy — that we wouldn't know how to recognize art at all if it were not autonomous. It is a thrillingly hopeless task to try to undo that knot. The dilemma of the post-avant-garde is sometimes sentimentalized as an aporetic stance, a proud refusal to compromise leading to a severe narrowing of the conception of the artistically permissible. Architecture, meanwhile, is clearly not an autonomous activity and the critic who persists in making the case for architectural autonomy is equally, symmetrically, obstinate. The sheer stubbornness and vanity of such arguments must be the source of their appeal within the architectural field, an appeal that is otherwise perplexing to an outsider.

Autonomy in architecture can never be more than one of the vectors of its force, one of the multiple frames of mind that make up the building process. That seems self-evident. Architecture cannot afford the aporetic disengagement of the post-avant-garde, which is essentially the fastidiousness of the mandarin, ultimately a gentlemanly ideal of withdrawal from the world. Architecture, in fact, has an appetite for the mêlée. All the theoretical talk of autonomy is surely a blind! Sincerity and authenticity, the criteria of ideal personhood that emerged in modern times alongside the doctrine of the pure and independent work of art, are only confusingly, unhelpfully imposed on a practical architect.[18] Architecture, the discipline and the practice, will build the right buildings not by presenting the world with the truth about buildings, but by convincing the world that the world itself knows which buildings are the right ones. Successful architecture calls for a certain political cunning and even duplicity.

The autonomous artwork, ultimately a religious ideal, is a beautiful modern contrivance. Architecture is perhaps best thought of as a pre-modern art.

I am grateful to Romy Golan for her thoughts on this topic.

NOTES

1   Martin Warnke, *The Court Artist: On the Ancestry of the Modern Artist* (Cambridge, Cambridge UP, 1993). esp. p.243–259.

2   Sarah P. Morris, *Daidalos and the Origin of Greek Art* (Princeton: Princeton University Press, 1992), esp. chap.8.

3   Horst Bredekamp, *The Lure of Antiquity and the Cult of the Machine: the Kunstkammer and the Evolution of Nature, Art, and Technology* (Princeton: Markus Wiener, 1995).

4   Benedetto Croce, *Estetica* (1909), cited in Edgar Wind, *Art and Anarchy* (London: Faber and Faber, 1963), p.114, n.57.

5   Konrad Fiedler, "Moderner Naturalismus und künstlerische Wahrheit," in Fiedler, *Schriften über Kunst* (Cologne: DuMont, 1977), p.125.

6   Alois Riegl, *Problems of Style: Foundations for a History of Ornament* (1893), trans. Evelyn Kain (Princeton: Princeton University Press, 1992); *Late Roman Art Industry* (1901), trans. Rolf Winkes (Rome: Bretschneider, 1985); *The Group Portrait of Holland* (1902), trans. Evelyn Kain and David Britt (Los Angeles: Getty Research Institute, 1999).

7   Margaret Iversen, *Alois Riegl: Art History and Theory* (Cambridge, MA: MIT Press, 1993), p.55–56.

8   Francesco Dal Co, *Figures of Architecture and Thought: German Architecture Culture 1880–1920* (New York: Rizzoli, 1990), p.108.

9   Roland Barthes, *Elements of Semiology* (New York: Hill and Wang, 1973), p.39.

10   Alois Riegl, *Historische Grammatik der bildenden Künste* (Graz and Cologne: Böhlau, 1966), a posthumous publication based on lecture notes; the concept of a "historical grammar" was Riegl's own.

11   Jonah Siegel, *Desire and Excess: The Nineteenth-Century Culture of Art* (Princeton: Princeton University Press, 2000), p.231.

12   Riegl, *Problems of Style*, p.207.

13   Alex Potts, *Flesh and the Ideal: Winckelmann and the Origins of Art History* (New Haven : Yale University Press, 1994), p.4.

14   Peter Eisenman, referring to Aldo Rossi and Robert Venturi, in *Autonomy and Ideology: Positioning an Avant-Garde in America* R. E. Somol ed. (New York: Monacelli Press, 1997), p.73.

15   R. E. Somol, "Statement of Editorial Withdrawal," *Autonomy and Ideology*, p.25–26.

16   Hans Sedlmayr, *Art in Crisis: The Lost Center* (1948) (Chicago: Regnery, 1958), esp. p.80–81, 95 ff. Emil Kaufmann, *Von Ledoux bis Le Corbusier: Ursprung und Entwicklung der Autonomen Architektur* (Vienna, 1933).

17   Sedlmayr, *Art in Crisis*, p.100, 101.

18   Lionel Trilling, *Sincerity and Authenticity* (Cambridge: Harvard UP, 1972).

K. MICHAEL HAYS
LAUREN KOGOD
THE EDITORS

Twenty Projects at the Boundaries of the Architectural Discipline Examined in Relation to the Historical and Contemporary Debates over Autonomy

The fundamental criteria for the selection of the twenty projects featured were that each would challenge, in some way, the conventional foundations of the architecutural discipline and engage a discipline outside its boundaries. Further, the choices were limited to contemporary, realized (or soon to be realized) buildings designed by architects. As is clear from the selection, however, each of these stipulations was violated at least once. This framework was valuable for refining and testing our ideas and for establishing a coherent, visible body of built work functioning in a critical context outside the autonomous center of the discipline.

The text that accompanies the selections is taken from discussions between the editors, K. Michael Hays, and Lauren Kogod which focused on the implications of the projects to the discourse on autonomy, in both historical and contemporary contexts. The nine essays listed at the left served as a textual framework for the discussion.

1   Robert A.M. Stern, "Gray Architecture as Post-Modernism, or, Up and Down from Orthodoxy," *Architecture d'aujourd'hui* Aug.–Sept. 1976.

2   Diana Agrest, "Design versus Non-Design," *Oppositions* 6, Fall 1976.

3   Peter Eisenman, "Post-Functionalism," *Oppositions* 6, Fall 1976.

4   Anthony Vidler, "The Third Typology," *Oppositions* 7, Spring 1977.

5   K. Michael Hays, "Critical Architecture: Between Culture and Form," *Perspecta* 21, 1984.

6   Autonomous Architecture, Special issue of *Harvard Architecture Review 3*, Winter 1984.

7   Stanford Anderson, "Critical Conventionalism in Architecture," *Assemblage* 1, October 1986.

8   K. Michael Hays, "The Oppositions of Autonomy and History," in *The Oppositions Reader*, (Princeton: Princeton University Press, 1998).

9   Peter Eisenman, "Autonomy and the Will to the Critical," *Assemblage* 41, April 2000.

K. MICHAEL HAYS When the issue of autonomy re-emerged in the 70s, architecture was in the peculiar situation of being eroded from within by having become a service industry completely determined by the building technology and programmatic demands of the time. On the other hand, it had been challenged from outside the discipline by behaviorisms, sociology, pseudo-positivist history and pseudo-scientific discourses that tried to explain architecture away in terms of how people behaved, or what response they checked off on a questionnaire. Formal issues had given way to these statistical and operational analyses. Architecture found itself without cultural or disciplinary specificity. The re-emergence of the autonomy debate in texts by Agrest or Anderson comes out of that situation. In contemporary vocabulary, we could say that architecture found itself de-territorialized. It lost its domain; it lost the cultural realm that it had controlled. It had to, therefore, re-territorialize itself by rediscovering, reasserting or reinventing its codes, and this is why I think the essays by Diana Agrest and Stanford Anderson are important.

LAUREN KOGOD The spatiality of what you are saying can't go unnoticed – there's an assumption of a legitimate "inside" and a dangerous "outside" here. The idea of autonomy that emerged in the 1970s didn't so much "reclaim" a territory as much as it produced one and normalized it. It produced the "inside" and "outside" that you mention. On the other hand, consider Gropius' "total architecture" and the "everything is architecture" of the late 60s. We can see a cyclical recurrence of critiques of disciplinary specificity, of limits to the discipline.

PERSPECTA 33 Is there a distinction between the autonomous object and the autonomous discipline? Or are they inseparable?

KMH I think they are certainly related and, yes, that which counted as inside or outside architecture certainly mattered. My understanding of the work in the 70s of Eisenman, Rossi, and Agrest and Gandelsonas, the people who were thinking about issues of autonomy, was that the very specificity of the discipline or the discourse was at stake. But certainly that implies that out of that discourse, out of the codes, out of the grammar, objects would be produced which in themselves had a high degree of technical specificity and a logic all their own. Eisenman's series of houses were explorations of purely autonomous objects and were generated by the discourse, the codes. So there's a distinction: the autonomy of the object required a degree of disciplinary autonomy, and the disciplinary autonomy had the expectation of generating autonomous objects. Let me be clear that I don't think architecture can ever really be autonomous. What interests me is that at one point in its history it very much desired to be.

P33 Are you saying that at that time the discipline actually relied upon the autonomous object to have its own discourse?

KMH To represent itself as a distinct mode of thought in a sort of self-identifying, self-criticizing operation.

P33 The architecture was the discourse.

KMH Yes. On the one hand, having accomplished the re-territorialization of the discipline and the construction of these objects, these architects had something through which the discipline could represent itself to itself. FOREIGN OFFICE ARCHITECTS' Yokohama Port Terminal and BILL MASSIE'S Big Belt House come out of that trajectory. JOEL SANDERS could also be related back to the autonomy of the 70s, even though his concern is more with identity and ambiance – concerns not usually associated with the autonomy project of the 70s. But there's something in the way you organize architectural form, whether the desire is to create effects that have to do with sexual or social identity, as in SANDERS, or whether the desired effects have to do with the sort of material experience or the sensuousness of materials. I think the way you organize material, the way you organize spaces, can still be traced back to the searches for, if not the achievement of, disciplinary autonomy in the 70s. But the situation has changed because now that we have recovered architecture's specificity relative to other modes of thought and experience, we ask of what use is it? How can you use it now to produce different sorts of effects? Many of the projects here could be classified as architecture producing very different sorts of experiential, aesthetic, visual, social, or programmatic effects from those that have been previously achieved.

P33 One observation that you made in the introduction to the *Oppositions Reader* was that Agrest, Gandelsonas, and Eisenman were trying to use autonomy and the codes of the discourse to break down or remove architecture from a system of ideology, so that it could speak against it. So when the project starts to be re-functionalized, to have an effect again, to come back into the world with an identity politics or to question the problem of low-income housing in Houston's Fifth Ward, for example, it then begs the question of ideology. At that point, is architecture playing a social role it had renounced in the 70s? If so, how do we trace the legacy of autonomy when architectural projects seem to be re-entering the social realm?

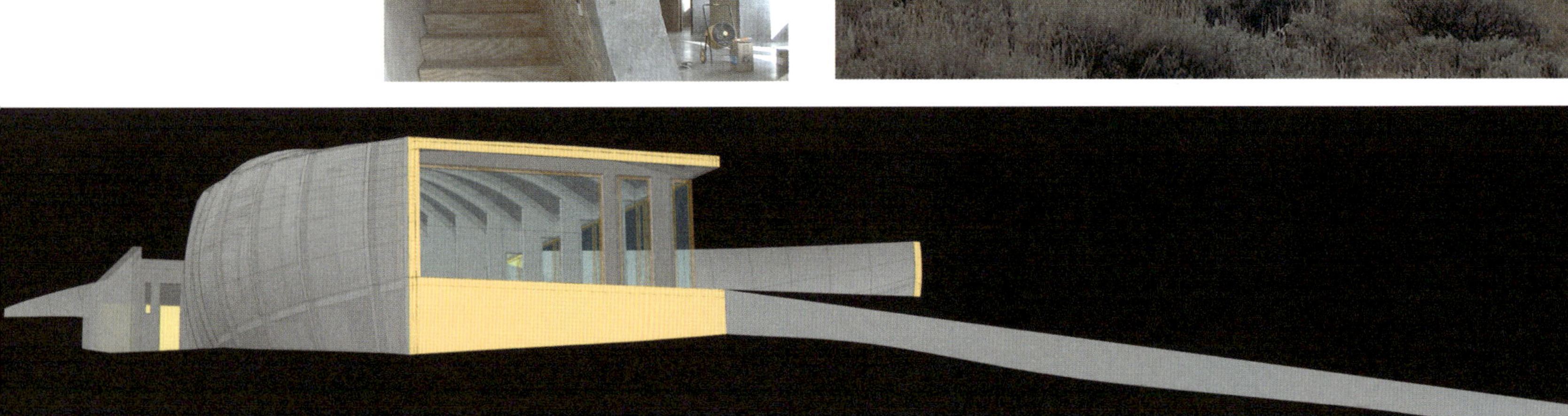

1 BIG BELT HOUSE, BOZEMAN, MONTANA, 2000
Bill Massie

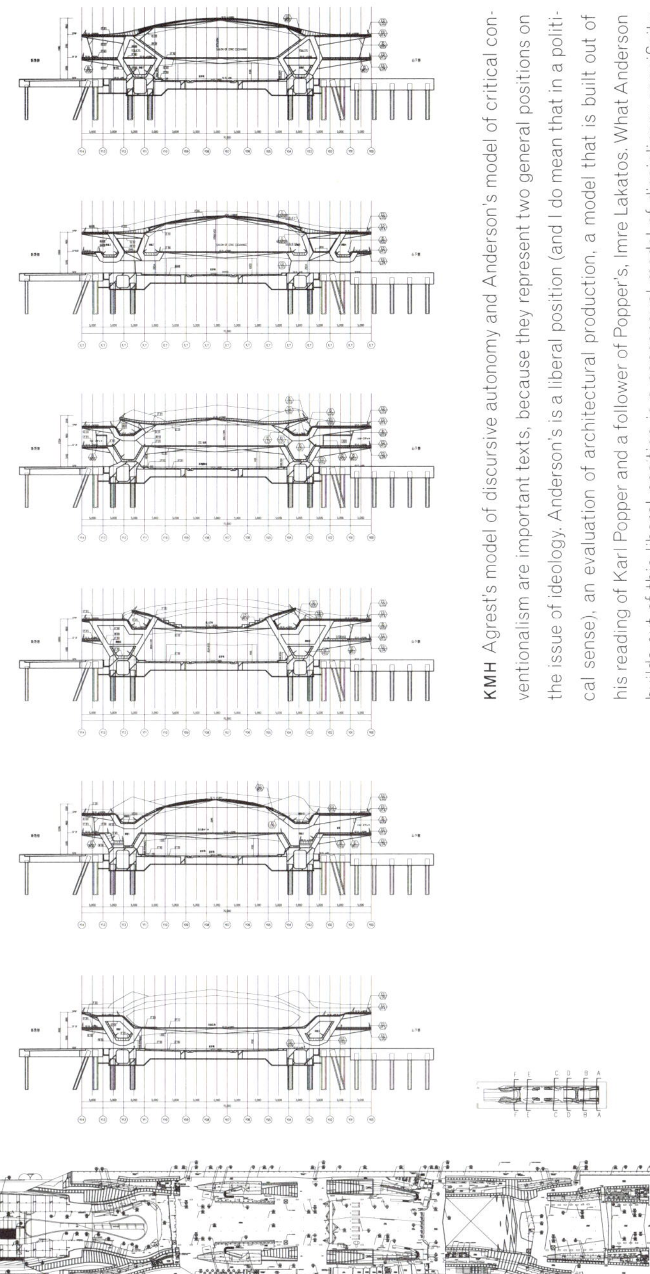

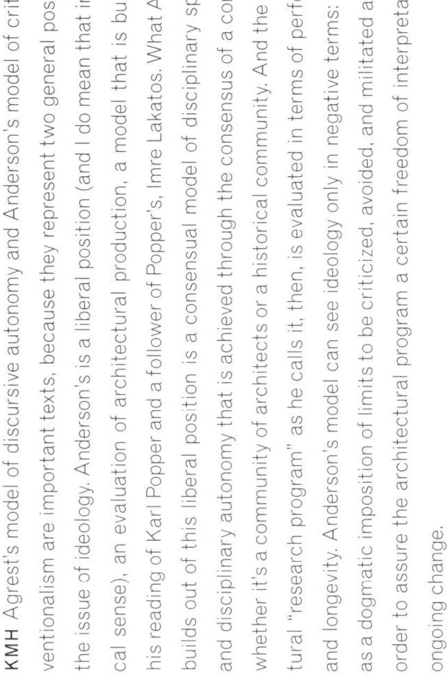

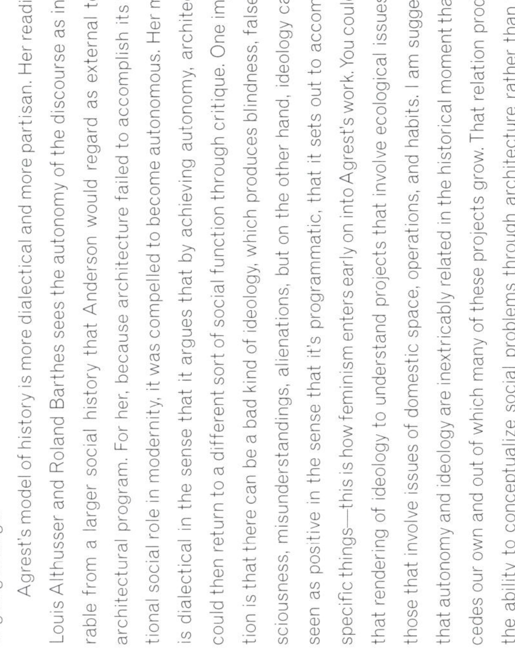

KMH Agrest's model of discursive autonomy and Anderson's model of critical conventionalism are important texts, because they represent two general positions on the issue of ideology. Anderson's is a liberal position (and I do mean that in a political sense), an evaluation of architectural production, a model that is built out of his reading of Karl Popper and a follower of Popper's, Imre Lakatos. What Anderson builds out of this liberal position is a consensual model of disciplinary specificity and disciplinary autonomy that is achieved through the consensus of a community, whether it's a community of architects or a historical community. And the architectural "research program" as he calls it, then, is evaluated in terms of performance and longevity. Anderson's model can see ideology only in negative terms: ideology as a dogmatic imposition of limits to be criticized, avoided, and militated against in order to assure the architectural program a certain freedom of interpretation and ongoing change.

Agrest's model of history is more dialectical and more partisan. Her reading of Louis Althusser and Roland Barthes sees the autonomy of the discourse as inseparable from a larger social history that Anderson would regard as external to the architectural program. For her, because architecture failed to accomplish its traditional social role in modernity, it was compelled to become autonomous. Her model is dialectical in the sense that it argues that by achieving autonomy, architecture could then return to a different sort of social function through critique. One implication is that there can be a bad kind of ideology, which produces blindness, false consciousness, misunderstandings, alienations, but on the other hand, ideology can be seen as positive in the sense that it's programmatic, that it sets out to accomplish specific things—this is how feminism enters early on into Agrest's work. You could use that rendering of ideology to understand projects that involve ecological issues and those that involve issues of domestic space, operations, and habits. I am suggesting that autonomy and ideology are inextricably related in the historical moment that precedes our own and out of which many of these projects grow. That relation produces the ability to conceptualize social problems through architecture rather than think

56

about each one separately. I would look at **MARK RAKATANSKY'S** Adult Day, prototype handrail. To the extent that these projects have a programmatic agenda – social, aesthetic, ecological, constructional, or technological – it is a positive notion of ideology. It is that notion of ideology that gets put into operation and brings with it some notion of disciplinary specificity. It's the autonomy argument, just modulated towards a certain audience or a certain social agenda. Without some notion of a specificity of practice, how can architecture have any cultural moment or effect?

P33 If Agrest and Anderson represent a certain type of critical position, what do we make of Robert Somol's notion of the post-critical relative to these other critical positions and their projects?

KMH I think what bothers Somol about what he calls "critical architecture" is that it depends on the forms having a certain legibility and, as such, restricts other dimensions of experience, like distracted aperception, or "lounging." I think he's right that that strain of architectural theory, related to architectural design production inherited from Eisenman, is a theory that is supposed to generate the architectural forms and also explain them. It is a self-confirming system of theoretical and intellectual legitimacy that is based fundamentally on the legibility of the artifacts, the legibility of the object. If you can't read the object and trace it back to the theory, then the object is inadequate to the theory. And if the theory cannot predict what the object is going to look like, then the theory has somehow failed.

LK It's interesting that this one-to-one correlation is demanded in the jury review system in schools. So often you hear, "these are good ideas, but it isn't what you've done." We try to read the theory directly into the project as a criterion of rigor.

KMH That's true and the result of the dominance of this model is a huge reduction of both the theoretical and the architectural project insofar as it delimits them to a very narrow range of formal generation and legibility. It's a repressive operation that puts a fig leaf over a range of sensuous, ludic, libidinal, ecological, material concerns. That's part of the stuff that Somol is interested in and sees "critical architecture" as having left out. My understanding, on the other hand, is that the term "critical" came from the critical theory of the Frankfurt School or critical theory in its Derridian mode, or critical theory in architecture itself that has its own larger history at least since Hegel. In my mind, critical theory asks how architecture can be irreducible to the conditions of its emergence – how it can have a dimension of autonomy – at the same time those conditions are determinate. More generally, "critical" simply means the constant imagination, search for, and construction of alternatives. If we accept that definition, then Somol's own project is still within the larger meaning of the term.

3 **HABITAT FURTIF**
Roche, DSV & Sie. P/B:L

4 **SCRAMBLED FLAT, EVOLENE, SWITZERLAND, 2001**
Roche, DSV & Sie. P/B:L

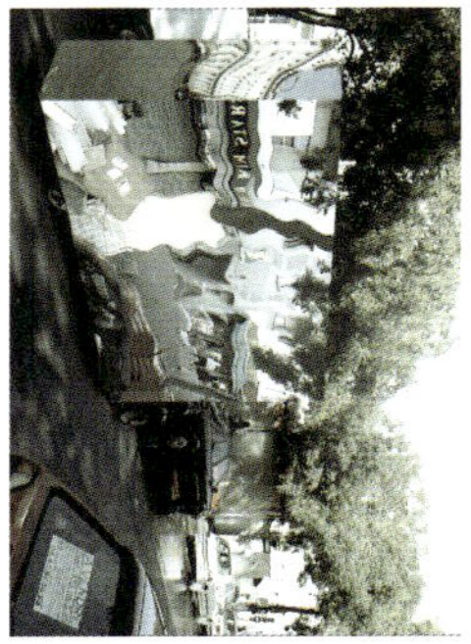

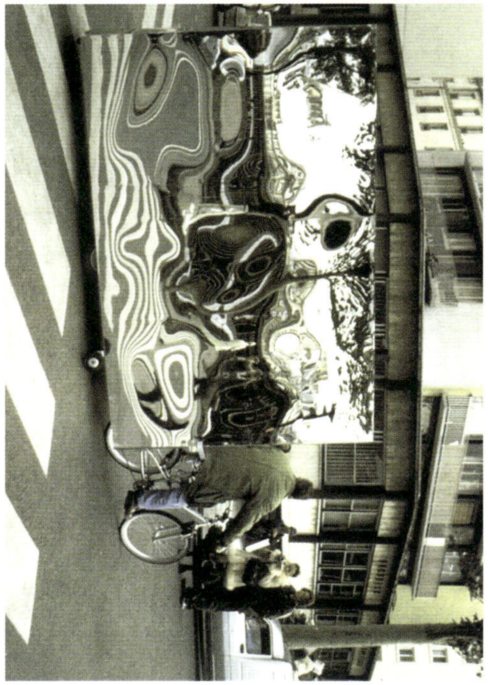

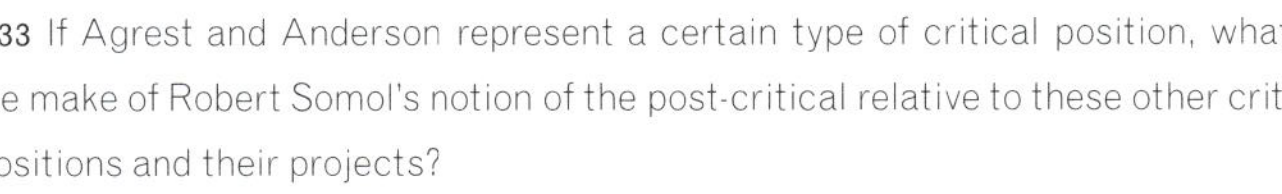

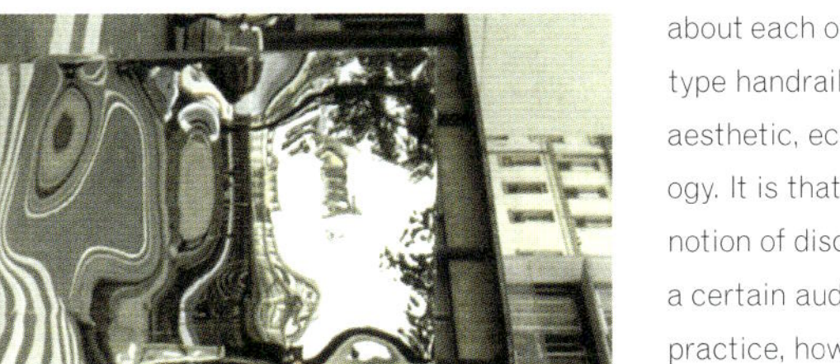

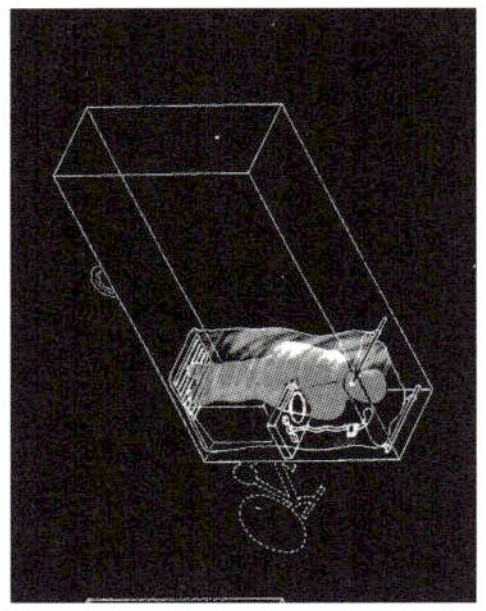

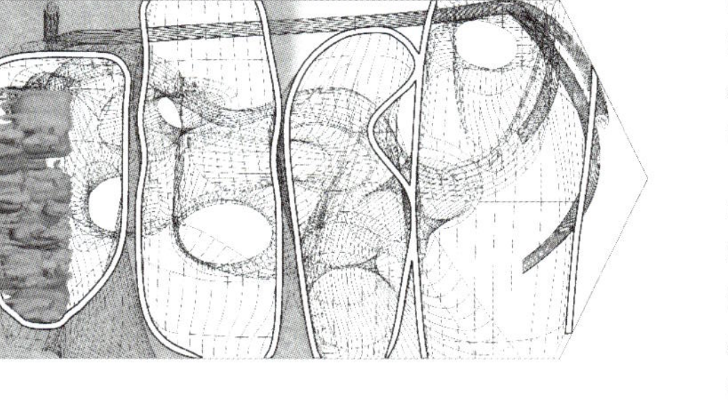

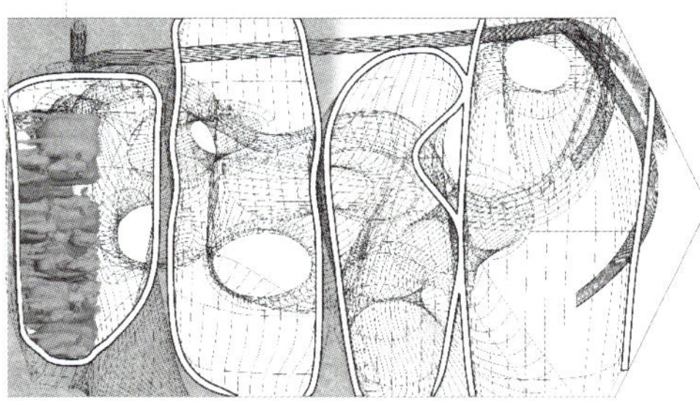

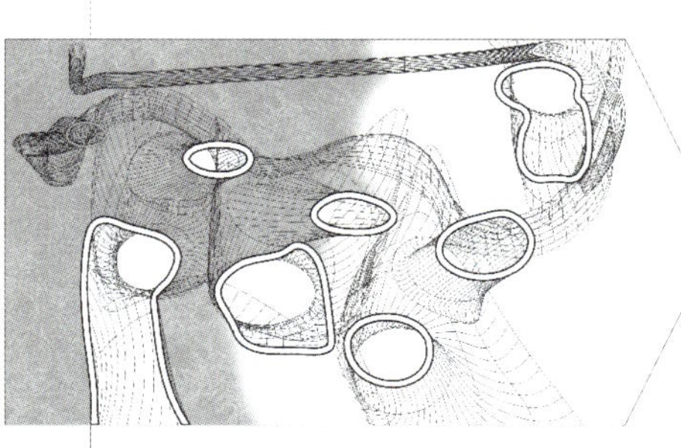

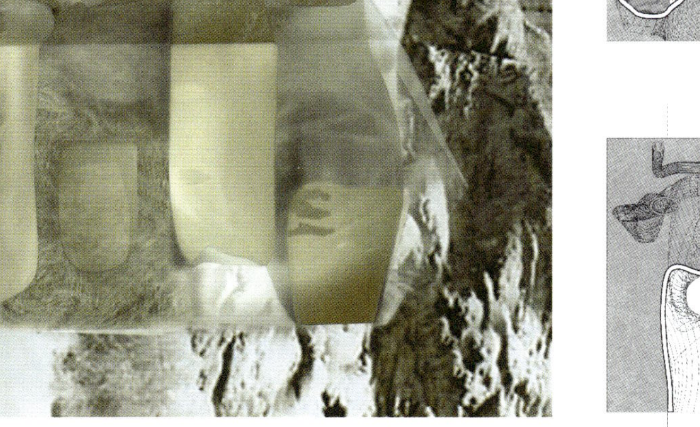

P33 Doesn't Somol assume that a critical project relies on a dialectical model, whereas his version – the projective – does not rely upon the dialectical, and therefore is capable of pure invention?

KMH Yes, he sees a critical project as a dialectical project, and I don't think he's wrong. He sees his ambient model as a way of accommodating other forces and effects that architecture can produce and organize beyond what can be read, beyond what could be encoded visually or formally. But I think he and I would disagree on the continued advantage of dialectics, as long as we understand it as a dialectics that never stops, that can never be resolved.

P33 In the last issue of *Assemblage*, Eisenman wrote about Jeffrey Kipnis and Rosalind Krauss and their opposition to normative architecture and their definition of critical architecture as a practice that destroys any notion of normative architecture. So if architecture is normatively built with four walls, critical architecture tries to renounce that. **ROCHE DSV'S** Habitat Furtif warps our perception of our environment through an object, but it doesn't stand in opposition to a normative condition.

KMH It's important to note that according to Eisenman, autonomy is bound up with the very idea of the modern. Modernism existed in painting and in music, but we never had a modern architecture because we never achieved disciplinary autonomy, never found architecture's intrinsic medium. The extension of the achievement of autonomy would be that architecture can only progress through a self-critical, self-negating procedure. If the norms of the discourse dictate that we have four walls, then the next step of any sort of progress would be the negation and deconstruction of that. Modernism entails autonomy and a way of calibrating progress. So, according to that model, the Habitat Furtif has no force. It doesn't emerge out of an existing formal problem, it simply visually distorts the existing condition.

P33 It has no force, but it still has an effect.

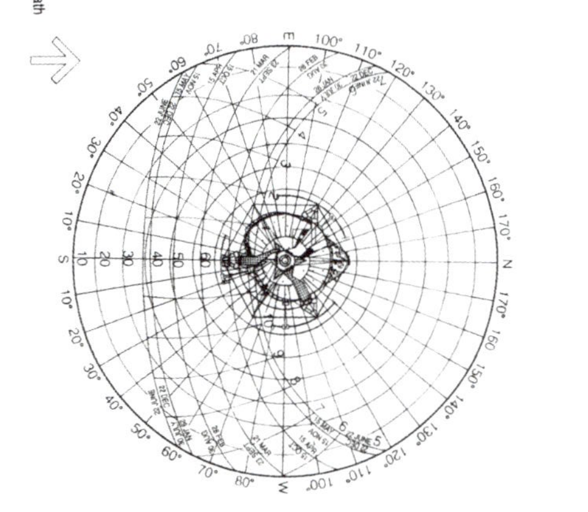

KMH The effect exists only in the momentary experience of it. It doesn't even exist in the photographs; the photograph is just an attempt to capture the experience. I think the same thing could be said about **KEN YEANG**; his architecture doesn't fit within a discourse of formal autonomy and progress through self-negation. It has no formal project. It's outside of architecture according to that model. The Roche and Yeang projects suggest the limits of that model.

Twenty years ago, we began to shift out of a concern solely with producing architectural objects to a concern with the ways in which architectural effects are received. So

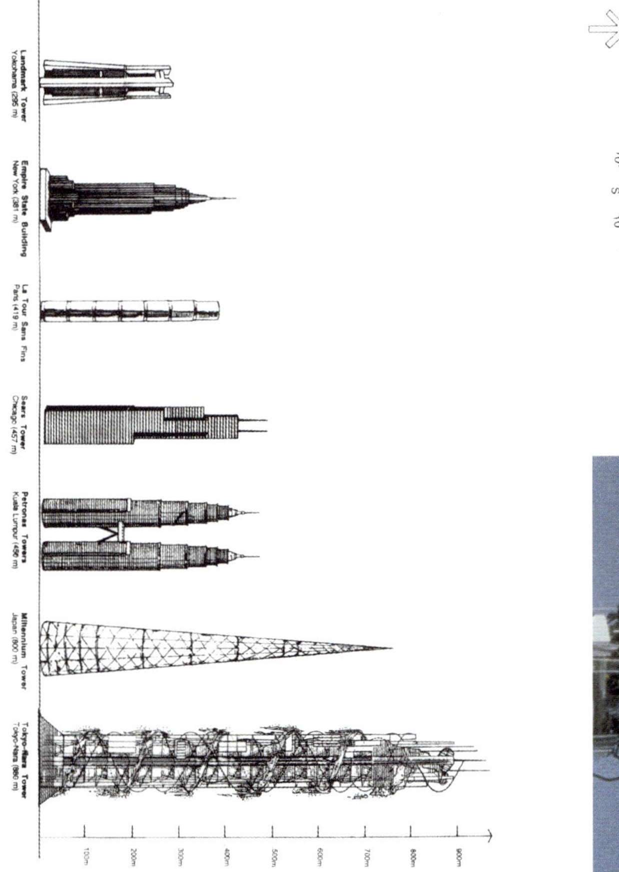

5 TOKYO-NARA TOWER, TOKYO, 1998
Hamzah & Yeang

some of these recent projects come out of the shift from production to reception, from object to effect. Somol and I completely agree on this point. For me it's a historical fact. For him it's polemical. For me it happened because of a convergence of large forces. It's just a historical shift that began to occur and to which architecture responded, and I think that's why these projects now find themselves here.

LK In whatever form, the models of production and reception are both based on a shared assumption about the centrality of the audience and the belief that architectural meaning is located there. But the difference between legibility-based models (both typological and those which inscribed their own processes of design) and effect-based or experiential models is the scale of the architecture in relation to the audience. Many – even most of the textual or legibility-based projects of the 70s and 80s – were as valid on the page as they were built, if not more so. Process and reference were read perfectly well in the drawings. Effect- or response-based work needs or wants to be tested at full scale. Maybe the economy as well as the proliferation of theory in the academies and journals have made more built work possible in recent years. But what could be understood as a backlash against theory in this rush to "make things" might also be seen as a desire to test theories and ideas, and to experience them in a more tangible way – to taste them, so to speak. So instead of seeing an anti-theoretical moment, we could be witnessing a certain victory or sublation of theory.

KMH One of the things that's exciting about this moment is that the territory of the discipline is now vastly expanding because of the perception that architecture can produce these effects. It involves sometimes purely conceptual or visual consequences, as in ROCHE DSV'S Habitat Furtif and as in KEN YEANG'S work, it involves some purely environmental concerns. In both cases form is not an issue, but architecture has expanded to be able to include those concerns. It also goes back to the fact that digital technologies are used to generate the project as well as represent, evaluate, and construct it.

P33 BILL MASSIE'S Big Belt House is a perfect example. He's got a CNC mill on the back of his truck. The frame of the object is completely dislocated; its territory is everywhere. The site is instantaneously inscribed into the project and has immediate effects on production.

6   IL GRANDE CRETTO, GIBELLINA, ITALY, 1968
Alberto Burri

KMH What concerns me about the talk around digitally-generated projects is the claim that they're spontaneous, that they're not authored, that they're not controlled, that they have their own Kunstwollen. What we're seeing in high-end digital imaging should make us suspicious because the projects all look like the software itself. The technology is overly controlling and overly determining. But what's interesting is when the look that emerges from technology can then be read back into, or rescaled, or reframed to have different spatial and material effects. I think **KENGO KUMA'S** Eco-particle Park is really interesting in that respect. He unabashedly starts from a kind of an arbitrary pattern, but reads it back into material and space.

P33 This ties into the work of **FRANCOIS + LEWIS** and **ROCHE DSV**. With **KENGO KUMA** it's a pixel and with **FRANCOIS + LEWIS** and **ROCHE DSV** it's actually an image. But they don't carry with them **KEN YEANG**'s functionally positivistic aim behind his project. Can one find the functional process of a pixel? **FRANCOIS + LEWIS** are not dealing with the ecological properties of the shrubbery around the house. At a certain point, does architecture have to be separated from its original intent and made into form and image?

KMH One thing that should be added to our vocabulary when we're talking about effect and image is the notion of conceptual frame. The **ALBERTO BURRI** project takes a found object, and not only reifies it, making it permanent, but it also conceptually frames it and causes us to rethink something that we might otherwise have never seen or would have forgotten. The **FRANCOIS + LEWIS** project may provide less an image than a conceptual frame. An anecdote that has always helped me is this: you come upon a place (presumably completely natural, in the woods) where there's a pond and some trees, and there's a little plaque that says "see Poussin." By providing a frame, suddenly that natural place in the woods becomes a picturesque garden. It provides an instruction, a conceptual frame that completely alters your perception. In some ways I think there is a dimension of that in the **FRANCOIS + LEWIS**, in the **ROCHE DSV**, and even in the **BURRI**. So, I think frame is related to image but different from it. Tschumi and Koolhaas discovered this early on. The retroactive manifesto theorized un-authored events; they became architecture only when they were framed as architecture.

P33 If the third typology, as defined by Anthony Vidler in the work of Aldo Rossi, is another sort of conceptual frame, how do projects like those of **ONE ARCHITECTURE**, **ANA**, or **KALHOFER & KORSCHILDGEN** relate to it? They seem to relate lifestyle to typology, and use it to criticize or discuss the implications of the Vinex project. We can see this also in **MICHAEL BELL'S** use of low-income housing to question the tradition of the glass house or **LEWIS TSURUMAKI LEWIS'** interrogation of suburban sprawl.

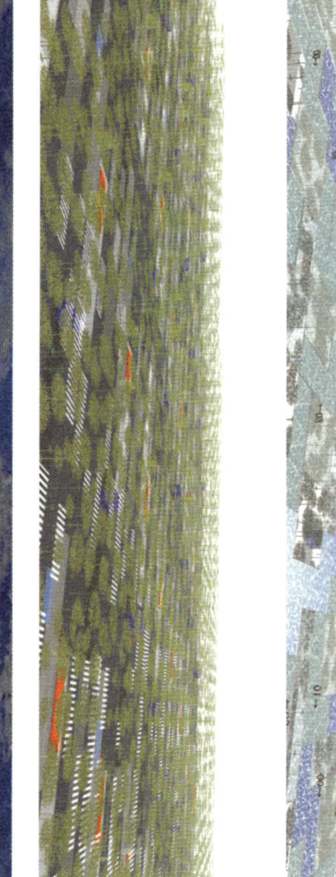

7 ECO-PARTICLE PARK, OSAKA, JAPAN, 1999
Kengo Kuma

8   HOUSE IN JUPILLES, FRANCE, 1998
Edward Francois & Duncan Lewis

KMH Vidler's understanding of typology and his reading of Rossi is that the city itself acts as a generative grammar producing certain objects that the city, as a system, has found useful over long periods of time. We're calling these objects types. Recently, with the work of KALHOFER & KORSCHILDGEN, ONE ARCHITECTURE, ANA, and LEWIS TSURUMAKI LEWIS, it seems that the issue of typology has shifted as architects have become more aware of the threat of the twin poles of market and academy. The typology argument that followed Rossi's work quickly became the hypothesized academic formula that allowed historians, designers, and urbanists to feel all warm and fuzzy about each other. It became a self-confirming academic formula, the polar opposite of the market. The other position is that the market should determine architectural types: that in this way a more spontaneous taxonomy of architecture is revealed. KALHOFER & KORSCHILDGEN, ONE ARCHITECTURE, and ANA are trying to look for a third term outside the bipolar condition of academy and market. They're trying to find it in lifestyle or in the suburban. The typology that spontaneously emerges out of this suburban condition can be retroactively fitted or reframed as an alternative to the architecture of the academy. It's a slightly different version of what we might have at some point called regionalism or the vernacular. MICHAEL BELL'S GLASS HOUSE should be recognized as peculiar. It may be thought of as typological because it's very reduced and basic in its form, but I think BELL and INTERLOOP, too, bring up an interest at the scale of the juncture of materials, a scale that may not be represented otherwise. For INTERLOOP it's at the scale of a hand tool, an appliance. For BELL, it's almost at a micro scale. He's concerned with how glass and metal inflect one another. It gets kind of elusive and ephemeral, but it produces certain effects that are both visual and social, and he would even say political.

65
65

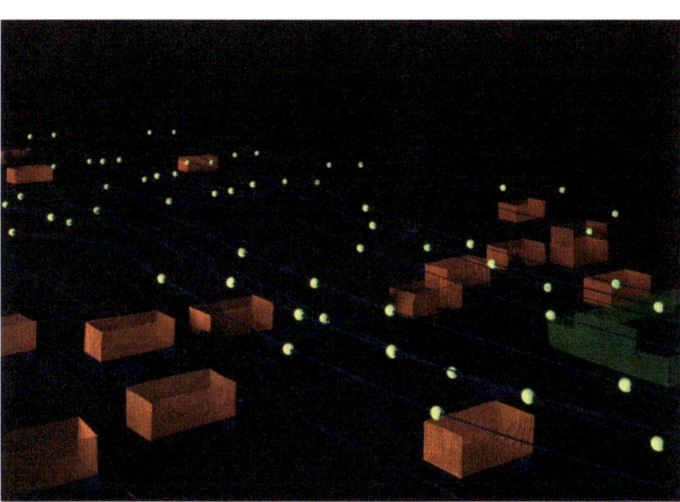

9 SIX UNDER A TENNIS COURT,
LIEDSCHERIJN, THE NETHERLANDS, 1996
One Architecture.

10 HUIS & AMSTERDAM, THE NETHERLANDS, 2000
ANA

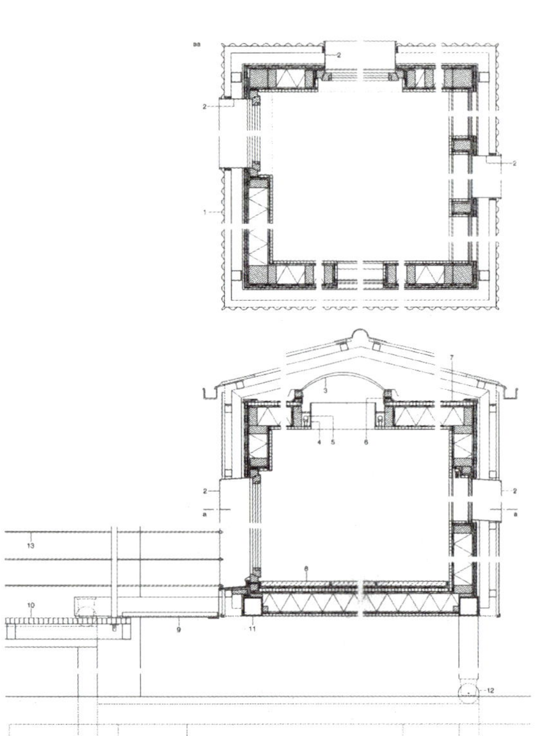

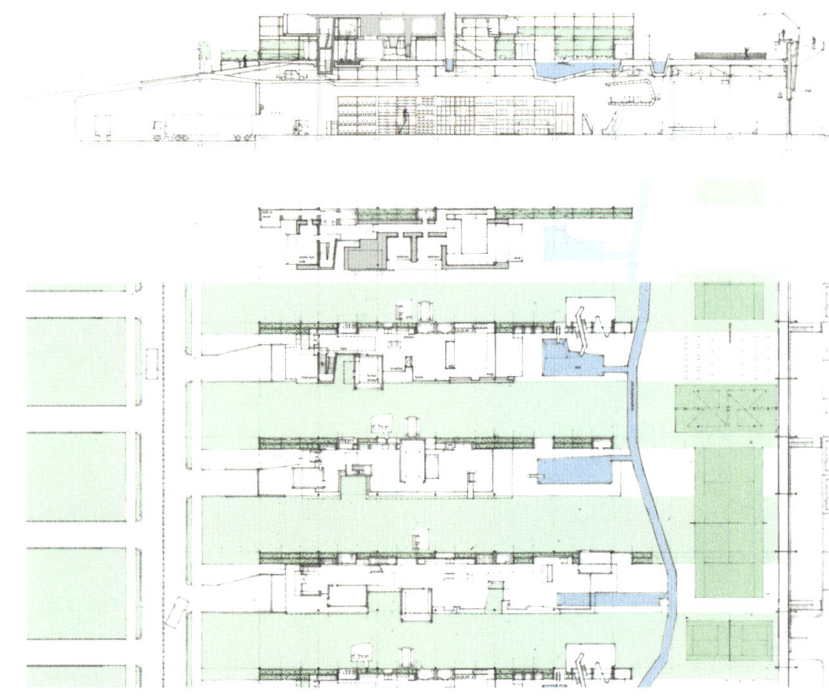

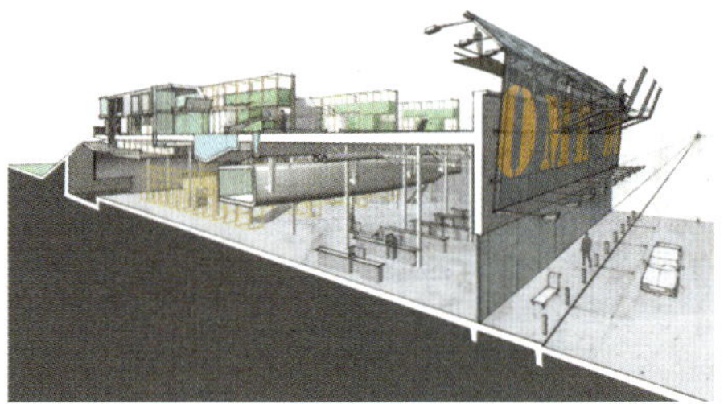

11 HOUSE ENLARGEMENT, GERMANY, 1997
Kalhofer and Korschildgen

12 SUBURBAN SPECULATION, 2000
Lewis Tsurumaki Lewis

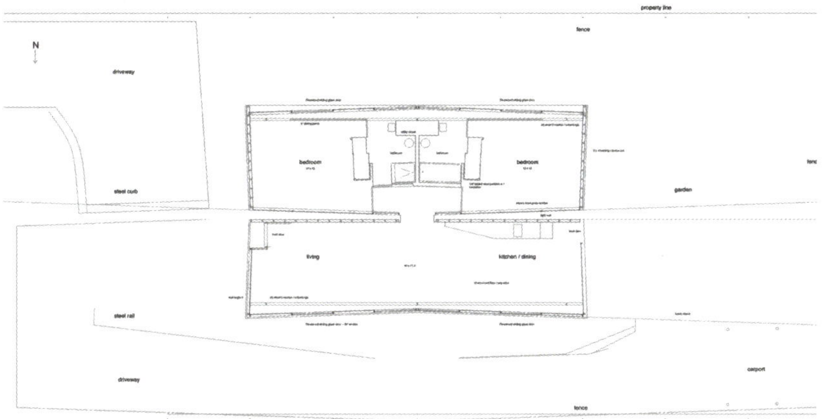

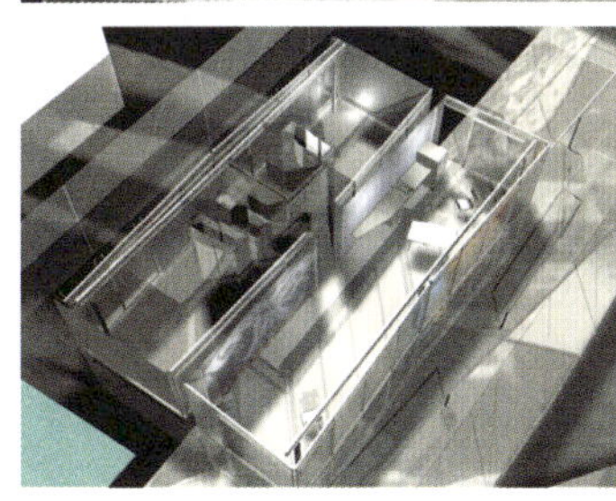

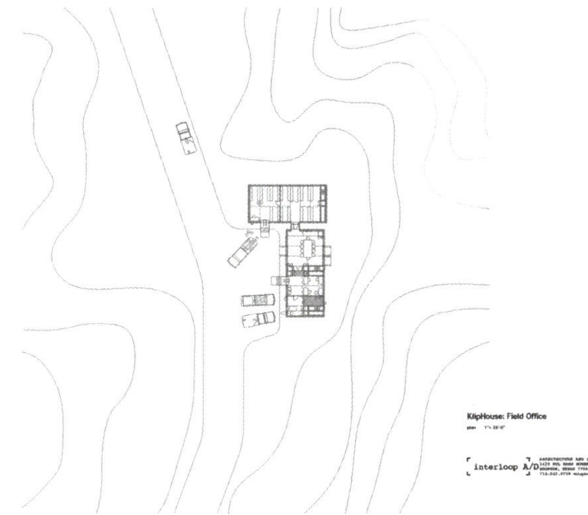

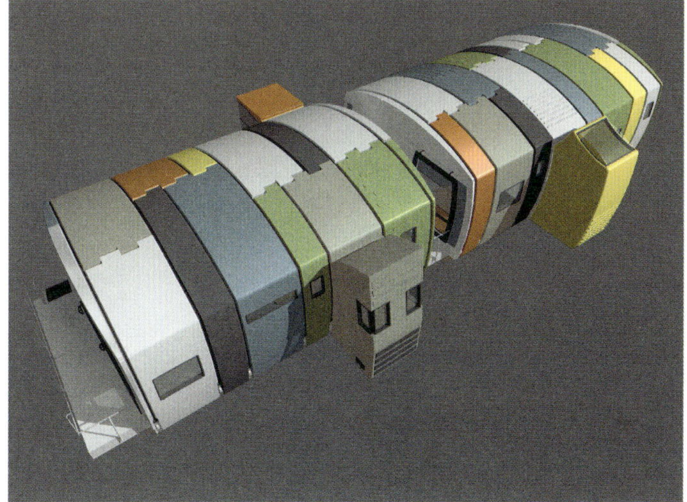

13 GLASS HOUSE @ 2°, HOUSTON, TEXAS 1998–2000
Michael Bell

14 KLIP BINDER HOUSE, HOUSTON, TEXAS, 1999
Interloop Architects

66 65

66   65 64

P33 Including the FUSCO AND KEGLI installation in Berlin it seems that the projects we've been talking about have urban pretensions and want to take on a larger social role. Are they appliances that are about to take over the city? Whereas for Vidler in the analogous city, the city becomes an object, here, the architectural object becomes a disturbance in the city, like an appliance.

KMH Or something inserted into the city as an object that can influence it. But now we're dealing with a different city. By the time the typology argument had been crystallized, the traditional European capital that provides the basic definition of urbanism had almost ceased to exist. But the city that INTERLOOP, FUSCO AND KEGLI, LEWIS TSURUMAKI LEWIS, and MICHAEL BELL seem to be interested in is a city that's not just physical. It's a city of modes of distribution, and it's a city that's not fundamentally European or not even fundamentally like a capital or urban center. It's a city that's much more dispersed, in which the hope of radical difference must be diminished.

P33 You've mentioned that Rossi's brand of typology is "mournful" because it refers back to something that has been lost.

KMH I do see Rossi as mournful – with a surreal, hollowed-out quality – and melancholy, subconsciously or not. I guess in **MICHAEL BELL, LEWIS TSURUMAKI LEWIS,** and **INTERLOOP,** I actually see a committed optimism. I see a commitment, still, to a transformatory architecture. I don't know the project well, but in **FUSCO & KEGLI'S,** I do see some cynicism, some wry commentary on domesticity and suburbia, which is continuous with **DILLER + SCOFIDIO,** and even with **JOEL SANDERS** – still critical if you want to insist on that word.

One of the things that concerns me about the so-called post-critical model is – and I don't think this is Somol's intention – it can too easily be misunderstood to be relinquishing the transformatory project. I think Somol insists on a post-critical dimension to his project in order to distinguish himself from Greg Lynn. By insisting on it, however, he comes to close to identifying his projects with the search for everyday architecture in the Steven Harris or Deborah Berke mode. I respect their work, but my concern is that an embrace of the everyday relinguishes architecture's transformative capability, and that Somol's "lounge" architecture may do the same thing. A distracted, smooth mode need not be uncritical.

P33 Instead of aligning themselves with the city as an object, **LEWIS TSURUMAKI LEWIS, INTERLOOP, MICHAEL BELL,** and **FUSCO & KEGLI** embed their projects within the network of the city. They actually act within that network; for them, architecture is a system of exchange. What is the potential of understanding architecture as a commodity and how does this shape its relationship to the city?

KMH Part of the plight of modern architecture in the broadest sense was its relationship to modes of production and systems of distribution – architecture's relationship to commodification and commercialism. Tafuri is fully part of the generation that thought that any meaningful baggage that architecture could carry would be necessarily contaminated by, if not fully complicit with, the mode of production – which is to say capitalism. I think Eisenman inherits this understanding. From Tafuri through Eisenman, even up to early Tschumi, there was an effort to do away with meaning itself because commerce had already created an excess of meaning, a kind of nausea, an anxiety. There's a recognition that architecture needs to search for meaning, and yet all meaning is contaminated and complicitous. There was a sense that we were in a condition that could be described only as absurd, and I think this

16 LOFT RENOVATION, NEW YORK, 1997
Joel Sanders

comes out in Eisenman's *Perspecta* 21 essay. Around that moment, there's a hinge between a sense of the absurd and ecstasy or euphoria. That's where Koolhaas, late Tschumi, and a different generation enter in with the recognition that the model of the recalcitrant negative object against the commercial city is an old model. At that point, the object goes away and begins to be replaced by program and experience. The word criticality is most thoroughly associated with this moment of absurdity. I think this may also be Somol's objection to the word criticality. It may be that we're moving through another hinge period toward something else–beyond the absurd but also beyond the euphoric. We are at a different moment when we both realize the limits of the architectural object and its power to effect change, but we also realize the wider-ranging domain in which architecture operates. So we're moving away from euphoria and hedonism and ecstasy to a more calculated swerving, adjusting, tuning, but always in a decentralized and multiple way, engaging the given, but not identifying with the given. These are not clean breaks. There are hinges. One idea folds into the other. So, I think it has something to do with the ecstatic in the way Jeffrey Kipnis uses the term, but it's different from an earlier moment of *Delirious New York* and *The Manhattan Transcripts*. That kind of perversity and hedonism is folding into a more programmatic, controlled, managerial mode.

One reason for thinking in larger chunks of time is not only to see the continuities, unfoldings, and transformations, but also to see that there has been a proliferation of positions. We're seeing that in the projects in the portfolio. It used to be that if you weren't participating in "the critical project," then you weren't really responsible as an intellectual and as an architect. Now we have a more decentralized model. **KEN YEANG** can work in one mode and **JOEL SANDERS** can work in another. They don't have to be doing the same thing. It's a huge liberation from an earlier moment where you had to be doing a certain kind of formal, critical, negational work. I think the expansion is healthy. Within the discipline there's also a proliferation of media and materials. It's an obvious corollary that there's going to be interaction with other discourses and other disci-

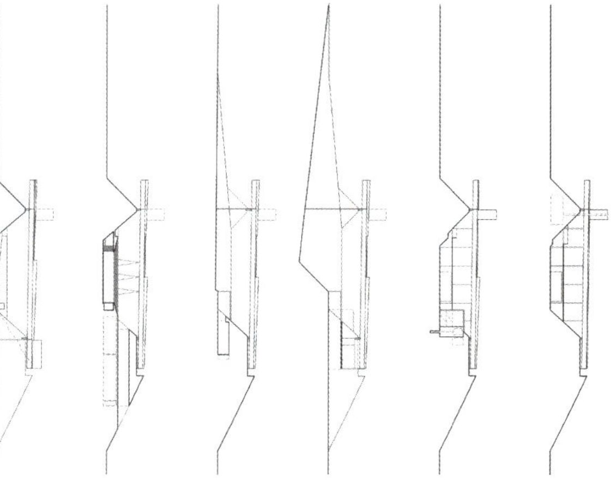

69

70

69

plines. The proliferation will break down boundaries, but there's still an architectural knowledge and specificity of practice that's irreducible. There's something that can't be explained away in terms of other discourses or other disciplines. You don't want to push that too far, you don't want to essentialize architecture, but I still think there's an identifiable though fuzzy core to the discourse – a structure that's very porous, but a structure, nonetheless.

P33 We chose the projects in the portfolio based on effect and not form. So, how do we deal with form when ultimately autonomy as described by both the Whites and the Grays overlaps on the question of form? If that's where architecture's domain lies, how does effect fit into that strict understanding?

KMH What's the project that's the least formal to you? Any of them?

P33 DILLER + SCOFIDIO'S or PETER LATZ'S.

KMH I think you're right that the Whites and Grays agree that architecture's autonomy is a formal issue, but we've decided that it's a vastly reduced definition of architectural form. We can talk about effects, we talked about projection, we can talk about ambience, but all those are organized and controlled and enabled by a form of some sort. The Blur Building maybe is the most formless, but it's visible, it's spatial, its material. It has to be. It controls the way you move through it; it organizes the experience through form; it produces differences, and PETER LATZ'S Landschaftspark has the same qualities. In any of the ecological projects, whatever their effects in time, those effects are organized, controlled and managed by some sort of form. I just think we have a very expanded notion of form. Form is not something we start with like an initial pattern or parti pris, but something we end with, as the final articulation of a deeper logic.

P33 That's a good way of saying that they don't devalue form, but can we locate a perceptual link that binds these projects together?

KMH I understand my job as requiring me to look at any of these projects as formal encodings of some deeper social-historical problem. Then I would ask: does the project

18 LANDSCHAFTSPARK, DUISBURG-NORD, GERMANY 2000
Latz und Partner

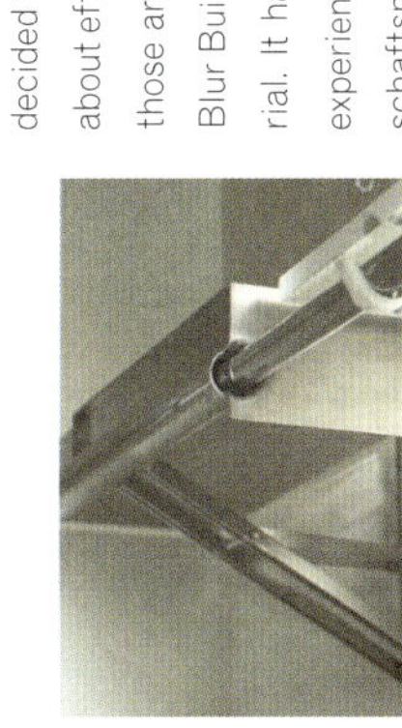

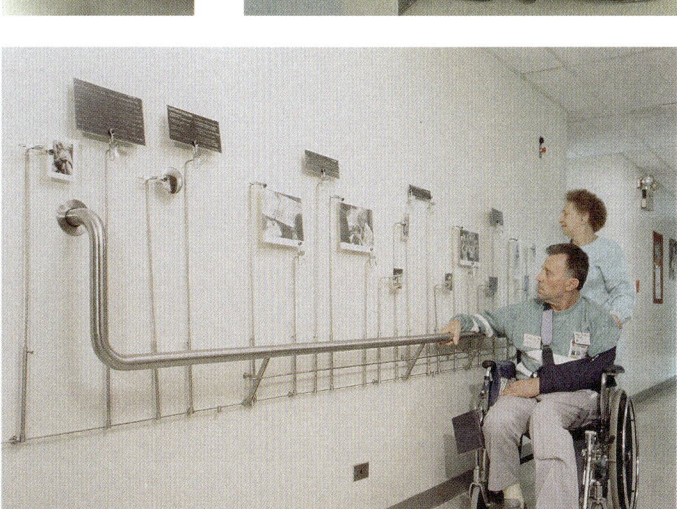

19 ADULT DAY, PROTOTYPE HANDRAIL, DES PLAINES, IL, 1992
Mark Rakatansky

simply replicate that determinate context or does it swerve, distort, and produce difference? Doing that is the long-term goal. At some point, we should be able to see any of these projects as wrestling with some underlying problem. The terms of that problem and the kinds of cracks that emerge would then be understandable in formal, material terms. I'm not arguing for the precise legibility that we talked about earlier. I'm just arguing that if we find those connections between architecture as a larger representational system and its underlying historical infrastructure, we have to be able to detect it in some formal way, and I think we can.

LK I think there's some discrepancy in the way we've defined "critical" architecture. What *Perspecta 33* understands as the critical interdisciplinary edges of architecture-plus, you seem to be annexing as territory for architecture in a disciplinary Anschluss. Also, I don't think they would agree with your definition of criticality because they see practices which question disciplinary autonomy as critical while you seem to be preserving an almost Eisenmanian criticality of autonomy.

KMH If Eisenman is thinking of an old New Critical model or of autonomy in an absolute sense, then I am far away from that. This is where I'm afraid I've become Hegelian. I actually believe that some larger set of collective forces – not a ghost of time but real material vectors operating at a fairly large scale – finds a way to represent itself through certain problems in architecture. I believe that as soon as it manifests itself in that way, the problem changes. Then architecture has to address a different kind of problem, and out of that problem a new architectural response emerges. I still believe in the deeply dialectical notion that it is not either/or, but it's both and neither - we have to continue to try to construct and think mutually contradictory things, not solve contradictions that already exist. There is an autonomous dimension to architecture, that we talked about. There are transformations that happen purely within the discourse that have their own logic and unfolding. But you can't separate that from the larger problem of social, economic, historical forces that control, influence and limit that discourse, that set its terms to a certain extent. I also think you can't separate that from the fact that this discourse is partly what informs and constructs larger historical, social and cultural forces even as it's constructed by them. I don't think architectural theory has a thorough model of that process. I don't think Anderson's semi-autonomy hit it. I don't think Tafuri got it. I don't think Rowe got it. I don't think we have it yet. Maybe it's not the kind of thing you can ever get fully. And I think that's the way history works: we can see only certain histories from where we are, but when we're in a different place, we are able to see different histories. The projects you've presented here will help us rewrite history because they open up concepts. In that sense they do the theory for us.

1 Bill Massie: Big Belt House, Bozeman, MT, 2000. Massie's project for a single-family house challenges traditional design and fabrication methods. Like other contemporary digital projects, its formal language is derived from the use of spline-based curves, in this case traced from the topography of the site. Using CNC (computer numerically controlled) technology for the physical construction of the building allows for the direct transfer from digital model/design to building – transforming the roles of design (designer) and construction (contractor).

2 Foreign Office Architects: Yokohama International Port Terminal, Yokohama, Japan, under construction. The designers used digitally-based bezier spline geometry to develop the original design proposal, but issues encountered in its construction have compromised these geometries. In their collaborations with Ove Arup structural designer Cecil Balmond, FOA have shown that it is possible to construct formally-radical proposals conceived of in the computer by opening architecture to the influence of ideas outside of its traditional domain.

3/4 Roche, DSV & Sie. P/B:L: Habitat Furtif, Paris, 1999. Scrambled Flat, Evolene, Switzerland, 2001. A primary focus of Roche's practice and theory is an investigation of the operation of digital mutation and its potential to forge new relationships between architecture and its physical context. Habitat Furtif is a mobile housing unit that reflects modulated images of its surroundings - the image of this dwelling is generated from any possible context it encounters. Scrambled Flat is a proposal for farm dwellings that contain living space as well as space for farm animals and the storage of wood and hay. The building takes its inspiration from the vernacular hay piles of the Evolene region.

5 Hamzah & Yeang, Tokyo-Nara Tower, Tokyo, 1998. Ken Yeang's work brings together architecture and environmental engineering. His central project is the Bioclimactic Sky Scraper, a rigorously engineered structure that uses large bands of continuous greenery to improve urban air quality. His buildings derive much of their form from the consideration of local climatic conditions such as wind and sun patterns.

6 Alberto Burri: Il Grande Cretto, Gibellina, Italy, 1968. This project was undertaken after the entire town of Gibellina was destroyed in an earthquake. Burri took the street pattern from the destroyed town and rebuilt it by casting it as a single-story relief in concrete. The Cretto generates a strong dialogue with the history of the destroyed town: it has been rebuilt yet evacuated of all life. Burri questions the very possibility of reconstruction after disaster while forcefully reminding us that history never completely disappears.

7 Kengo Kuma: Eco-Particle Park, Osaka, Japan, 1999. Kuma's design for an urban park with housing combines a contemporary preoccupation with digitally-derived form and environmentally-based urbanism. The site plan functions with the logic of pixels on a computer screen – each point carrying the same weight, regardless of its function as building or park. Sectionally, the planes between building, landscape and waterscape shift, creating a considered interaction between figure and ground. The project blurs the boundaries between built form and landscape through its strategy of proximity.

8 Edward Francois & Duncan Lewis, House in Jupilles, 1998. Francois & Lewis' house in Jupilles addresses the relationship between architecture and its natural environment. At first glance, the dense grove of trees in which the body of this house sits seems to dictate the form of the project, implying a dominance of the natural over the man made. Further inspection, however, reveals that the foliage is bound and formed by architectural elements such as windows and an orthogonal wood and wire frame. This relationship reveals the fallacy of thinking of the natural as untouched by man and questions architecture's recent green fascination (have political and scientific environmental discussions developed into functional strategies or aesthetic trends?)

9 One Architecture: Six Under A Tennis Court, Liedscherijn, the Netherlands, 1996. A planning proposal for the million-unit Dutch housing initiative known as V.I.N.E.X., this project is an attempt to address V.I.N.E.X.'s social and ideological implications. In the proposal, the standard suburban street patterns and typical Dutch housing arrangements are discarded in favor of the organizational logic of tennis courts. This principle makes explicit the upper-middle class bias implicit in V.I.N.E.X's developer-determined housing typologies. By placing public facilities above private homes, the divisions between public and private, as important in suburban culture as they are in socialist societies, are seriously skewed.

10 ANA: Huis &, Amsterdam, Netherlands, 2000. The houses are designed as assemblies of compartments, each specifically designed to maximize a certain lifestyle program. In their combination, the specificity of the lifestyle of their inhabitant can be formally approximated. As such, the house can be both highly customized and mass produced. This project does not divide the traditionally distinct operations of architecture and urban design, but combines them at the single-family house.

11 Kalhofer + Korschildgen: House Enlargement, Germany, 1997. Kalhofer + Korschildgen's addition to a small, traditional house in Germany functions as a domestic prosthesis. Although formally sharing the same geometries of massing and pitched roof as the original portion of the house, the addition has a moveable, hinged connection to the existing piece – the addition is able to function between the private domesticity of family and the semi-public, yet autonomous, individual.

12 Lewis Tsurumaki Lewis: Suburban Speculation, 2000. Building housing on top of big-box retailers is a radical proposition that attempts to alter the essence of mainstream American suburban fabric. The increased density of the proposal can be interpreted as direct criticism of land use in the U.S. that has allowed the development of sprawling suburban communities to alarming proportions.

13 Michael Bell: Glass House @ 2°, Houston, 1998-2000. Providing high design for low-income housing and challenging the elitist legacy of the glass-house type, Michael Bell is rethinking the traditional social boundaries of architecture. Situated in a medium-density neighborhood in Houston, the house is subject to concerns of privacy and climate suitability that question the role of architecture in the development of normative housing alternatives.

14 Interloop Architecture + Design: Klip Binder House, Houston, 1999. Developing housing units that can be sold as individual components is an affordable housing solution that takes advantage of mainstream marketing, financing, fabrication and shipping techniques. Because the parts are made by large companies (and in fact are branded, like the Nike Klips that attach the components to the binder) they can be custom ordered, fabricated and shipped to the client in a short time period. Interloop has also introduced the idea of flexible leasing and sell-back options, viewing housing as a commodity rather than the time-honored specialty generated by architects. Designers: Mark Wamble, Dawn Finley. Project Team: Ana Miljacki, Blaine Brownell, James Spearman, Peter Koehler, Wyatt Frantom.

15 Filomento Fusco & Victor Kegli: Weiss 104, Berlin, Germany, 2000. Installing a series of laundry machines in Schlossplatz, a public square in central Berlin, Fusco & Kegli draw our attention to the highly volatile nature of such spaces. The political and historical metaphors are clear, but in addition, the installation presents an instance where public and private space has been reversed. The organized distribution of laundry machines brings a level of informality and everyday utility to what might otherwise function as simply monumental.

16 Joel Sanders, Vitale Loft Renovation, New York, 1997. Sanders directly questions traditional separation of public and private in the domestic realm. This project's visual proximity of kitchen and bathroom (separated only by a translucent panel) juxtaposes normally separate spatial and functional distinctions.

17 Barkow Leibinger Architekten: Biosphere and Flower Pavilion, Potsdam, Germany, 2001. In nineteenth-century projects such as Paxton's Crystal Palace, architecture simply enclosed nature in a neutral glass box Barkow Leibinger, however, allows these hierarchies to become more ambiguous; the landscape and architecture take turns defining the volume of enclosure. Further, within the biosphere, the circulation and programmatic separations are all achieved through subtle manipulations of the landscape's form, color and textural qualities.

18 Latz und Partner, Landschaftspark, Duisburg-Nord, Germany, 2000. Peter Latz converted a derelict steel mill into a public park, complete with gardens, public squares, bike paths and a climbing wall. This recycling urbanism not only cleans and beautifies an otherwise hazardous industrial site, but it also provides a valuable resource of public space. By 'recreating' this factory as 'recreation', Latz is addressing the problem of how the post-industrial world deals with its industrial heritage.

19 Mark Rakatansky: Adult Day, Prototype Handrail, Des Plaines, IL, 1992. Rakatansky's prototype, designed for an adult day-care center, shifts the valence of the common handrail from pure functionality to engage questions of identity. The handrails have been designed with vertical poles, each topped with a clamp to hold photographs and other personal items. The reoriented handrail blurs the functional, aesthetic and bodily.

20 Diller + Scofidio: Blur Project, Swiss Expo, 2000. Diller + Scofidio's use of technology to guide visitors through their 'blur' building (where one is surrounded by fog) by means of voices that come into focus only as the visitor follows a certain trajectory erases architecture's traditional reliance on the visual, thereby heightening the awareness of other senses.

Notes around the Doppler Effect and other Moods of Modernism

No matter how often I tell myself that chance happenings of this kind occur far more often than we suspect, since we all move, one after the other, along the same roads mapped out of for us by our origins and our hopes, my rational mind is nonetheless unable to lay the ghosts of repetition that haunt me with ever greater frequency. Scarcely am I in company but it seems as if I had already heard the same opinions expressed by the same people somewhere or other, in the same way, with the same words, turns of phrase and gestures . . . Perhaps there is in this as yet unexplained phenomenon of apparent duplication some kind of anticipation of the end, a venture into the void, a sort of disengagement, which, like a gramophone repeatedly playing the same sequence of notes, has less to do with damage to the machine itself than with an irreparable defect in its programme.

W.G. SEBALD, THE RINGS OF SATURN

I would like to show that these unities form a number of autonomous, but not independent domains, governed by rules, but in perpetual transformation, anonymous and without a subject, but imbuing a great many individual works.

MICHEL FOUCAULT, THE ARCHAEOLOGY OF KNOWLEDGE

ROBERT SOMOL
SARAH WHITING

FROM CRITICAL TO PROJECTIVE

In 1984, the editors of *Perspecta*, Carol Burns and Robert Taylor, set out an ambitious agenda for issue 21: "Architecture is not an isolated or autonomous medium, it is actively engaged by the social, intellectual, and visual culture which is outside the discipline and which encompasses it … It is based on a premise that architecture is inevitably involved with questions more difficult than those of form or style." While this orientation bears a curious connection to the "realist" or "grey" tradition of an earlier Yale generation, it also serves as a sign of the nascent mixture of a critical, neo-Marxism with a celebration of the vernacular or everyday with which Yale would soon become synonymous.[1] Published in that same issue, K. Michael Hays's canonic essay "Critical Architecture: Between Culture and Form" offered a useful corrective to the editorial position of the issue by indirectly implying that the editors were insufficiently dialectical in their understanding of engagement and autonomy. Hays's sophistication has always been to recognize that autonomy is a precondition for engagement. Using Mies as a paradigm, Hays argued for the possibility of a "critical architecture" that would operate between the extremes of conciliatory commodity and negative commentary.

Twelve issues and seventeen years later, the editors of issue 33 have returned to the theme of interdisciplinarity. This time, however, the topic is explicitly underwritten by the terms established in Hays's 1984 essay: "*Perspecta* 33 is built around the belief that architecture stands in the critical position between being a cultural product and a discrete autonomous discipline." Yet, while Hays was suggesting that only critical architecture operated in his privileged "between" position, the editors of 33 imply that all architecture now automatically occupies a de facto critical status. What for Hays was then an exceptional practice, has now been rendered an everyday fact of life. If nothing else, however, this inflation of critical practice by the editors of 33 has perhaps unconsciously identified a fact of the last twenty years: namely, that disciplinarity has been absorbed and exhausted by the project of criticality. As Hays's first articulation of critical architecture was a necessary corrective to the realist position of *Perspecta* 21, it may be necessary (or, at least, useful) to provide an alternative to the now dominant paradigm of criticality, an alternative that will be characterized here as projective.

As evidenced by Hays's insightful polemic, critical architecture, under the regime of textuality, required the condition of being "between" various discursive oppositions. Thus "culture and form" can alternatively be figured as "kitsch and avant-garde" (Clement Greenberg), "literal and phenomenal" (Colin Rowe), "objecthood and art" (Michael Fried), or "capitalist development and design" (Manfredo Tafuri). Within architecture, Rowe's and Tafuri's discourses most fully enable, if never completely realize, the critical project of "betweeness," whether within history/theory, as with Hays, or in terms of design, as with the work of Peter Eisenman.

It is from Rowe's and Tafuri's conceptual genetic material that architecture's critical project has been formulated. For both authors, there is a requisite assumption of contradiction or ambiguity, regardless of whether it is subsumed or sublated (dialectical materialism) or balanced (liberal formalism). Even before examining the various reconfigurations of Rowe and Tafuri, however, it is important to recognize that the opposition between them is never as clear as would be imagined: Rowe's ostensibly formal project has deep connections to a particular liberal politics, and Tafuri's apparently engaged practice of dialectical critique entails a precise series of formal a prioris as well as a pessimistic prognosis with regard to architectural production. Seen in this way, there is no more political writer than Rowe, and none more formalist than Tafuri.

The criticality of Hays and Eisenman maintains the oppositional or dialectical framework in the work of their mentors and predecessors, while simultaneously trying to short-circuit or blur their terms. In their various attempts to hybridize Rowe and Tafuri in order to fashion a critical position,[2] both Hays and Eisenman rely on dialectics — as is immediately evidenced in the titles of the journals each was responsible for founding: *Oppositions*

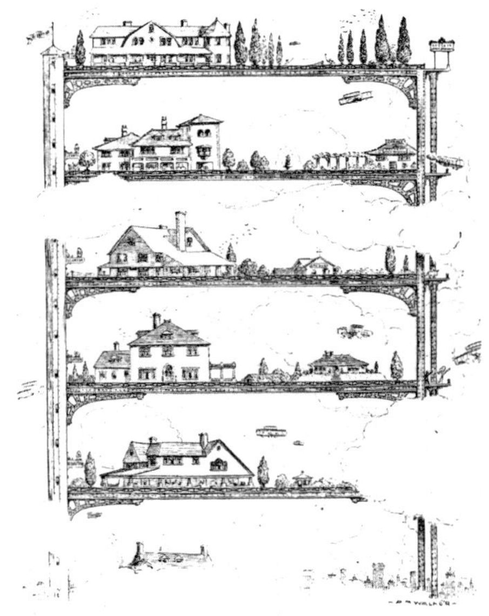

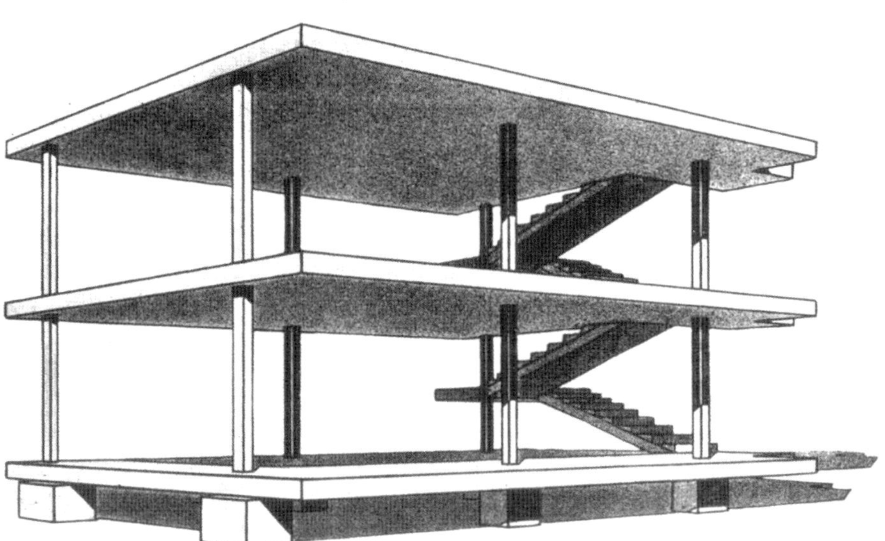

and *Assemblage.* Despite their implicit critiques of Michael Fried's aesthetics,[3] both Eisenman and Hays ultimately fear literalism as much as Fried does; both warn against the isomorphic remapping of life and art. For both, disciplinarity is understood as autonomy (enabling critique, representation, and signification), but not as instrumentality (projection, performativity, and pragmatics). One could say that their definition of disciplinarity is directed against reification rather then toward the possibility of emergence. While reification concerns itself with the negative reduction of qualitative experience to quantification, emergence promises that serial accumulation may itself result in the production of new qualities. As an alternative to the critical project – here linked to the indexical, the dialectical and hot representation – this text develops an alternative genealogy of the projective – linked to the diagrammatic, the atmospheric and cool performance.

FROM INDEX TO DIAGRAM

In the significant production of both Hays and Eisenman, as parallel realignments of Rowe and Tafuri, the critical project is inevitably mediated; in fact, it is perpetually obsessed by, and inextricably linked to, reproduction.[4] This obsession manifests itself both in Hays's account of Mies van der Rohe's Barcelona Pavilion and Peter Eisenman's rereading of Le Corbusier's Dom-ino, where both authors adopt the technique of the index.[5] The index emerges as the most opportune mediator (or critical instigator of the between) in part because it automatically combines materialism with signification: in other words, it exists as a physically driven sign, one that is not culturally or visually determined, as are the symbol or icon. For Hays, Mies's architecture situates itself "between the efficient representation of preexisting cultural values and the wholly detached autonomy of an abstract formal system."[6] This status of being in the world yet resistant to it is attained by the

way the architectural object materially reflects its specific temporal and spatial context, as well as the way it serves as a trace of its productive systems. Hays describes the Barcelona Pavilion as "an event with temporal duration, whose actual existence is continually being produced," or whose meaning is continually being decided. This act of decision is both in fact and etymologically the critical gesture par excellence.

In Eisenman's discussion of the Dom-ino, it is the design process itself that is being registered rather than the material productive and technical systems or specific context discussed by Hays. In marking the status of its existence, in its ability to function as a self-referential sign, the Dom-ino is one of the first modernist and critical gestures in architecture: "Architecture is both substance and act. The sign is a record of an intervention – an event and an act which goes beyond the presence of elements which are merely necessary conditions." For Eisenman and Hays, the Dom-ino and Barcelona Pavilion are at once traces of an event, indices of their procedures of design or construction, and objects that potentially point to a state of continual transformation. In both cases, the critical forms of self-referentiality are demonstrated via serial reproductions: be they Eisenman's re-drawn axonometrics of the non-existent Dom-ino perspective, or the historical photographs Hays uses to extract the experience of the defunct, original Barcelona Pavilion. Just as the architectural artifacts are indices of a missing process or practice, the objects themselves are also significantly missing in both cases, so that a series of reproductions must stand in as their traces. This process of infinite regress or deferral is constitutive of the critical architectural project: architecture inevitably and centrally preoccupied by its status as representation, and its simultaneous commentary on that condition.

As an alternative to Eisenman's reflections on the high European frame, which situated the frame within the context of the critical-indexical project of the 1970s, one might look to Rem Koolhaas's appropriation of the mass cultural American frame at the same moment. As suggested above, Eisenman understands Le Corbusier's Domino as the trace of a transformative process, and in so doing he deviates from Rowe by animating the grid. Just as the indexical project assumes or invents a particular kind of reading subject for architecture, its imagination of architectural movement relies on a narrative for the grid. Thus, although the indexical program for architecture may proceed through diagrams, it is still tied to a semiotic, representational and sequential ambi-

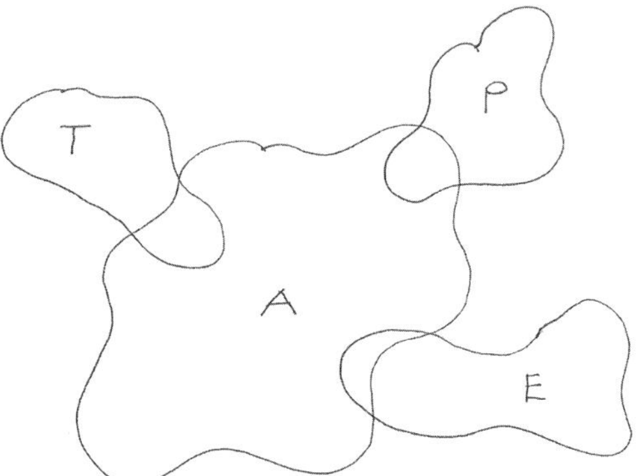

tion. Koolhaas's invocation of the "cartoon-theorem" from *Life* magazine — as well as the section cut from the Downtown Athletic Club — alternatively enlists a vision of architecture as contributing to the production and projection of new forms of collectivity. These New York frames exist as instruments of metropolitan plasticity and are not primarily architecture for paying attention to; they are not for reading, but for seducing, becoming, instigating new events and behaviors. The skyscraper-machine allows the projection infinitely upward of virtual worlds within this world, and in this way extends Michel Foucault's reflections on heterotopias and prisons. Gilles Deleuze argues that Foucault understands Jeremy Bentham's Panopticon not simply as a machine for surveillance, but more broadly and productively as a diagram which "imposes a particular form of conduct on a particular multiplicity." Koolhaas's investigation of the frame structure is diagrammatic in the same way.

From these two inventions of the frame structure in mid-70s architectural discourse, one can discern two orientations toward disciplinarity: that is, disciplinarity as autonomy and process, as in the case of Eisenman's reading of the Domino, and disciplinarity as force and effect, as in Koolhaas's staging of the Downtown Athletic Club. Moreover, these two examples begin to differentiate the critical project in architecture, with its connection to the indexical, from the projective, which proceeds through the diagram. The diagram is a tool of the virtual to the same degree that the index is the trace of the real.[7]

FROM DIALECTICS TO DOPPLER

Rather than relying upon the oppositional strategy of critical dialectics, the projective employs something similar to the Doppler Effect – the perceived change in the frequency of a wave that occurs when the source and receiver of the wave have a relative velocity. The Doppler Effect explains the change in pitch between the sound of a train as it approaches and then moves away from the listener.[8] If critical dialectics established architecture's autonomy as a means of defining architecture's field or discipline, a Doppler architecture acknowledges the adaptive synthesis of architecture's many contingencies. Rather than isolating a singular autonomy, the Doppler focuses upon the effects and exchanges of architecture's inherent multiplicities: material, program, writing, atmosphere, form, technologies, economics, etc. It is important to underscore that this multiplying of contingencies differs greatly from the more dilute

notion of interdisciplinarity, which seeks to legitimize architecture through an external measuring stick, thereby reducing architecture to the entirely amorphous role of absorber of heterogeneous life. A projective architecture does not shy away from reinstating architectural definition, but that definition stems from design and its effects rather than a language of means and materials. The Doppler shifts the understanding of disciplinarity as autonomy to disciplinarity as performance or practice. In the former, knowledge and form are based on shared norms, principles, and traditions. In the latter, a more Foucaultian notion of disciplinarity is advanced in which the discipline is not a fixed datum or entity, but rather an active organism or discursive practice, unplanned and ungovernable, like Foucault's "unities form[ing] a number of autonomous, but not independent domains, governed by rules, but in perpetual transformation."[9] Rather than looking back or criticizing the status quo, the Doppler projects forward alternative (not necessarily oppositional) arrangements or scenarios.

A projective architecture does not make a claim for expertise outside the field of architecture nor does it limit its field of expertise to an absolute definition of architecture. Design is what keeps architecture from slipping into a cloud of heterogeneity. It delineates the fluctuating borders of architecture's disciplinarity and expertise. So when architects engage topics that are seemingly outside of architecture's historically-defined scope – questions of economics or civic politics, for example – they don't engage those topics as experts on economics or civic politics, but rather, as experts on design and how design may affect economics or politics. They engage these other fields as experts on design's relationship to those other disciplines, rather than as critics. Design encompasses object qualities (form, proportion, materiality, composition, etc.) but it also includes qualities of sensibility, such as effect, ambiance, and atmosphere.

An example of a projective architecture that engages the strategy of the Doppler effect in lieu of that of the dialectic is ww's IntraCenter, a 40,000 ft.[2] community center located in Lexington, Kentucky. The IntraCenter's client provided ww with a program list of dizzying operational heterogeneity: daycare, athletic facilities, social services, café, library, computer center, job training facilities, shops, etc. Rather than figuring these multiple programs so as to provide each with its own formal identification, or rather than establishing a neutral field so as to allow the programs to define the project, the IntraCenter elides the expected

Above
Projective Architecture: diagram of overlap of A (architecture) with P (politics), E (economics) and T (theory).

Middle
The Doppler Effect.

overlap between form and program. Their lack of alignment leads to a perpetual Doppler shift between the two. This strategy of non-concentricity generates other Doppler Effects, including the many reverberations among overlapping constituencies as well as material and structural conditions. The IntraCenter is projective rather than critical in that it very deliberately sets into motion the possibility of multiple engagements rather than a single articulation of program, technology or form (contemporary architecture's commodity, firmness and delight).

The Doppler Effect shares some attributes with parallax, which, as Yve-Alain Bois notes, comes from the Greek parallaxis, or "change": "the apparent change in the position of an object resulting from the change in the ... position from which it is viewed."[10] Claiming that Serra consciously responded to the possibilities of parallax, Bois cites as an example Serra's description of his sculpture entitled Sight Point: "[It seems at first] to fall right to left, make an x, and straighten itself out to a truncated pyramid. That would occur three times as you walked around."[11] In other words, parallax is the theatrical effect of a peripatetic view of an object. It takes into account how the context and the viewer "complete" the work of art.

Where the Doppler differs from parallax is in that it is not purely optical. Predicated on waves that can be auditory or visual, the Doppler suggests that the optical and conceptual are only two of many sensibilities. Additionally, it is not a reading strategy – that is, it is not just an unfolding reading of an artwork – but an atmospheric interaction. It foregrounds the belief that both the subject and the object carry and exchange information and energy. In short, a user might be more attuned to certain aspects of a building than others. He or she might understand how the building responds to a formal history of architecture or deploys a specific technology or he or she might have particular associations with

a building's material palette or site. As the novelist W.G. Sebald explains, each one of us experiences moments of repetition, coincidence or duplication, where echoes of other experiences, conversations, moods and encounters affect current ones. Such momentary echoes are like tracks out of alignment, hearing and seeing out of phase that generate momentary déjà vus, an overlap of real and virtual worlds.

FROM HOT TO COOL

Someone should establish an anthropology of hot and cool ...

Jean Baudrillard

Overall, one might characterize the shift from critical to projective modes of disciplinarity as a process of cooling down or, in Marshall McLuhan's terms, of moving from a "hot" to a "cool" version of the discipline. Critical architecture is hot in the sense that it is preoccupied with separating itself from normative, background or anonymous conditions of production, and with articulating difference. For McLuhan, hot media like film are "high-definition", conveying very precise information on one channel or in one mode. By contrast, cool media, such as television, are low-definition and, since the information they convey is compromised, they require the participation of the user. In this regard, the formalist-critical project is hot in its prioritization of definition, delineation and distinction (or medium specificity). One alternative, minimalism, would be a cool art form; it is low-definition and requires the context and viewer to complete it, lacking both self-sufficiency and self-consciousness. Minimalism explicitly requires participation and is related to Smithson's promotion of entropy. While cooling suggests a process of mixing (and thus the Doppler Effect would be one form of cool), the hot resists through distinction, and connotes the overly difficult, belabored, worked, complicated. Cool is relaxed, easy. This difference between the cool and the hot may be

amplified by briefly examining a medium McLuhan does not discuss: performance.

In his obituary on the actor, Dave Hickey writes that with Robert Mitchum you get performance,[12] and performance, he says, not expressed (or represented), but delivered. The Mitchum effect relies on knowing something is back there, but not being sure exactly what it is. Hickey says that what Mitchum does, then, is always surprising and plausible. And it's exactly this trait of surprising plausibility that might be adapted as a projective effect, one which combines the chance event with an expanded realism. There are two kinds of actors, Hickey argues. First are some who construct a character out of details and make you believe their character by constructing a narrative for them. One could say that this is the school of the "Method," where the actor provides gesture and motivation, and supplies a sub-text for the text of the script. The second group of actors create plausibility by their bodies; Hickey says they are not really acting, but rather "performing with a vengeance." While Robert De Niro is an actor in the first category, Mitchum is in the second.

In the nineteen-eighties and nineties, architecture's relationship to philosophy was like that of De Niro to his character. In other words, a kind of Method acting, or Method designing, where the architect expressed a text or where architecture represented its procedure of formation. As with the "critical project," Method acting was connected to psychoanalysis, to calling up and reenacting memories and past events. In contrast, Mitchum, Hickey says, is,

Like Coltrane, playing a standard, he is investing the text with his own subversive vision, his own pace and sense of dark contingency. So what we see in a Mitchum performance is less the character portrayed than a propositional alternative: What if someone with Mitchum's sensibility grew up to be a sea captain? a private eye? a school-teacher?[13]

In De Niro's acting, one witnesses the struggle, not just within the character, but between the actor and the character, such that the trace of the construction of the character is visible. There is no other way to say this except that, when watching De Niro, it looks like work (think of the signature mugging and concentrated gestures). The opening scenes in both versions of *Cape Fear* are instructive in this regard. The 1991 remake begins with De Niro working out in prison, exercising or rehearsing, where the sweat rolling off his back is visible. In the original, Mitchum is in no rush: rakish, lascivious, enjoying a cigar and checking out two women as they leave the courthouse, cool as the breeze. He makes it look easy. So "De Niro architecture" is hot, difficult, and indexes the processes of its production: it's clearly labored, narrative, or representational, or expresses a relationship of the representation to the real (the provision of a psychic subtext from a real event for a fictional text). Mitchum plays a cameo role as a detective in the remake, and as he is watching De Niro/Cady strip-searched he sees his body covered with biblical proverbs and comments with a degree of reproach (as much for the Method-acting De Niro as the character Cady?): "I don't know whether to look at him or to read him." In contrast to this narrative mode, "Mitchum architecture" is cool, easy, and never looks like work; it's about mood or the inhabitation of alternative realities (what if?, the virtual). Here, mood is the open-ended corollary of the cool-producing effect without high definition, providing room for maneuver, and promoting complicity with subject(s). With Mitchum, there are scenarios, not psychodramas. The unease and anxiety of the unhomely has been replaced with the propositional alternative of the untimely.

Within architecture, a project of delivering performance, or soliciting a surprising plausibility, suggests moving away from a critical architectural practice – one which is reflective, representational, and narrative – to a projective practice. Setting out this projective program does not necessarily entail a capitulation to market forces, but actually respects or reorganizes multiple economies, ecologies, information systems, and social groups.

Our thanks to Ron Witte, Linda Pollari and Adam Ruedig for their help and patience with this endeavor.

NOTES

1 See the collection of essays, *Architecture of the Everyday*, edited by Deborah Berke and Steven Harris (New York: Princeton Architectural Press, 1997).

2 Formulating their own critical positions, both Hays and Eisenman misread Rowe and Tafuri, according to Harold Bloom's understanding of misreading as poetic influence: "Poetic influence – when it involves two strong, authentic poets – always proceeds by a misreading of the prior poet, an act of creative correction that is actually and necessarily a misinterpreation." Harold Bloom, *The Anxiety of Influence: A Theory of Poetry* (NY: Oxford University Press, 1973; 1997): 30.

3 Significantly, the "between" for Fried was a theatrical anathema that undermined modernist specificity.

4 Mediated here refers both to Fredric Jameson's theorization of mediation as an active between – that is, as an engaged interaction between two subjects or between a subject and an object, rather than a passive between that operates as pure conciliation between two terms – and to Marshall McLuhan's understanding of mediation as mass media's translatable reproducibility.

5 "Repetition thus demonstrates how architecture can resist, rather than reflect, an external cultural reality." K. Michael Hays, "Between Culture and Form," *Perspecta* 21 (Cambridge, MIT Press, 1984): 27. Also see Peter Eisenman, "Aspects of Modernism: Maison Dom-ino and the Self-Referential Sign," *Oppositions* 15/16 (Winter/Spring, 1979).

6 Hays, ibid: 15.

7 For more on this distinction, see Deleuze and Guattari: "Diagrams must be distinguished from indexes, which are territorial signs, but also from icons, which pertain to reterritorialization, and from symbols, which pertain to relative or negative deterritorialization. Defined diagrammatically in this way, an abstract machine is neither an infrastructure that is determining in the last instance nor a transcendental Idea that is determining in the supreme instance. Rather, it plays a piloting role. The diagrammatic or abstract machine does not function to represent, even something real, but rather constructs a real that is yet to come, a new type of reality." *A Thousand Plateaus* (Minneapolis: University of Minnesota Press, 1987), p.142.

8 The Doppler Effect was discovered by the Austrian mathematician and physicist, Christian Doppler (1803–1853).

9 Michel Foucault, *Archaeology of Knowledge*.

10 Yve-Alain Bois citing Webster's Dictionary, "A Picturesque Stroll Around Clara-Clara," in Richard Serra, Hal Foster with Gordon Hughes, eds. (Cambridge: MIT Press October Books, 2001): 65.

11 Ibid.: 66.

12 Dave Hickey, "Mitchum Gets Out of Jail," *Art Issues* (September/October 1997): 10–13.

13 Ibid: 12.

Opposite page
IntraCenter, WW, 2001.

Form-Program Diagram 1,
IntraCenter, WW, 2001.

Left
Robert Mitchum.

Notes on

ELIZABETH GROSZ

This argument is presented in the form of postulates, or rather provocations, a manifesto on the thing.

The thing has, in the West, always been conceived as the passive, inert, unresisting other or counterpart to the subject, consciousness, or mind, that is, as matter, substance, or noumena. The thing is that against which mind is understood, its other or object.

There is another less systematic and more submerged tradition of the thing within the history of philosophy, which arguably dates from the work of Darwin, and meanders through Nietzsche, to Peirce, James, Bergson to Rorty and Deleuze. This counter-tradition conceives of the thing, not as other, but as provocation or incitement for the subject: the thing is that which prompts us to act, to invent, to practice, to extend ourselves beyond ourselves.

Within this later tradition, the thing itself is divided or duplicated. It is both resource or raw material, the given or starting point of life and the human (Heidegger's standing reserve or Lacan's Real), and it is also the product, effect, or construct of the living (Marx's commodity, Bergson's object). The thing is both pre- and post-technological, that which technology finds given and remakes as its own. In this sense, technology must be understood to be the second-order thing, the thing that finds and makes other things, as it itself has been made.

Within the pragmatist tradition, the world itself, and our being positioned within it, generates questions, problems, provocations for life: what to eat? How to attain it? How to live? By what means? Things are the way in which life responds to these provocations. Both instinct and intelligence, blind animal and intelligently directed (primate or mammal) behaviors, are incited by the real and produce things, the division of the real, as their mode of acting in the world and rendering it manageable. The thing is a cutting out of the real, the solidification of what exists in the flux of the real. It is an outline imposed on the real by our purposes and needs.

This cutting of the world, this whittling down of the plethora of the world's interpenetrating qualities into objects amenable to our action, is a fundamentally constructive process: we make or fabricate the world of objects as an activity we undertake by living with and assimilating objects. We make objects in order to live in the world. Or, in another, Nietzschean sense, we must live in the world artistically, as homo faber.

This process of fabrication of the world into things, objects with clearly delimitable and determinable relations, finds its natural inclination directed to solids. Things are solids, conceived progressively as more and more minute in their basic constitution, as physics itself elaborates more and more minute fundamental particles. Yet physics itself remains incapable of understanding what is fluid, innumerable, outside calculation without reduction to solids. It is this flux, though, sometimes recognized in philosophy, that provides the condition for the generation of new things from old things. Our "artisticness," as Nietzsche puts it, our creativity, in Bergsonian terms, consists in nothing else than the continuous experimentation with the world of things, to produce new things from the fluidity or flux, which elude everyday need, or use-value.

Technology, as metaproduction, is the result of the living being's capacity to utilize the non-living (and the living) prosthetically. This prosthetic existence is the living's dependence on and capacity to harness and incorporate the non-living into its bodily practices. What pragmatism entails is a recognition that the technological is and always has been the condition of human action, as necessary for us

This paper was first presented as part of the conference entitled *The Pragmatist Imagination: Thinking about Things in the Making* held at the Temple Hoyne Buell Center for the Study of American Architecture at Columbia University, in Spring 2000.

The Thing

as things themselves. Technology can be conceived as the cultural correlate of the thing, which is itself the human or living correlate of the materiality of the world.

Bergson claims that the intellect transforms matter into things, which render them as prostheses, artificial organs, and in a surprising reversal, at the same time as it humanizes or orders nature, it appends itself as a kind of prosthesis to inorganic matter itself, to function as its rational supplement, its conscious rendering. Matter and life become reflections, through the ordering the intellect makes of the world. Things become the measure of life's action upon them, things become "standing reserve," life itself becomes extended through things.

Inorganic matter, transformed into an immense organ, a prosthesis, through the intellect, is perhaps the most primordial or elementary definition of architecture itself, which is, in a sense, the first prosthesis, the first instrumental use of intelligence to meld the world into things, through a certain primitive technicity, to the needs of the living. The inorganic becomes the mirror for the possible action of the living, the armature and architecture necessary for the survival and evolution of the living.

The limit of the intellect is in a sense the limit of the technical and the technological. The intellect functions to dissect, divide, atomize: contemporary binarization and digitalization are simply the current versions of this tendency to the clear-cut, the unambiguous, the opposition or binary impulses of the intellect, which is bound by the impetus to (eventual or possible) actions.

Thus technology is not the supercession of the thing, but its ever more entrenched functioning. The thing pervades technology, which is its extension, and extends the human into the material. The task before us is not so much to make things and resolve relations into things, more and more minutely framed and microscopically understood. Rather, it may be to liberate matter from the constraint, the practicality, utility of the thing, to orient technology not so much to knowing and mediating as to experience and the rich indeterminacy of duration. Instead of understanding the thing and the technologies it induces, through intellect, in the Bergsonian sense, perhaps it can also be developed through intuition, that Bergsonian apprehension of the unique particularity of things, and of the time within which things exist.

Perhaps the question ahead of us now is this: what are the conditions of digitization and binarization? Can we produce technologies of other kinds? Is technology inherently simplification and reduction of the real? What in us is being extended and prosthetically rendered in technological development? Can other vectors be extended instead? What might a technology of processes, rather than things, look like?

BERNARD CACHE

Gottfried Semper: Stereotomy, Biology, and Geometry

Our point of departure is what is known in mathematics as a double point. This particular point is constituted by the two statues — one of George Cuvier[1] and the other of Alexander von Humboldt,[2] the German disciple of Etienne Geoffrey Saint-Hilaire[3] — Gottfried Semper placed at the top of the Naturhistorisches Museum (1872–1881). The fact that Semper did not place one, but two biologists at the summit of his representation of science should act as a question mark within Semper's *Der Stil*. His insistence on placing a statue of a disciple of Geoffroy Saint-Hilaire betrays a doubt in Semper that in turn reveals a blind spot in *Der Stil*.

The four technical arts of *Der Stil*'s table of contents, the four pillars, are treated far from equally. Semper's emphasis on textiles is of course very well known, but what is rarely discussed is the weakness of the chapters on stereotomy.[4] The numbers of pages dedicated to each of the technical arts in *Der Stil* are: Textile, 550 pages;

Ceramique, 200; Tectonique, 135; Stereotomy, 123. But at issue is not merely the number of pages, nor is it that the majority of what is actually discussed is dedicated to tectonics in stone rather than to stereotomy proper. In the pages of *Der Stil* devoted to stereotomy, Semper goes so far as to assert that the whole history of architecture is signified by the victory of the vault (usually considered the primary territory of stereotomy) over the tectonic frame, but then hardly mentions any more about it. This absence of the core of stereotomy is even more surprising considering that Semper lived and studied in France, where architecture was strongly rooted in stereotomy. How could such a well-informed scholar as Semper write about stereotomy without mentioning figures such as Philibert de L'Orme[5] or Girard Desargues?[6] Was Semper acknowledging the fall of French building traditions? Was he drawing conclusions from Soufflot's controversial Sainte-Geneviève church, where tra-

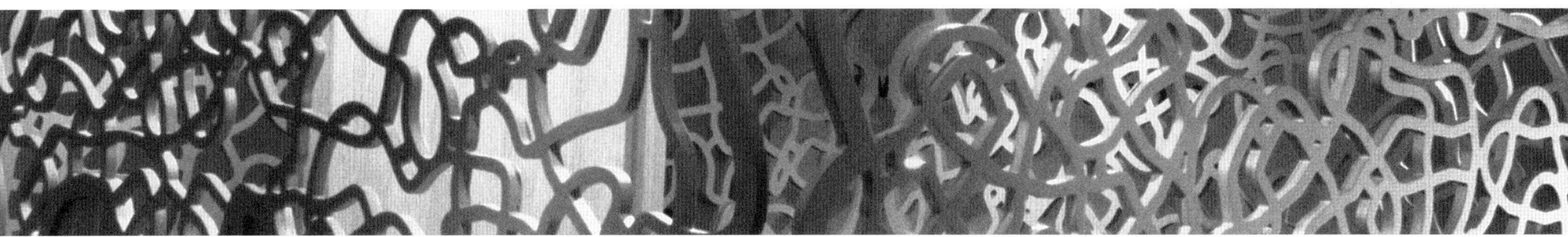

ditional French geometric methodology was supplanted by a physical approach based on statics and the strength of materials? Did Semper feel these traditions were unable to cope with the technological challenges of the time?

These reasons cannot fully explain why Semper made no mention at all of what appears to be the most 'Semperian' piece of architecture in Paris, the wonderful stone interlacing of the roodscreen within Saint-Etienne du Mont, only a hundred meters behind Sainte-Geneviève.[7] No other piece of architecture so clearly embodies the architectural motif of the Semperian knot and the theoretical concept of stereotomy, the transposition from textile to stone. Could it be that what really puzzled Semper was not only that Philibert de l'Orme was the presumed architect of this roodscreen,[8] as well as of so many other Semperian pieces of architecture, but that an architect could be the initiator of projective geometry,[9] the branch of mathematics forming the conceptual background of Geoffroy Saint-Hilaire's work?

One could object that these questions were of little relevance to Semper's architectural project, and that he could have very well ignored projective geometry and its connections to Saint-Hilaire's biology. But we should remember that Semper actually studied mathematics with Carl Friedrich Gauss, the man who first accepted positively the consequences of the negation of Euclid's fifth postulate, and in so doing initiated the field of "non-Euclidean geometry." Semper's interest in mathematics was strong enough for him to write at the age of fifty a technical essay on differential calculus applied to the shape of projectiles.[10] It is my hypothesis that Semper had the capacity to fully understand projective geometry, but he repressed it in *Der Stil* because it implied a reformulation of geometry that had yet to be achieved by mathematicians themselves.[11] Until this reformulation was achieved, the architectural reading of geometry was bound to remain neo-classical in a manner similar to Winckelmann's reading of Greek architecture as pure, ideal, white form. Gottfried Semper, whose first serious job in life had been to re-establish a non-neoclassical reading of Greek architecture based upon color, was unable to conduct the same type of operation on form.[12]

Such a hypothesis relies upon two assumptions. The first is that projective geometry was an important feature of Geoffroy Saint-Hilaire's background — so prominent a feature it could not be ignored by someone like Semper with strong interests in architecture, biology, and geometry. The second is that projective geometry could imply a non-neoclassical reading of geometry that would have enabled Semper to pursue his work begun on color by applying it to shape. Such an accomplishment would have enabled Semper to adequately write his missing text on stereotomy.

BIOLOGY

What was the core of the debate between Cuvier and Saint-Hilaire that excited contemporaries such as Goethe and Balzac? The two biologists were initially good friends who worked together on vertebrate classification in order to corroborate Saint-Hilaire's theory of a single organizational plan that would inform the whole of the vertebrate family. Since 1796, Geoffroy Saint-Hilaire had worked with the concept that there existed a single organizational plan for all animals.[13] Saint-Hilaire's research began with mammals and then extended the concept to tetrapods. An 1808 essay by Saint-Hilaire on fish generalized the single plan to all vertebrates.[14] Until that point Cuvier still enthusiastically supported Saint-Hilaire. But in 1812, Cuvier announced his own thesis, classifying animals into several branches or "embranchments": Vertebrata, Articulata, Mollusca, Cnidarians, and Echinoderms. For Cuvier, these embranchements were fundamentally different from each other and could not be connected by any evolutionary transformation. Cuvier's "fixist" view of biology posited that every single part of an organism is so well fitted to its surroundings that there is only one way in which each part can be connected to the whole organism. For those who would think that this is far away from architecture, remember, it is Cuvier who wrote the famous sentence taken as a principle of functionalist architecture, "give me any single piece of an animal and I will draw you the whole body." According to this view, each embranchment has its own organization and there can be no way of connecting parts in any manner other than that described in each of the categories.

Until 1820, Cuvier and Saint-Hilaire lived and worked peacefully in the same institution, le Musée d'Histoire Naturelle, in Paris. During this time, Jules-Câesar Savigny, who had been in Egypt with Saint-Hilaire on the Napoleonic Expedition, studied the comparative anatomy of an insect's mouth. Another of Saint-Hilaire's peers, Pierre Andre Latreille, applied the principle of unity of composition to all of the Articulata.[15] Until that point, the work of Cuvier and Saint-Hilaire remained compatible because neither Saint-Hilaire nor his followers broke any frontiers between Cuvier's sacrosanct embranchments. But in 1820, Saint-Hilaire suggested a unity of plan between Vertebrata and Insects. Cuvier's critiques began at this point and only increased when Saint-Hilaire, leaning on works by Laurencet and Meyrand, extended his unity of composition to Mollusca as well.[16] Saint-Hilaire had unified three of the embranchments; an accomplishment Cuvier was unable to accept.

But as one examines Saint-Hilaire's unification of Vertebrata and Insects, the relation between the two embranchments seems far from obvious, since each has a thoroughly different relationship to the ground. All Vertebrata have their digestive organs facing the ground, located underneath the vertebral column, which in turn houses the nervous system. In contrast, Insects have digestive systems in an inverted position facing the sky, with the spinal cord located underneath the body. To address these differences in orientation, Saint-Hilaire makes use of a torsion operation, a tool from projective geometry, to explain how insects have their belly upward and their back downward. Semper uses a similar vectorial organization in *Der Stil*, comparing the composition of biological vectors in various species with the vector of gravity in architecture.

In terms of validating his research, however, Saint-Hilaire committed an error when he went so far as to posit that "each animal lives either inside or outside its spine" – effectively assimilating all carapaces from Insects to Vertebrata. Eventually, he would even compare the legs of shellfishes to the ribs of Vertebrata. It was no difficult task for Cuvier to take advantage of this hypothesis in order to invalidate the whole of Saint-Hilaire's categorization. As a result, Cuvier appeared the winner of a crucial series of highly-publicized debates that took place between the two biologists in 1830, at the very time that Semper was studying in Paris.[17] Cuvier retained the victory mantle until very recently, when the scientific publication *Nature* published an article by E.M. de Robertis and Y. Sassai which used contemporary biological studies to assert the validity of Saint-Hilaire's original theory.[18] Modern biology has found genes that code the orientation of organs backward and forward, as well as downward and upward.[19] As a result, the most plausible hypothesis now is that indeed Insects and Vertebrata had a common ancestor from which they bifurcated some 540 million years ago.

GEOMETRY

To return to the nineteenth century and the geometric concepts in use by Saint-Hilaire, it should be understood that a crucial concept for Saint-Hilaire was inversion, which is also a key transformation in projective geometry.[20] Through inversion, the closed quadrangle, as used in projective geometry, can be taken as a conceptual equivalent of an ant in Saint-Hilaire's work, insofar as an insect is a

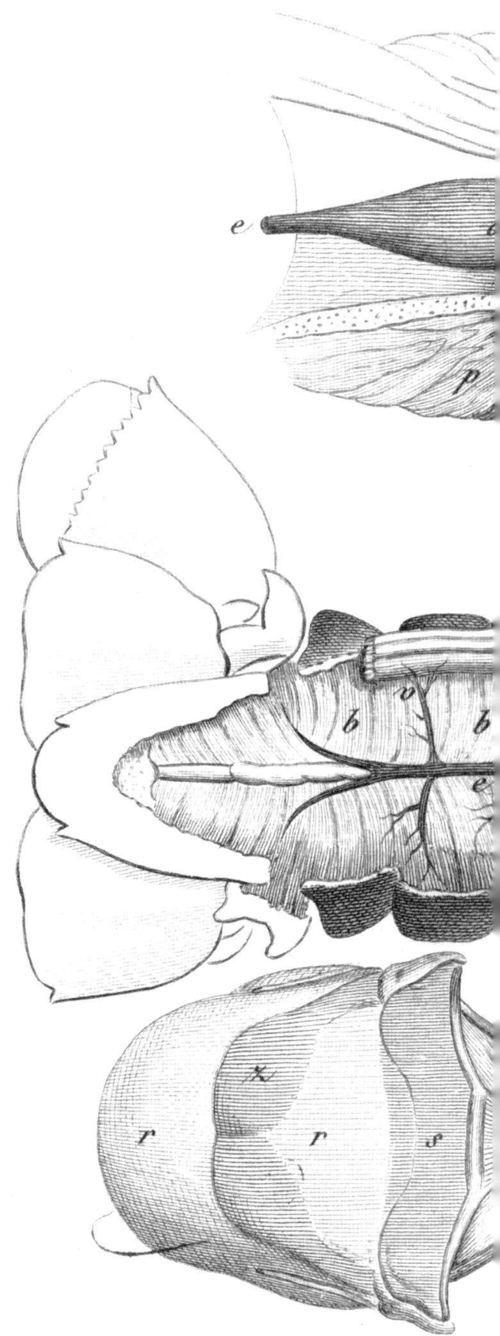

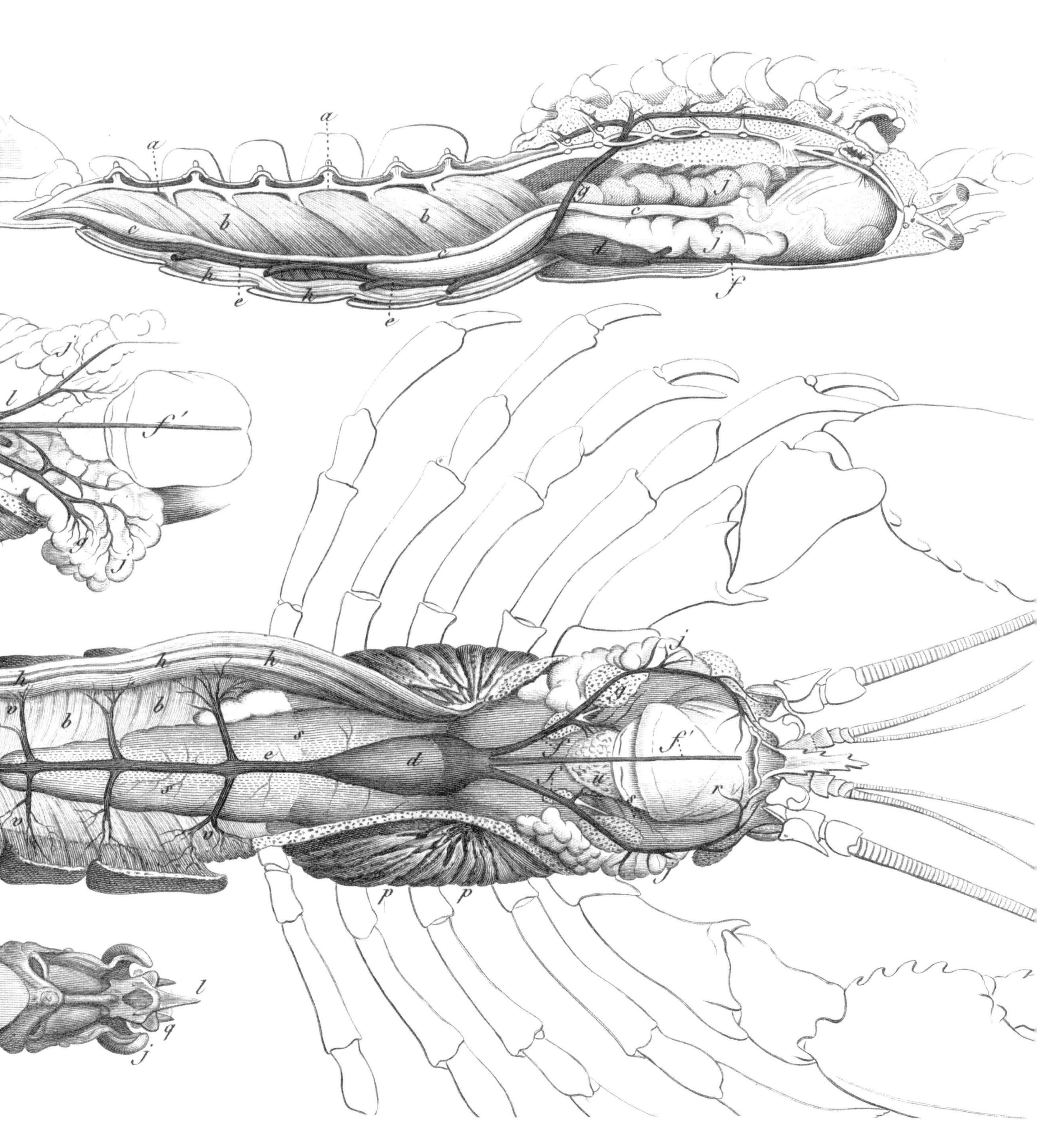

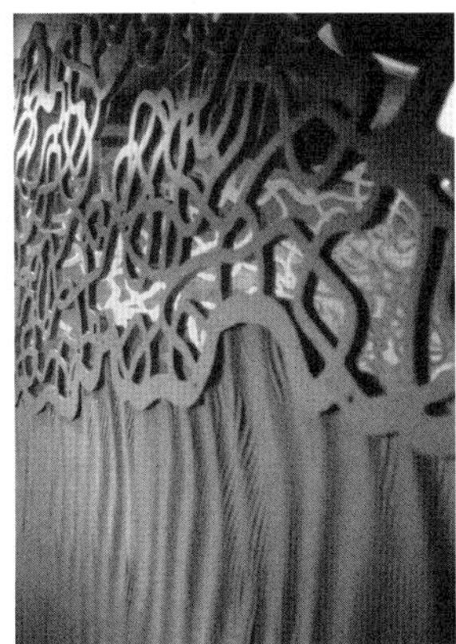

Left and below
Views of the Semper Pavilion.

Top to bottom

Interior of Sainte-Etienne Du Mont showing stone interlacing of the roodscreen, Paris, Philibert de l'Orme.

Detail of the roodscreen, within Saint-Etienne du Mont, Paris, Philibert de l'Orme.

crossed (or inverted) vertebrate. This conceptual equality establishes a common ground between Geoffroy Saint-Hilaire and Gaspard Monge,[21] the rediscoverer of projective geometry.

Monge, who taught at the Ecole de Mézières and was closely connected, in 1794, to the Ecole Normale, where the young Geoffrey Saint-Hilaire had arrived, believed in descriptive geometry's ability to become a universal language. Monge was also one of the organizers of the scientific portion of Napoleon's Egypt expedition, and would later become the Chair of the Institut d'Egypte. It is likely that Monge and Saint-Hilaire had plenty of opportunity to discuss their shared interests. Within a year of their overlap at the Ecole Normale, Saint-Hilaire was to formulate his principle of "unity of plan."

Interestingly, Monge developed projective geometry by teaching stereotomy. His interest in architecture went so far as to lead to a proposal for an ellipsoidal vault – the joints of which were lines of curvature that admit two limit points, called "umbilics."[22] Inversion and umbilic are only two among many other hybrid concepts shared between biology and geometry.[23] There is also great overlap in Saint-Hilaire's use of the terms "homology" and "plane of composition," both of which are significant and well-defined terms within projective geometry. Saint-Hilaire didn't use the word "homologue" as a vague synonym to "analogue", nor did he use "plan" as a vague synonym to "organization."[24] He intended these terms to carry their full mathematical meanings, such as those used by the mathematician Girard Desargues, in 1638, to formulate the theorem "if two tri-

angles have a center of homology, then they have also an axis of homology." This theorem would become a cornerstone of projective geometry.

Abstract elements such as the 'center' and the 'axis of homology' were certainly the kind of invariants Saint-Hilaire was looking for in the continuation of the work of his teacher René Just Hauy.[25] Just Huay founded crystallography – another scientific domain not at all foreign to the history of art, especially when one considers that the crystal was to become the paradigm of the abstract "Kunstwollen." Just as, having dropped a crystal, René Just Hauy found that the broken pieces showed planes intersecting at a constant angle, Saint-Hilaire was looking for the equivalent plane, the invariant element, on the basis of which various animals could be said to belong to the same "forme primitive," in the language of Just Huay, or to the same "urmotiv," using the language of Gottfried Semper. It is on the basis of this unique plane that one would be able to generate any species by varying the proportions of an "urtier." While Semper hints at notions of varying proportions in his chapter on stereotomy, he remains far from considering such notions as the proportions which appear to be constant in projective transformation.

PROJECTIVE GEOMETRY

The fate of projective geometry was to be developed by mathematicians and used by technicians while simply ignored by most people in other fields. Projective geometry is commonly thought of as only a set of drawing tools, when it has historically involved much wider practical goals than simply representation. Alongside stonecutting and gnomonics,[26] perspective was only one field of development for projective geometry. In mathematics for example, projective geometry had a much deeper significance than as just the codification of a practice. It led to the structuring of geometry into categories – isometry, similitude, projection, and topology. The problem is that the history of projective geometry is rather slippery. It developed independently in the three practical fields mentioned earlier – stereotomy, perspective and gnomonics – until Desargues invented general theorems to be used commonly by all of the fields. Unfortunately Desargues's theorems were widely ignored with the exception of a few eminent readers.[27]

Although many reasons can be invoked to explain the rejection of Desargues's work, it is at least worthwhile to mention three of them and their implications in various fields. In mathematics, Desargues's theory of projective geometry appeared at the same time as Descartes' theory of analytic geometry, which was to give way to differential geometry. At the time, the path was already open for a progressive eclipse of geometry as a whole, to the advantage of algebra. By the end of the nineteenth century, Euclid's *Elements*, which for two thousand years had been the model of all rational discourse, ceased to be a teaching reference. In stereotomy, Desargues had the same type of trouble that Philibert de l'Orme had already experienced, and that Monge would face in his turn as a teacher of stone-cutting at the Ecole de Mézières; the three threatened the division of labor in architecture – revealing technical knowledge that was considered the secret, autonomous property of workers on site. In painting, Desargues also encountered strong opposition from the "art" milieu, but perhaps for social rather than theoretical reasons. Yet strangely enough, one of Desargues's main opponents, Charles Lebrun, was still able to anticipate, artistically, Geoffroy Saint-Hilaire's notion of establishing continuity between remote species by progressive deformation.[28] So even though Desargues never enjoyed the success he deserved, his work had sufficiently pervaded several areas of society enough to prepare his revival at the beginning of the nineteenth century, just before Semper's arrival in Paris.[29]

Semper arrived in Paris in 1830, when it could be said the era of projective geometry there had already begun to pass. Algebra had supplanted geometry at the Ecole de Polytechnique, and eventually, the consequences of projective geometry were to be drawn not in France, but in German countries, by von Staudt, Plucker, and Felix Klein.[30] Still, at the time Semper was studying mathematics, projective geometry was considered to be primarily French. What was Semper's understanding of geometry? And what could he have learned from Frederick Gauss? It's a difficult question because Gauss was known for keeping secret most of his work until he was sure of all its conclusions. In fact, he rarely made public the methods he used to discover his theorems. His demonstrations were so deprived of all traces of method that they displayed only their final structure. Gauss would explain: "When a beautiful building is achieved, one must not see what has been the scaffolding."[31] Such a sentence is so close to Semper's conception of architecture that it quite probably was inspired by Gauss.

Ian Stewart presents Gauss very well by stating that he was at the same time the first of the modern mathematicians and the last of the classical ones. "His methods were modern, while his choice of problems was classic." Most probably, Semper inherited from Gauss this classical approach to geometry that read Euclid's *Elements* as a text oriented towards a Platonic theory of polyhedrons (as it is espoused in the *Timée*). Semper's *Prolegomena* begins with images of the sphere and the polyhedron as they appear in crystals. This polygonal conception shows up again in Semper's text on stereotomy, where blocks of stone are conceived as polyhedrons. Chapter 166, "Gestalt des Unterbaues als Ganzes betrachtet," reproduces this "kristallinisch-eurhythmisch" conception: "auf den Kreis, das Polygon, das Rechteck."[32] Geometrically speaking, Gottfried Semper is an unusual case, his conception of textiles clearly anticipates topology and knot theory, and it revives the main geometrical concept of Anaximandre,[33] the apeiron. But his conception of stereotomy is entirely based upon the transposition of wood tectonics into stone, and as such it remains anchored in a neo-classical reading of Euclid. Semper missed the intermediary level between the polygons of Euclid and the knots of William Thomson.[34] Had Semper read Desargues he would have discovered a language of geometry close to Philibert de l'Orme's architectural language – not only in its knots and stone interlacing, and not only in the projective cone of the Trompe d'Anet, but in the vocabulary of its French order – a trunk, with knots, branches, and thinner ramification.[35] Instead of restricting his view to regular convex polygons, Semper could have realized that they are only a very particular case within a whole variety of concave and crossed figures. Moreover, Semper would have realized that non-regular polygons could have interesting projective properties, like the alignment of the intersection of the opposed sides evidenced in Pascal's theorem of the hexagon.[36] Geometry takes on a new appearance when one doesn't focus solely on the last chapters of Euclid's *Elements* and instead allows it to combine with Menelaus's theorem. This geometrician of the first century established the first projective properties upon the base of Thales's theorem.[37] Moreover, it is possible to deduct all the fundamental theorems of projective geometry, Pappus, Ceva, Desargues, Pascal, and Brianchon, on the basis of this single theorem of Menelaus.

Are we not today in a situation similar to Semper's? Piling up topology on top of classical geometry, are we not missing the intermediary step? Are we not putting things too simply when we oppose the cube to the blob? Is there no other solution than the modernist grid and the contemporary free form? Can't we find supple regularities? To be sure, morphing software enables us to link anything with any other thing. But isn't it the path that matters? By simply rejecting polygons to promote NURBS, don't we miss a geometry for our projects, a projective geometry?

NOTES

1 Cuvier, Georges, Baron – (1769–1832) Cuvier's theories were based upon the notion that function determines biological form. As such, form was deemed immutable within the restraints of function. From this assumption, Cuvier developed a system of classification that assigned all species of animal to one of four distinct categories and denied the existence of evolution.

2 Wilhelm Alexander von Humbold, Friedrich – (1769–1859) A German naturalist, Von Humbold was a pioneer in the field of Biogeography. His exhaustive account of the structure of the then known universe, *Kosmos*, was widely translated and influential.

3 Geoffroy Saint-Hailaire, Etienne – (1772–1844) French naturalist who developed the principle of "unity of organic composition." This theory proposed that the anatomical structure of all animals could be traced back to a single form from which all other organic form is derived.

4 Stereotomy is defined as the cutting of solids, in particular stone.

5 de L'Orme, Philibert – (1512–1570) Court architect for Henry II, de L'Orme was considered one of the fathers of French Neo-Classical architecture. He is known for, among other things, the development of innovative stone cutting and vaulting techniques, which made use of unique geometric methods.

6 Desargues, Girard – (1591–1661) French mathematician who developed the foundations of projective geometry. His work, which depended heavily on a unique mathematical symbolism and derived from botanical notation, was not widely accepted by other mathematicians until the second half of the nineteenth century.

7 Philippe Potie has already hinted at the "Semperian-ness" of Philibert de l'Orme's architecture in his brilliant book, *Figures de la Pensee Constructive*. In a way, this text is a reciprocal essay on the "non-de l'Orme-ness" of *Der Stil*.

8 Attributed to Philibert de l'Orme by Anthony Blunt

9 Projective Geometry is the branch of mathematics that deals with the relationships between geometric figures and the images, or mappings, of them that result from projection. Common examples of projections are the shadows cast by opaque objects, motion pictures, and maps of the Earth's surface.

10 Gottfried Semper, 'Uber die bleiernen Schleudergeschosse der Alten und zweckmässige Gestaltung der Wurfkörper im Allgemein', (Frankfurt, 1859).

11 Not to be achieved by mathematicians until 1872.

12 Color and surface (which as Aristotle remarked are two closely related words, chroia and chroma) bear witness to a pre-Euclidean polychrome geometry where surfaces could not been thought of without color.

13 This chronology of the development and relation of Geoffroy Saint-Hilaire and Cuvier comes from Le Guyader, Hervé, *Théories et histoire en biologie* (Vrin, 1988).

14 "Description de deux singes d'Amerique, sous les noms d'ateles arachnoids et d'ateles marginatus."

15 Le Guyader, Hervé, *Théories et histoire en biologie* (Vrin, 1988).

16 Laurencet and Meyrand's concept was that the layout of the organs of a Cephalopod was analogous to that of a Vertebrata, thanks to a folding operation already suggested by the etymology of the word "Cephalo-pode."

17 At the very time Semper was making visits at the Jardins des Plantes while studying architecture in Paris.

18 "A common plan for dorso-ventral patterning in Bilateria", *Nature*, 1996.

19 Le Guyader, Hervé, *Geoffroy Saint-Hilaire*, Berlin, 1998.

20 Specifically, an inversion of power "k", relative to a pole O, is the transformation which associates to a point M the point M1 such as OM*OM1 = k. One immediately sees that:
  1 Every single point of the plane has an inverse, except from the pole O whose inverse is rejected at infinity.
  2 If M1 is the inverse of M, then reciprocally, M is the inverse of M1
  3 The circle with center O and radius Vk remains invariant
  4 Any two points and their inverse constitute a quadrangle inscribed on a circle.
  5 This circle cut the invariant circle at right angle
  6 The quadrilateral of the quadrangle has one external vertex on the center of the invariant circle
  7 The other external vertex goes on the crossing of the two other opposed sides when M comes into the invariant circle while N keeps remaining outside.

21 Monge, Gaspard, Comte De Peluse – (1746–1818) French mathematician who developed the fields of descriptive and analytical geometry. Both of which now form branches of projective geometry.

22 Joël Sakarovitch, *Epures d'architecture* (Birkhäuser, 1998).

23 In mathematics, an umbilic is a point on a curved surface where all normal sections have the same curvature. In biology, an umbilic is the connection between the embryo and the mother through the umbilical cord.

24 The mathematical definition of homology is, if between two figures, composed of points and straight lines, one can establish such a correspondence that couples of associated points are located on converging lines, those figures have a center of homology where the lines converge. If the correspondence is such that couples of associated lines intersect in points located on the same line, this line is the axis of the homology which transforms one figure into another.

25 René Just Hauy taught physics at the Ecole Normal at the same time Monge taught geometry.

26 Gnomonics pertains to the measuring of time by means of the projection of the sun – most commonly using a sundial.

27 The first of whom was Blaise Pascal. Indeed, Pascal should be given the right to share the paternity of projective geometry

28 Jurgis Baltrusaitis, "Les perspectives depraves," Part I.

29 After Monge's codification of descriptive geometry in 1795, in 1810 Brianchon announced his astonishing principle of duality. According to Brianchon's principle, all theorems of geometry have a "shadow" theorem, which can be deduced by simply exchanging the word "point" with "straight line", and the word "intersect" with "being aligned." In 1822 Poncelet published "Traité des propriétés projectives des figures," so it is no surprise that Sainte-Hilaire thought of biology in terms of projective geometry, one of the hot topics among the scientific community at that time.

30 von Staudt, Karl George Christian – (1789–1867), Pluker, Julius – (1801–1868), Klien, Felix – (1849–1925) – German mathematicians who contributed significantly to the development and solidification of projective geometry among other branches of mathematics and physics.

31 Biography of Carl Friedrich Gauss by Ian Steward in *Les Mathématiciens* (Berlin, 1996).

32 'From the circle, the polygon, the rectangle'

33 Anaximandre – (610 BC–545 BC) Greek philosopher who developed a systematic philosophical view of the world based on the concept of the aperion, which was the unified, and undifferentiable state in which all things existed before they were separated into discernible entities.

34 William Thomson, Lord Kelvin (1824–1907) proposed that different elements consisted of different configurations of knots, or knotted vortices. Knot theory led many scientists to believe that they could understand the chemical elements by studying different types of knots and thus this led to a completely new field of study in math. A knot is defined as a closed 3-Dimensional curve that does not intersect itself.

35 Projective geometry appears tightly connected to biology since the very beginning of its theorization. At the time Desargues was writing, biology was essentially botany, hence the vegetal nature of the terms projective geometry borrows from natural science. At the time of its rediscovery by Monge, Poncelet and Brianchon, biology began focusing on the animal reign. But this time, the direction of the borrowing seems to have gone mainly the other way round – from geometry towards biology.

36 Even more surprisingly, those properties are kept invariant when the polygons happen to be crossed, or degenerated. Degeneration is another key concept of projective geometry that also happens to be central to Geoffroy Saint-Hilaire's work.

37 Menelaus also initiated spheric trigonometry, which would provide one of the Euclidean models of non-Euclidean geometry.

Digital de l'Orme

BERNARD CACHE AND PATRICK BEAUCÉ

Translation from Spanish by JORGE ZAPATA

The de l'Orme Pavilion is the product of a design and fabrication studio taught by Bernard Cache and Patrick Beaucé at the L'Escola Superior d'Arquitectura of the Universitat Internacional de Catalunya in Barcelona, Spain. The studio was an exercise in utilizing the basic operations of a numerically controlled machine for full-scale production of an architectural object as well as an attempt to push the limits of the new suite of software and machinery that have become increasingly available to architects.

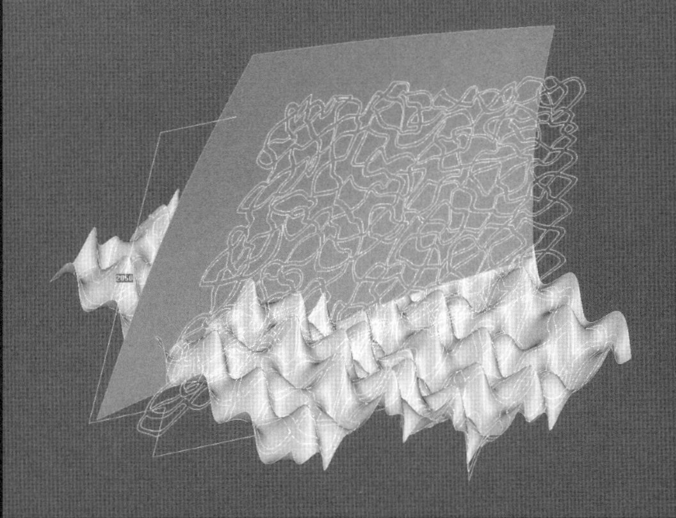

In 1999, Objectile presented the Semper Pavilion in two international expositions, Batimat 99 and Archilab 99. The Semper Pavilion revealed how digital textures elaborated on simple flat panels could be molded into an architectural ensemble. At the same time, this technological object strived to reach a dialogue with Gottfried Semper's principal thesis asserting that interlacing constitutes a fundamental architectural motif in the sense that the art of construction is derived from the art of sewing, or textiles.

Recently, Objectile has attempted to benefit from the consequences of a new generation of cad-cam software that has established a truly reciprocal relationship between conception and digital production – the de l'Orme Pavilion is an application of advanced technologies in this field. All documents and research in the project are combined in the architectural object in such a way that the first drawing hypotheses may be modified by events in the later stages of production. The changes in these hypotheses will, in turn, have consequences throughout the chain of production, up to and including the actual mechanized fabrication.

PHILIBERT DE L'ORME
AND THE CONCEPT OF TRANSPOSITION

The step from Semper to de l'Orme brings to light a question on the surprising absence of any mention of the French architect in the texts of the German architect. As I have written elsewhere, there is no more "semperian" architecture than the architecture of de l'Orme, who makes such intense use of the interlacing motif. There are plenty of instances of the interlacing motif in Philibert de l'Orme's work that demonstrate his mastery of transposition from textile to stone. De l'Orme's invention of the carpentry technique à petit bois is another example of his use of transposition – in this case from stone to wood. Thus, Philibert de l'Orme provides us with illustrious examples of the main concept of the Semper's treatise, *Der Stil*.

In a sense, Semper did nothing except augment the nucleus of Vitruvian theory. Instead of delimiting architecture to the transposition of the stone temple to the wooden hut, Semper broadened the concept of transposition to the full range of materials for each method of construction: textile, ceramics, carpentry, and stone. Correspondingly, Semper proposed an interesting relation to history, where the oldest motifs are capable of transposition to the newest materials and procedures. Interestingly, the fundamental advantage of the de l'Orme trompe l'oeils over the Gothic cul de lampes was that the trompe l'oeils could afford to intervene in ancient buildings, changing the distribution without changing the structure. Today's digital procedures permit us to take the interlacing motif and methods of transposition to levels of complexity difficult to attain without the possibilities of construction presented to us by computer controlled machines. We are better able to consider a field of research in which it is not clear if we are constructing the new with the old, or the old with the new.

Top
CAD CAM image of de l'Orme pavilion.

Left and below
De l'Orme pavilion in production.

Opposite
Interlacing pattern for de l'Orme pavilio

PHILIBERT DE L'ORME
AND THE CONSTRUCTIVE ORIGIN
OF PROJECTIVE GEOMETRY

The drawing of the pavilion is based upon the concepts of projective geometry, of which Philibert de l'Orme was a pioneer. The pavilion is circumscribed in a cube whose edges, instead of being parallel, converge in a vanishing point in finite space. This use of a point of convergence as a point of construction instead of as a vanishing point of representation reminds us that perspective is merely one of the results of projective geometry. Philibert de l'Orme had previously used this concept for the drawing of trompe l'oeils, such as the Trompe d'Aneth. In the development of this drawing technique, de l'Orme perfected stereotomy techniques originating from the South of France (Provence and Languedoc) and the North of Spain (see the trompe l'oeil of the Catalonia Library in Barcelona). This development parallels the contemporary focus on geometry in the field of mathematics catalyzed by computers – allowing the construction of ever more complex forms. Today's architecture will benefit from digital technology as the discipline evolves its own internal notions of geometry.

The Ledoux Effect:

GEORGE WAGNER

ultrasuede

1

THE PREMISE

The instrumental vision of the modernist architect seems to have panned easily from the piece of furniture to the design of the city, and to have done so by subjecting diverse scales to the binding operations of aesthetic unity. This unity came at the price of the autonomy of the individual design disciplines, which were silenced by the ambitions and economic imperatives of larger orchestrations. This paper reflects broadly on the subject of textiles, the body, furniture, and buildings in postwar North America. At a moment of material invention and spatial expansion, the dialectical possiblities of architecture's constituent elements were overwhelmed by a broad complicity. As a result, the enveloping continuity of the whole and its governing surfaces subsumed and refigured the parts. My speculations begin with a discussion of materials but ultimately grounds itself in the social culture of postwar North America, in the animated jostlings between rebellion and freedom, institutional deliberation and bodily improvisation.

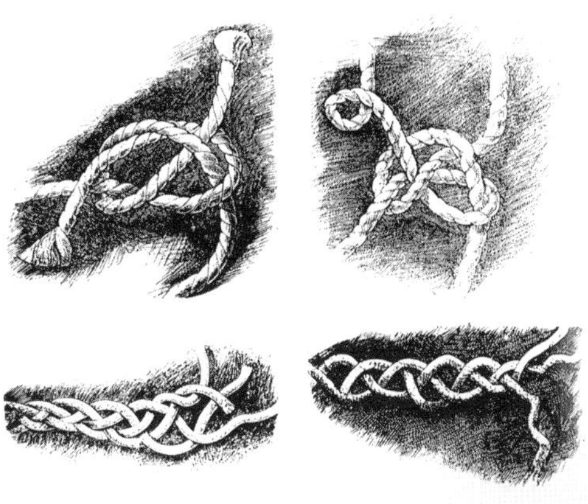

BETWEEN THE WAIST AND THE FLOOR

In 1958, articulating motives for the design of his pedestal furniture, Eero Saarinen wrote:

I wanted to clear up the slum of legs.[1]

Pondering this remark forty-four years later, I find it notable that the space under the dining table would be described using the physical and social context of the decaying postwar American city. But after the war, social issues and the domestic realm were frequently viewed together, just as the resettlement of the U.S. in the form of rampant suburbanization was an attempt to increase the physical distance between the two.

Saarinen's slum – the discordant collection of table and chair legs – was to be erased and the domestic landscape renewed with the elegant white cast-aluminum bases of his pedestal furniture. In nine words, Saarinen pans from city to interior, describing the broad scope of engagement in his practice of architecture. The form of the city is invoked to criticize the formal disunity of the dining set.

At least as interesting as the analogies Saarinen was drawing, is that he was looking: at the space under a table surrounded by chairs. It's not hard to imagine him as a child, sitting on the floor, cross-legged under the table, taking in the squalor, or perhaps, as an adult, with greater detachment and a taciturn gaze, regarding the havoc from a comfortable chair across the room. But that space, between table top and floor, waist and foot, is a charged zone of ergonomic action in the human body, and that action is projected onto the inhabitation of buildings, where it must accommodate and support multiple body postures and their functional needs.

Historically the wainscot demarcated the space of the body in the room. But the wainscot was merely a veneer applied to the wall in a building composed of planar surfaces. In an architecture that engaged monolithic materials for the purpose of generating plastic space and form (as Saarinen's became), another, more radical and discontinuous method was necessary.

Some of Saarinen's most innovative buildings fused floor and program, furniture and field – inflecting the floor itself to model a dynamic landscape for the body. Banishing furniture and its clutter, Saarinen designed conversation pits, as at the Noyes House of Vassar College, carving seating from the depth of the floor. At a larger scale, the continuous and organically-modeled ground surface of the TWA terminal further reflects a conception of the floor as more than inert surface, but as a domain actively inflecting to the project's functional and aesthetic dimensions.

Eero Saarinen came by this concentration on floor and furniture honestly. His father Eliel had been the Michelangelo of carpet, allowing it to transgress its place on the floor and actively mediate between horizontal and vertical. At Hvittrask, the elder Saarinen fixed a traditionally-patterned carpet to the wall, which allowed it to fall over a bench and onto the floor, serving as backrest, seat and floor covering. This carpet was not used, as carpets had been historically, as a unit of measure that figured and defined the space of the room, but as a textile that engaged and defined a localized space of the body and the zones of its tactile encounter. The rugs marked the body's posture in the room as it mediated between three different spatial zones.

ORIGINS: BUILDINGS, TEXTILES, BODIES

Eliel Saarinen's grafting of the carpet between wall and floor allows us to see some of the provocative issues of textiles and architecture after the war. Because he used the carpets with the sensibility of a collagist, they animated the room because he brought his own intentions to bear

against the authority of an authentic artifact. The carpets he used were traditional and handcrafted, and the significance of their unconventional position was registered through the conventions of their form.

Made by hand, knotted carpets have been venerated as folk artifacts that conjure and reflect the body through their crafting, pattern, pile and position. Their individuality is sufficient to suggest the muted presence of a narrative of their creation. The patterns of these carpets are discrete and individual. They bind space and give it scale, even as they declare their own formal autonomy.

Gottfried Semper theorized textiles in general, and wickerwork and carpets in particular, as important material artifacts – or motives – through which we can comprehend the origins of architecture. Semper hoped that this journey back to an elemental understanding of building materials and logics of fabrication would foster the preservation of meaning and continuity in architectural design. His writing did not focus on the carpets' appearance or pattern, but on the incremental technique of their fabrication – the knot, and the role it played in scenarios describing the evolution of prehistoric building. His was a way of figuring architecture that fuses decoration, structural forces, spatial dimension and human presence. His theories polarized the material distinctions between frame and wall, mass and space, seen and unseen, and imagined architectural origins in the gentle craft of textiles.

Hanging carpets remained the true wall, the visible boundaries of space. The often solid walls behind them were necessary for reasons that had nothing to do with the creation of space; they were needed for security, for supporting a load, for their permanence and so on ... Even where building solid walls became necessary, the latter were only the inner, invisible structure behind the true and legitimate representatives of the wall, the colorful woven textiles.[2]

In the most sophisticated version of this scenario, the building's perceived reality and essential spatial unit are defined by the carpet. Other realities are unseen and buried within, behind the textile surface, perhaps inside the wall. Conceiving the origins of architecture through textiles did not offer a holistic model for architectural theorization, but did offer one that was necessarily complex and discursive in the relation of the parts. While Semper's writing implied the perceptual immediacy of the spatial liner before the hidden facts of structure, in *The Principle of Cladding* (1898), Adolf Loos recognized of the differences between the two as driving the architectural process.

Carpets are warm and livable…But you cannot build a house out of carpets. Both the carpet on the floor and the tapestry on the wall require a structural frame to hold them in the correct place. To invent this frame is the architect's second task.[3]

Loos' reading of Semper did not attempt to imbue an ethical relation between wall covering and building structure; it is not an argument for articulation, or an ethical orchestration of parts. He wanted to theorize the surface itself, the covering, which he called "the oldest architectural detail." For him, the detail is not a point of connection or inflection, but a continuous veneer more a mask than a joint.

The ultimate strategy for manipulating this surface and the space to which it gives life, is described by Loos:

But the artist, the architect, first senses the effect that he intends to realize…He senses the effect that he wishes to exert upon the spectator…These effects are produced by both material and the form of the space.[4]

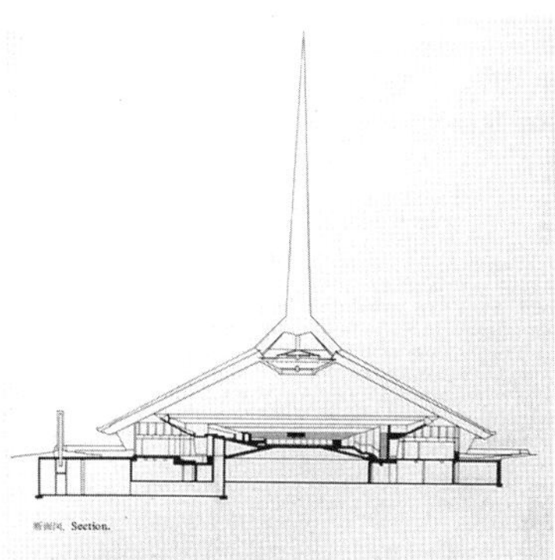

Loos offers a way of conceiving architecture unburdened from responsibilities of ethical expression, from the belief that the rhetorical articulation of the material facts of building somehow lie within the territory of honesty or truth. The celebrated corner of Schinkel's Altes Museum projects onto the surface a description of the building's internal parts and juxtaposes them against the figure of the monolithic whole. Loos suggests it is neither the responsibility nor the duty of the architect to bring to the surface the elements that reside privately within the deep space of architecture.

Schinkel's lucid reasoning and the clarity with which he hybridized building morphologies never impeded but only heightened his skills in scenography and creating effect. These were his other avocations. His tented room at Charlottenhof (1826–33) used stretched and hung fabric to devise a purely local space suspended from the architectural motives of the building that encased it. Its atmospheric reverie invokes a realm beyond the villa, to the suggestion of a Roman campaign tent. It is the isolated world of monolithic and indulgent decoration, unlike the analytic and historicizing theory of Semper.

DOMESTIC SPACE AND INTROSPECTION: DETACHED AND SUSPENDED

The detached reveries of Schinkel's tent room suggest most clearly the role that textiles came to play in the second half of the twentieth century: producing a purely local reality in a space with a continuous surface, eminently spatial and inwardly focused – a space for mental reflection and bodily suspension. In the 1970s, *Vogue* published a number of tented rooms as part of its monthly review of glamorous domesticity. The rooms are like boudoirs, and celebrate the possibility of an enclosed, bodily suspension from time and place. The character of these rooms is nothing like the images or sensibilities circulating through popular culture, the high arts, or the other pages of *Vogue*. They present their occupants in isolation from the world.

The decorator Billy Baldwin produced comparably detached interiors for his clients in New York. The element of separation from the world was the very commodity these spaces offered. The means employed to produce these effects were always similar: the room's interior surface was treated as continuous, and fabric, mirror or canvas (when paintings were used) were applied. Baldwin described Diana Vreeland's salon as "a garden in hell."[5] The bathroom of Mrs. Harding Lawrence (the advertising executive Mary Wells) was a hall of mirrors that surrealistically captured the movement of the city in an intimate space. "The only passers-by are birds, she bathes in full view of the elements; lying back in her tub, she can look up in the mirrored ceiling and watch reflections of barges on the river and the traffic roaring fourteen floors below."[6]

The walls and ceiling of Baldwin's bedroom for Si Newhouse were covered in brown velvet, "a cave."[7] The floor was taupe wall-to-wall carpeting. Paintings by Morris Louis and Mark Rothko on adjacent walls spanned from floor to ceiling, so that the architectural space of the room was subsumed by the pictorial space of the pictures. A print by Barnett Newman hung beside the Louis. The interiority of the room's soft enclosure found its visual foil in the two color field paintings in which the depth was as hermetic as the paintings were introspective. Clement Greenberg called this depth "color-space."[8] Greenberg admired another aspect of the spatiality of color field painting, calling it "openness."

Yet the ultimate effect sought is one of more than chromatic intensity; it is rather one of an almost literal openness that embraces and absorbs color in the act of being created by it. Openness, and not only in painting, is the quality that seems most to exhilarate the attuned eye of our time.[9]

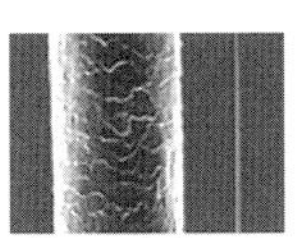

THE SCIENCE OF ULTRASUEDE®

From an architectural standpoint (and it seems clear that Greenberg hoped that the relevance of his term would extend beyond painting), this openness is abstract, referring as it does to mere paint on canvas. The paintings in question, a Newman or a Rothko, are legible as metaphors for space because of their relative blankness. And while Greenberg wrote of chromatic intensity, the openness of color field painting is more a product of chromatic restraint than intensity. Openness and its spatial implications are derived more from the field than from the image, and more from monochromatic subtlety than from chromatic intensity.[10]

The openness that Greenberg found can realistically be described in terms of enclosure, interiority and delimitation. With even greater conviction, Barnett Newman described the perceived opening of his paintings in their projection of a two-dimensional spatiality. Newman saw inside his work a "space-dome" and hoped that the viewer would "feel the vertical domelike vaults encompass him to awaken an awareness of his being alive in the sensation of complete space."[11] He described without irony the architectural space of the room that held his painting as both "chaotic and empty." The space-dome of his painting "should make one feel . . . full and alive in a spatial dome of 180 degrees going in all four directions. This is the only real sensation of space."[12]

The content of paintings mattered to Barnett Newman. Most paintings, he said, are full of "object-matter", a term borrowed from Meyer Schapiro, which can be applied either to the narrative subject matter of realist painting or to the emergent forms of the abstract; it is clutter either way. What Newman wanted to avoid he called the anecdotal and the episodic. Both terms seem to imply the presence of the narrative, the verbal, and the temporal. Its seems clear that the enemy for Newman was the presence within the work of a specificity that might inhibit the spatial expanse. "Instead of working with the remnants of space, I work with the whole space." Ultimately, Newman's insistence on the visual perception of this imagined space (and against talking), might offer "its assertion of freedom, its denial of dogmatic principles, its repudiation of all dogmatic life."[13]

But what is of interest is the impulse to read pictorial blankness as space, and the possibility that the motive to do so might have corollaries in other disciplines, as Greenberg suggested. Certainly the Newhouse bedroom, with its textile surfaces and large canvasses was an attempt to conflate the space of architecture and painting – and to do so through the treatment of the room's surface. It could be that this openness required of architects a recalibration of the relation between buildings and their furnishings, with the result that the space of the building absorbed the furniture and the accessories of daily life – just as the openness of color field painting soaked up color according to Greenberg.

This absorption of furniture into architecture initiated a new formal economy. While previously architecture and furniture had mirrored each other, each with its own discourse and formal vocabulary, these new interiors erased furniture, and replaced it with an inflection between a reprogrammed architectural shell and its object – throbbing space. Paul Rudolph made referred to this energy, identifying the presence of "spatial velocity," the visible and generative force "escaping from the room."[14]

The North Christian Community Church (1959–63) was designed by Eero Saarinen for the new postwar suburbs of Columbus, Indiana where his father had completed the First Christian Church in 1942. The interior of Eliel Saarinen's church is stark white, and lit by a large concealed window flanking the altar.

Eero Saarinen's church is a sort of space dome, caught between a molded floor and an inflected roof, two shells in tension, pulled away so that they never touch. Religious iconography has been minimized, reduced in scale and made discreet, no larger than a body. The space is full of little but light, dim and wavering, filtering down through a baffled oculus and washing up under the eaves across the soft, porous plaster. As little as a passing cloud can produce tremulous modulations. The ceiling reads like canvas that absorbs all the light and reflects all the color. The interior is monolithic, monochromatic and very subtle.

UBIQUITOUS TEXTILES AND FREE BODIES

This paper examines some aspects of the dynamic relations between architecture and textiles, and to focus those musings on the thirty years that followed the Second World War. The war effort itself had induced an era of material innovation, as natural resources became more difficult to obtain and expensive to use. Among the effects of the unprecedented economic and spatial expansion that followed in North America were numerous innovations in production that revolutionized textiles and carpeting, the scale at which they could be deployed, and the boundaries and thresholds of their use.

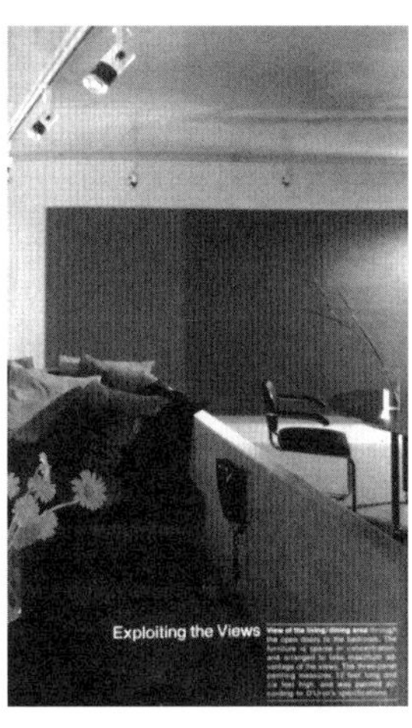

Government programs, new wealth, and entrenched social divisions revised urban patterns. The form of institutional and commercial buildings changed in response to decentralized regional expansion and the resulting transportation imperatives. New precincts of standardized single-family housing emerged, capturing vast markets.

At the same time as the physical landscape was being remade, the social fabric of North America also approached fundamental transformation. Political dissent, racial conflict, and the struggles for gender parity and against sexual oppression, caused almost every assumed orthodoxy of social behavior to be challenged and reexamined. This had enormous impact on attitudes towards the built environment, from the ease with which the historical city was "renewed" to the way in which the posture and presence of the human body were anticipated by form and material.

What catalyzed these phenomena most completely was unprecedented experimentation in the arena of human freedoms. This emergence and fetishization of the free self must be understood against the burgeoning markets of the postwar capitalist economy and the deliberate consolidation of the myths of freedom with the repetitive exhortations of a media-fed consumer culture.

The cult of the free and empowered individual allows each person to realize his potential as a consumer. Around this principle – the maximization of consumption – the new "urban" landscape was engineered. That engineering extended into the cultivation of daily life as a series of micro sites onto which the empowering negotiations of choice and product could be projected. Freedom became a market strategy.

In the 1960s and '70s, the idea of the self as an individuated increment of freedom took on new forms. Identity was refined and cultivated internally through psychological interpretation, sexual politics, alternative religions, drugs and self-help regimes.[15] This new self appeared outwardly as a visible artifact in the public landscape, available to represent affiliations and sympathies. Sartorial freedom became a point of leverage that allowed an individual to project identity as a demonstration of political alignment.

Posture – how we stand and sit, figuring our bodies interaction and response to the physical and social world – is another demonstration of individual alignment.[16] Just as furniture dictates posture, and so figures propriety, individuals can determine their posture as a reaction to the already-figured, ergonomically-fixed expectation of building and furniture. These are the battles of adolescent identity and independence, between parent and child and the battles move freely from the public to the private realm. Posture is portable, figured as much by the real forms that anticipate our interaction as by the abstract ones – the attitudes and auras we wish to project.

Even as individual identity was being cultivated in various strains of non-conformism, architectural spaces were often becoming more generalized and neutral. Readymade "shells," Eero Saarinen called them:

Usually the problem of interior design is limited. It begins within the existing framework of an office, apartment, or ready-made house. The shells of these living and working units have to answer the needs of hundreds of thousands of people. They have become completely anonymous shells. And thank God this is so! It is when they stray from strict impersonality – and try to anticipate some personal idiosyncrasy by mass producing some kind of fancy door-moulding or mantelpiece – that these living and working shells for a mass market fail both practically and esthetically. Likewise, furniture has moved . . . into a mass-production era, and so to a greater or lesser degree, have other items of the interior. The result is that the major equipment or furnishings of the interior have an impersonal character. As with the architectural shells, it is essential, in fact, that a mass-produced item must have this impersonal character.[17]

The impersonality that Saarinen espouses was often rendered by monolithic and monochromatic surfaces. Of course, the concrete of the shell was one. Textiles were others. Textiles are a provocative agent of industrial progress in a consumer culture. Their presence nearly always indicates the tactile intervention of the human body. Unlike most commercial products, they are not discrete, but necessarily continuous, anonymous in their ubiquity.

As an element that could provide spatial continuity and render the inconsequential even and continuous, carpeting was rivaled only by paint. Carpet could extend through the building, and like the kudzu vine in the Southern forest, neutralize and subsume everything in its path. Carpet, concrete, gypsum board and paint were all that were needed to render physical the desired anonymity.

ULTRASUEDE AND DENIM

Since the technological advances of the mid-nineteenth century, modern materials have been seen as significant representations of cultural progress and have frequently been engaged to serve nationalist ends. The historian Jeffrey Schnapp, in his essay "The Fabric of Modern Times" has chronicled the way in which the Futurists in Italy celebrated rayon in songs and poems, infusing the fabric with powers that allowed it to become "a site for elaborating a complex physics and metaphysics of sovereignty."[18] Marinetti wrote poems entitled "The Poem of the Milk Dress" and "The Poem of the Viscose Tower." The Fascists built a new town in Friuli around a rayon mill and named it Toriviscose. Speaking generally, Schnapp states that:

modern materials emerge as autonomous forces within an overarching modernist prosopopoeia. Beyond even their symbolic import, they become protagonists and heroes endowed with powers of agency and moral value, capable of sharing in the particular and universal attributes of human subjects and/or serving as prosthetic extensions of humanity.[19]

Schnapp's observations are particularly relevant when applied to North America in the decades following the Second World War, an era marked by innovations in manufacturing and rapid social change. Textiles became the tangible interface among industrial progress, politicized ideas about the body, and the public exercise and display of free will. Popular taste and the fashion industry often transform textiles into a mass-marketed medium, a veneer connected to the propulsion of advertising and entertainment. An aggressively-marketed fabric can become a form of wrapping that does not contain signs even as it manages to be one.

Beginning in the 1960s, denim was a highly visible textile, a throwback that catalyzed social movements. Kennedy Fraser's essay of 1973, "Denim and the New Conservatives," articulates the irony of denim, the ubiquitous textile which, appropriated from the world of labor, came first to represent social change in the 1960s, and later, the commercialization of fashion.

Theorists of blue jeans in the sixties claimed that one's individuality was made more apparent when it was contrasted with the sameness of denim, and that the malleable clay of blue jeans brought out the touching differences in human bodies.[20]

By recognizing denim's monochromatic emptiness as "malleable clay," Fraser lucidly describes how its sameness can be used to qualify and make visible the differences between bodies. Her perception is not unlike Saarinen's dictum "that a mass-produced item must have an impersonal character." The suggestion is of a rhetorical energy between sameness/impersonality and the dynamics of individuality. One frames the other, and renders visible differences of form and identity. Freedom and personal expression are relative.

Fraser goes further and drolly places denim in a category of architectural materials like "wicker, chromium, bare wood, brick and Lucite,[21]" that made up the venerated palette of surfaces of the era. While there definitely is some taste-bashing going on here, she parenthetically adds: "Perhaps this unthinking veneration of surfaces and substances is related to the use of drugs."[22] The cynical aside elegantly poses the conundrum of personal expression in a mass culture. Drugged or sober, free or conformist, the world of surfaces and reification always facilitates the identification of alignments in industrial society. Products are products, issued without ideology. Taken up by groups, they acquire a representational veneer.

Fraser's discussion identifies two "elites" wearing blue jeans, and in doing so, posits how one material can be employed to serve differing values.

The first group consists broadly, of the middle-aged, the middle class, and those who are still in revolt against the old sartorial rules but continue to be concerned with the way they dress. The second, and more exquisitely fashionable group is slightly younger, though well out of its teens (the very young have no impact on fashion any more), and its members long ago turned their backs on the idea of "fashionable" clothes. The first group continues to move vaguely toward self-expression; the second, and more evolved, group is in retreat from the flamboyance it courted some years ago. The first seeks out denim under the illusion that denim brings freedom, the second, more self conscious, adopts denim precisely for the its uniformity and as a purge.[23]

Coexisting between these groups are motivations for both freedom and uniformity, and the sense that these needs can be expressed through fabric. Freedom, at a sartorial level at least, suggests a release from the conventions of formal dress, from its physical constraints and class references — emancipation for the body. Uniformity of dress offers an erasure of an elemental discourse of parts. Parts are replaced with a monotony of form, one that refers to social pretension and position within a standardized structure, and then does no more.

Speaking in *Vogue*, the designer Halston saw monotony coming:

I don't like the idea, but I think people will dress more and more alike because there will be less and less opportunity for individuality. And this is because there will be fewer natural fabrics that one can choose from.[24]

Halston was the champion of ultrasuede, a synthetic fabric that acquired fame because he used it to make a shirt dress in 1972, model number 704, which sold 78,000 units at prices from $185 to $360. Halston, whose stated ambition was to "clean up fashion," was frequently quoted as saying, "less is more." In the popular press he was often called fashion's first minimalist.[25]

Ultrasuede is a brand name, patented in 1971 by a Japanese company, Toray Industries. It is 60 percent polyester and 40 percent polyurethane. This non-woven fiber is extremely strong and durable and was originally used for upholstery and wall covering. In the 1970s ultrasuede was the fabric of the future – a sort of anti-denim. It was the only fabric one needed. Ultrasuede is both cool in warm weather and warm in cool weather. Its virtues are practical:

It is the first product to offer the rich aesthetics of suede with benefits no animal product could offer. Ultrasuede is soft, supple, and sensuous to the touch. Yet it is also resistant to stains and discoloration. It is even machine washable, and never needs ironing.[26]

Its commercial allure was supported by the promise of technology to produce a material both eminently practical and immediately sensual. As a prestigious fabric, ultrasuede was unusual. No logo was required, since the fabric itself was the logo.

Unlike denim, ultrasuede had no affiliation with the counter-culture, but it was also easily adopted as a uniform by Halston's affluent customers. Halston's ultrasuede designs became the garments that confirmed social class and economic position, but remained casual and discreet. Model number 704, the shirt-dress, is purely typological (a shirt long enough to be a dress), but its invention is based upon the soft and neutral continuity of the fabric. The relative thickness of the fabric demanded simplicity of cut to minimize heavy seams, and precluded the use of either linings or interfacing.

Ultrasuede is always made in solid colors and so guarantees a monochromatic appearance. The body was typically concealed in Halston's designs. Sensuality was conferred not in making the body visible, but through the qualities of the fabric, which became a kind of sensual layer, draped between the wearer and the world, equally available to both sides. Suede is, after all, a second skin.

Ultrasuede was used by Halston as a fetish product and the luxury of the material was counterposed by the simplicity of the garment's tailoring: it was monochromatic, recessive and understated and its classic color was beige. While the elegance of his designs was often reinforced by the quality and sensuality of the fabrics he used, Halston's clothes were often neutral and appropriate. Over the years he designed numerous official uniforms in ultrasuede: for Braniff Airlines, for the Girl Scouts, for the 1976 Olympics, and for Avis Car Rental.[27]

Halston lived in a house in New York on East 63rd Street originally designed by Paul Rudolph and constructed for the real estate attorney Alexander Hirsch in 1966. The tall central living spaces of the house were furnished in monochromatic shades of dark gray fabric, which unified carpets and built-in seating banquettes in a continuous and low landscape. The subdued and minimal continuity of the room was broken by the rare flash of color: Halston's bright red socks, a vase of orchids, the white caftan of his barefoot valet.

Another practitioner whose work was described as minimalist in the 1970s was the interior designer Joe D'Urso. Like Halston, he experimented with textiles. D'Urso's interiors were notable for their restraint; he used both furniture and color minimally. He configured the space through the installation of low platforms covered in dark gray industrial carpet.[28] The effect, juxtaposed against high-gloss white walls, was to produce a continuous and abstract landscape which did not dictate or reveal the exact nature or posture of preferred human interaction. D'Urso's residential projects were often sited in anonymous residential buildings or the raw space of loft conversions. These conditions prompted him to question constructions of specificity and interaction.

Most interior design today is based on a kind of fake individuality in which the designer seeks to interpret his client's personality. I feel that what space is really all about is incompletion – unlike a drawing, say, where if you take a sheet of paper you're responsible, in a sense, for its completion. But a designer is not a fine artist. What I attempt to do is simply to equalize all the elements in a space. I don't want my work to look spontaneous. Rather I try to create firm, clear backgrounds for my clients. They are then responsible for giving them life.[29]

D'Urso purposely indulged the ability of carpet to erase specificity from the space, and to relocate the question of the body's appropriate position and engagement. These abstractions are motivated to stimulate the will of the clients, to solicit interaction, to figure their freedom to choose.

Both D'Urso and Halston were auteurs on the edge of the lifestyle revolution. And yet the sort of aura their work manufactured was not a product of excess, but instead the mute allure of materials engaging bodies. They employed abstraction to prompt engagement.

CARPET IS A VERB

Following the Second World War, the cost-efficiency, supply stability and performance characteristics of man-made fibers contributed to a steady reduction in broadloom carpet prices. The first viable replacement for wool was nylon, introduced in carpet manufacture in 1947.

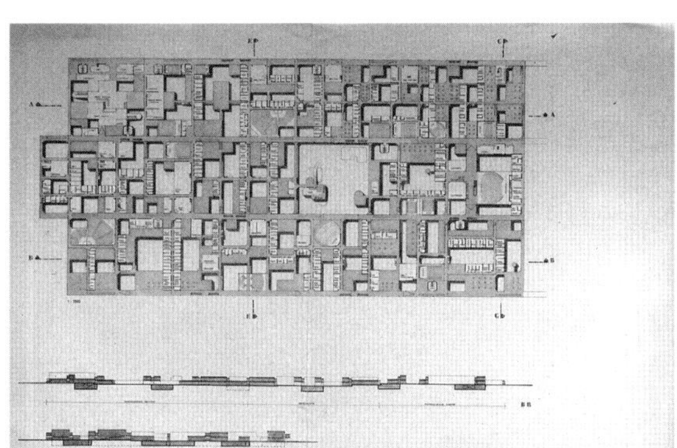

Whereas wool was primarily imported, nylon could be produced domestically, thereby ensuring a stable supply. Availability, along with low cost, resilience and brilliant colors, contributed to the rapid acceptance of nylon in the marketplace. By the late 1950s, it had secured the position as the second most popular carpet material in the industry, exceeded only by wool. ther synthetic fibers further accelerated the erosion of wool's market share. Acrylic, introduced in

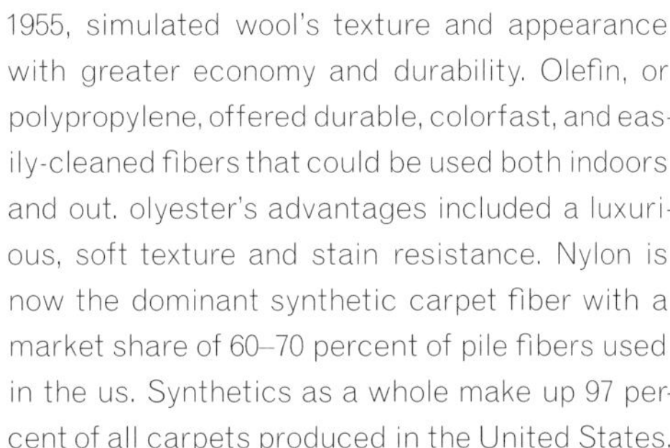

1955, simulated wool's texture and appearance with greater economy and durability. Olefin, or polypropylene, offered durable, colorfast, and easily-cleaned fibers that could be used both indoors and out. olyester's advantages included a luxurious, soft texture and stain resistance. Nylon is now the dominant synthetic carpet fiber with a market share of 60–70 percent of pile fibers used in the us. Synthetics as a whole make up 97 percent of all carpets produced in the United States.

The proliferation of carpeting following the war was significantly enabled by the rapid mechanization of the industry and the development of increasingly efficient production techniques. Carpet mills turned to a process developed in 1946 that stemmed from the production of candlewick bed covers. In this process (tufting) a needle presses looped fibers (tufts) through a backing fabric. Its main advantage is that it eliminates the complicated techniques required for the production of woven carpeting. Not only is it simpler and faster, but also the operating personnel require much less training. With their lower production costs, tufted carpeting rapidly came to dominate the industry in the US. Its market share grew from 9 percent in 1951 to 42 percent in 1956 to 72 percent in 1961. By 1971 tufted carpets amounted to over 90 percent of the total yardage of all types of carpets.

Subsequent developments were not nearly as revolutionary and did not go much farther than accelerating or expanding production capacity. The first variations on the tufting process widened the machines or added more rows of needles. Following these, sophisticated patterning and dyeing attachments were introduced that broadened the scope of design possibilities, including the production of landscaped carpets, or multi-level pile carpets, which are achieved through several methods. One method uses gears of different sizes that determine the stroke of the needle and therefore the length of the pile. Another changes the speed of the yarn being fed into the machine. When the yarn is introduced at a lower speed, the piles will be shorter because some of the yarn is pulled or robbed from the previous tuft. The final significant development was the honesty machine. This employs a pneumatic insertion of tufts as a stream of compressed air is shot through a hollow needle to punch the yarn through the backing fabric. Production was increased significantly by the removal of the mechanical needle.[30]

DOMESTICATING RAW SPACE, UNIFYING DISPARITY

In the postwar years, there was abundant building in North America. Builders produced houses as if they were breeding rabbits and the houses became test sites for the latest materials and appliances. The varied types of the new carpeting allowed the floor to become an arena of expression, sometimes acquiring the quality of mottled landscape, coherent enough to hold together random distributions of furniture and rooms while inviting children to sprawl out before the low cabinet that held the television.

In high design, carpeted platforms appeared in domestic interiors of downtown lofts, and sometimes even suburban boxes. The continuous monochromatic carpets displaced furniture and history, with the promise of a spontaneous life unhampered by regularized enclosure, good posture or dust bunnies. The new domestic landscape seemed to encourage conviviality and improvisation. Carpet unified the space, and gave the interior coherence and presence enough to rival the objectified identity of the single-family house.

Urban patterns changed, away from the dense center of the nineteenth century, towards a galactic regional urbanity strung across the landscape it consumed. Victor Gruen's Fort Worth Plan attempted to weave together the central city through the construction of underground service tunnels. The disparity of the city and its parts was to be given the continuous private infrastructure of a building.

Similarly, the urban web theories fostered by the members of Team 10 proposed a sort of soft, expansive tissue to hold together the dynamic elements of building and city. The web proposals intentionally abstracted architectural and urban planning orthodoxy, refusing the visualized representational dimensions of objectification in favor of a continuous spatial network. Berlin Free University, built by Team 10 members Candilis Josic and Woods, elevated carpeting and its color to demarcate location and address, a device common in an era that professionalized way-finding.[31]

As the size of institutional programs increased, and the megastructure emerged, carpeting became the inevitable interior finish of choice. The increased availability of carpeting transformed the nature of its use, replacing other materials fastened to the building in more integral ways, like wood, masonry, or linoleum. Both monolithic and friendly in its anticipation of the body, carpeting did not hinder the inherently abstract and schematic nature of large-scale building projects. It generalized space and prevented the development of an articulated specificity.

Companies such as Forms and Surfaces of California, marketed feature elements such as tile veneers, planters and grills which offered specificity to vast and undifferentiated spatial fields. Furniture companies produced sectional seating units that could expand to thirty units or contract to five, depending on the particular needs and general configuration of its placement.

Large megastructural projects, typified in North America by the work of Paul Rudolph (Southeastern Massachusetts University 1966–76) and Arthur Erickson (Lethbridge University 1972, Simon Fraser University 1965), represented the advent of large public commissions. These projects, produced by legislative initiative, organized mammoth square footage of raw space on isolated non-sites – reclaimed farmland, badland ravines and forested mountaintops.

While the site and architectural strategies of Erickson and Rudolph were different, both architects used carpet to soften the texture of concrete. Carpet was the only material that could mediate between the extent of the space and the position of a body. Rudolph configured his site plans and buildings into a contorted particularity, echoed by the corduroy finish of hammered concrete. Erickson strove to do much less, to reduce the building's aura to the specifics of a landscape situation, and let abstraction follow.

In the megastructures of both architects, carpeting is used as a veneer of semantic erasure, silencing the parts in deference to the work's larger gestures. Mesmerized by the toxic brew of geometry in the service of passionate artistry, Rudolph's interiors are reduced to corduroy concrete walls and orange carpet covering floors and benches. Erickson was seemingly less afraid of the building's vast expanse of banality. Lethbridge University is all situation, bridging a ravine as might a dam or large log.[32] The long, seemingly endless, central concourse of the monochromatic interior is punctuated by unarticulated carpeted seating platforms.[33] The fact that the whole of the building, seems more important than a part suggests virtues Donald Judd ascribed to artworks in his early description of minimal art:

It isn't necessary for a work to have a lot of things to look at, to compare, to analyze one by one, to contemplate. The thing as whole, its quality as a whole, is what is interesting. The main things are alone and are more intense clear and powerful. They are not diluted by an inherited format, variations of a form, mild contrasts and connecting parts and areas. European art had to represent a space and its content as well as have sufficient unity and aesthetic interest.[34]

One could argue that the muteness of these platforms that seem to betray no anticipation of an engagement with the human body besides the fact they are covered in carpet, is a call to passers-by. They may be like a request, for instance, that they make something of this absence and improvise a use, a posture, an engagement with their body, that they respond to this silence by figuring their own freedom, mobility or collectivity. Alternatively, another argument might posit that real architecture cannot be made at this magnitude, in this abbreviated time frame, with such schematic, ultimately bureaucratic programs that kill the city while making simplistic space out of simplified form. The arguments, of course, have all been made. But one has to ask, all these years later, what it means to make furniture endure like architecture, and whether, like the sheets on a bed or a dirty slipcover, the carpets have been changed yet.

IMAGE NOTES

1 Eero Saarinen, "pedestal" chair, 1955–57 Saarinen, Eero, *Eero Saarinen on His Work*, ed. Aline B. Saarinen (New Haven CT: Yale University Press, 1968) p.67.

2 Eliel Saarinen, Hvittrask, 1902, www.greatbuildings.com.

3 Eliel Saarinen, Hvittrask, 1902, www.greatbuildings.com.

4 Gottfried Semper, examples of knots Semper, Gottfried, Der Stil vol. 1 p.172–75.

5 Karl Friedrich Schinkel, Schloss Charlottenhof, Potsdam, 1826–33 Bergdoll, Barry, *Karl Friedrich Schinkel: An Architecture for Prussia*, (New York NY: Rizzoli International Publications, 1994) p.154.

6 "...in a garden overhanging the sea, with Zefferelli at Positano," *Vogue*, 1974, p.118.

7 "Summer living and cool surprises at Valentino's on the Appian Way" *Vogue*, 1974, p.116.

8 Billy Baldwin, apartment interior for Diana Vreeland, Baldwin, Billy, *Billy Baldwin Remembers* (New York NY: Harcourt Brace Jovanovich, 1974) p.137.

9 Billy Baldwin, bathroom interior for Mrs. Harding Lawrence, Baldwin, *Billy Baldwin Remembers*, p.229 Billy Baldwin, apartment interior for S. I. Newhouse, Baldwin, *Billy Baldwin Decorates*, p.198–199.

10 Eero Saarinen, sanctuary, North Christian Church, Columbus, Indiana Saarinen, Eero, *Eero Saarinen on His Work*, ed. Aline B. Saarinen (New Haven CT: Yale University Press, 1968) p.101.

11 Eero Saarinen, sanctuary, North Christian Church, Columbus, Indiana, Eero Saarinen, *Architecture and Urbanism*, April 1984, p.173.

12 Eero Saarinen section, North Christian Church, Columbus, Indiana, Eero Saarinen, *Architecture and Urbanism*, April 1984, p.175.

13 Eero Saarinen, sancutuary, North Christian Church, Columbus, Indiana,1959–63, *Eero Saarinen, Architecture and Urbanism*, April 1984, p.173.

14 Genuine Tenpelle advertisement.

15 The Science of Ultrasuede. www.ultrasuede.com.

16 Halston and Ultrasuede uniforms designed for Braniff Airlines flight crew, Gross, Elaine and Rottman, Fred, *Halston: An American Original* (New York NY: Harper Collins Publishers, 1999) p.32.

17 Halston, Ultrasuede shirtdress style #104, 1972, Gross, Elaine and Rottman, Fred, *Halston: An American Original* (New York NY: Harper Collins Publishers, 1999) p.173.

18 Living room of the East 63rd Street house, *The Architecture of Paul Rudolph*. Introd. by Sibyl Moholy-Nagy. Captions by Gerhard Schwab. With comments by Paul Rudolph. New York, Praeger, 1970.

19 Halston in the living room of his East 63rd Street house designed by Paul Rudolph, Gross, Elaine and Rottman, Fred, *Halston: An American Original* (New York NY: Harper Collins Publishers, 1999) p.17.

20 Joseph D'Urso Manhattan apartment interior, 1980, *Interior Design*, "Exploiting the Views," January 1981, p.263.

21 Joseph D'Urso Manhattan apartment interior, 1980, *Interior Design*, "Exploiting the Views," January 1981, p.266.

22 Joseph D'urso Manhattan apartment interior, 1980 *Interior Design*, "Exploiting the Views," January 1981, p.261.

23 from High-TechHigh-Tech, "Designer Tim Romanello used movers' pads to cover the bed, floor and cabinets in his one bedroom apartment." *High-tech : the industrial style and source book for the home* by Joan Kron and Suzanne Slesin; foreword by Emilio Ambasz New York : C.N. Potter New York 1978 p.135.

24 from High-TechHigh-Tech, "Diving board cocoa matting covers floor and bed platform of Renny Reynolds bedroom." *High-tech : the industrial style and source book for the home* by Joan Kron and Suzanne Slesin; foreword by Emilio Ambasz New York: C.N. Potter New York 1978 p.137.

25 "Breckenwood by Milliken show a sculptured shag (also called a cut and loop)." Ellis, Robert, *The Complete Book of Floor Coverings* (New York NY: Charles Scribner's Sons, 1980) p.32.

26 Wall to wall carpet – the new domestic landscape. Ellis, Robert, *The Complete Book of Floor Coverings* (New York NY: Charles Scribner's Sons, 1980) p.29.

27 A "painted" carpet Ellis, Robert, *The Complete Book of Floor Coverings* (New York NY: Charles Scribner's Sons, 1980) p. 32.

28 "Here real imagination creates a dramatic effect by combining 2 carpet styles in the same room." Ellis, Robert, *The Complete Book of Floor Coverings* (New York NY: Charles Scribner's Sons, 1980) p.35.

29 "Tampa International Airport seating areas have shag-carpeted islands in bright warm colors." Shoshkes, Lila, *Contract Carpeting* (New York NY: Whitney Library of Design, 1974) p.119.

30 "After the dyeing process and before the drying oven, the carpet is rinsed to remove chemical residue and ensure uniform wetness so that it will dry evenly. In the drying ovens, temperatures are monitored to maintain uniformity of drying that ensures constant color levels throughout the roll. The carpet is now ready for backing with either jute or foam cushion." Shoshkes, Lila, *Contract Carpeting* (New York NY: Whitney Library of Design, 1974) p.44.

31 "Before the carpeting enters the finishing ovens, it is steamed and beaten to erect the pile for shearing. Huge rollers laminate the backing." Shoshkes, Lila, *Contract Carpeting* (New York NY: Whitney Library of Design, 1974) p.45.

32 Victor Gruen, Fort Worth plan, before, A Greater Fort Worth Tomorrow, Victor Gruen & Associates, Greater Forth Worth Planning Commission, 1956.

33 Victor Gruen, Fort Worth plan, after, A Greater Fort Worth Tomorrow, Victor Gruen & Associates, Greater Forth Worth Planning Commission, 1956.

34 Interior Corridor, Berlin Free University, Candilis, Josic and Woods, Schiedhelm, Berlin, 1978, unpublished, Charles Tashima, photgrapher.

35 Competition project model, Candilis, Josic and Woods, Schiedhelm, Berlin Free University, Berlin Free University Berlin, Candilis, Josic and Woods, Schiedhelm, Architectural Association, London, 1999, p.18.

36 Arthur Erickson, Museum of Anthropology, University of British Columbia, Vancouver, British Columbia, 1972, G. Wagner photograph.

37 Enkalure II advertisement.

38 Arthur Erickson, student lounge, Simon Fraser University, Burnaby British Columbia, 1966, G. Wagner photograph.

39 Forms and Surfaces advertisement *Interiors*, July 1972, p.35.

40 Forms and Surfaces advertisement *Interiors*, August 1976, p.77.

41 Forms and Surfaces advertisement *Interiors*, August 1976, p.77.

42 Arthur Erickson, University of Lethbridge, Lethbridge, Alberta, 1968 Erickson, Arthur, *The Architecture of Arthur Erickson* (Montreal: Tundra Books, 1975) p.157.

43 Arthur Erickson, interior, University of Lethbridge, Lethbridge, Alberta, 1968 Slide Library, Department of Fine Arts, University of British Columbia, or: *The Architecture of Arthur Erickson*, Douglas & McIntyre, Vancouver, 1988, p.67.

44 Arthur Erickson, University of Lethbridge, Lethbridge, Alberta, 1968 Erickson, Arthur, *The Architecture of Arthur Erickson* (Montreal: Tundra Books, 1975) p.157.

45 Paul Rudolph, Christian Science Student Center, University of Illinois, 1962–66 *The Architecture of Paul Rudolph*. Introd. by Sibyl Moholy-Nagy. Captions by Gerhard Schwab. With comments by Paul Rudolph. New York, Praeger, 1970, p.141.

46 Paul Rudolph, students' lounge, Southern Massachusetts University, 1966, *The Architecture of Paul Rudolph*. Introd. by Sibyl Moholy-Nagy. Captions by Gerhard Schwab. With comments by Paul Rudolph. New York, Praeger, 1970, p.163.

47 Skidmore, Owings and Merrill Louis Jefferson Long Library, Wells College, seat and tables on the top floor. Drexler, Arthur and Menges Axel, *Architecture of Skidmore Owings & Merrill, 1963–1973* (New York NY: Architectural Book Publishing Co., 1974) p.209.

48 Skidmore, Owings and Merrill Louis Jefferson Long Library, Wells College, lounge on the first floor. Drexler, Arthur and Menges Axel, *Architecture of Skidmore Owings & Merrill, 1963–1973* (New York NY: Architectural Book Publishing Co., 1974) p.215.

NOTES

1 Eero Saarinen, *Eero Saarinen On His Work* (New Haven: Yale University Press, 1968) p.66. "The undercarriage of chairs and tables in a typical interior makes an ugly, confusing, unrestful world."

2 Gottfried Semper, "The Four Elements of Architecture," *The Four Elements of Architecture and Other Writings*, trans. Harry Francis Mulgrave (Cambridge: Cambridge University Press, 1989), p.104. See also "The Textile Art" p.215–263.

3 Adolf Loos, "The Principle of Cladding," in *Spoken into the Void* (Cambridge: MIT Press, 1982), p.66.

4 Ibid.

5 Billy Baldwin, *Billy Baldwin Remembers* (New York: Harcourt Brace, 1974), p.136.

6 Ibid., p.225.

7 Billy Baldwin, *Billy Baldwin Decorates* (New York: Chartwell Books, 1972), p.200.

8 Clement Greenberg, "After Abstract Expressionism," *Art in Theory 1900–1990*, ed. C. Harrison and P. Wood (Oxford: Blackwell Press), p.768.

9 Ibid., p.768

10 Donald Judd wrote about this spatiality in his essay "Specific Objects" of 1965: "The main thing wrong with painting is that it is a rectangular plane placed flat against the wall. Almost all paintings are spatial in one way or another. Anything on a surface has space behind it. Two colors on the same surface almost always lie on different depths. An even color, especially in oil paint, covering all or much of a painting is almost always both flat and infinitely spatial. The space is shallow in all of the work in which the rectangular plane is stressed. Rothko's space is shallow and the soft rectangles are parallel to the plane, but the space is almost traditionally illusionistic. In Reinhard's painting, just back from the plane of the canvas, there is a flat plane and this seems in turn indefinitely deep. Pollock's paint is obviously on the canvas, and the space is mainly that made by any marks on a surface, so that it is not very descriptive and illusionist. Noland's concentric bands are not as specifically paint on a surface as Pollock's paint, but the banks flatten the literal space more. As flat and unillusionistic as Noland's paintings are, the bands do advance and recede. Even a single circle will warp the surface to it, will have a little space behind it.

11 Barnett Newman, "Interview with Dorothy Gees Seckler," *Art in Theory 1900–1990*, p.765.

12 Ibid., p.765.

13 Ibid., p.766.

14 Paul Rudolph, in lecture at Roger Williams College, 1984.

15 Rollo May, *Freedom and Destiny* (New York: Norton, 1981), p.175–6 "In America we have traditionally associated freedom, especially in the form of leisure, with space. . . . We expressed our freedom of the body by moving to a new space. So we remained extroverts, concerned with our muscles." See also William L. Ewens, *Becoming Free: The Struggle for Human Development* (Wilmington: Scholarly Resources, 1984).

16 Eero Saarinen noted this: "There is the fact that people sit differently today than in the Victorian era. They sit lower and they like to slouch. In my first post-war chair, I attempted to shape the slouch in an organized way by giving support for the back as well as the seat, shoulders and head. The "womb" chair also has three planes of support." In *Eero Saarinen On His Work*, p.66.

17 Ibid., p.11.

18 Jeffrey T. Schnapp, "The Fabric of Modern Times," *Critical Inquiry*, Autumn 1997, p.194.

19 Ibid., p.192.

20 Kennedy Fraser, "Denim and the New Conservatives," *The Fashionable Mind*, (New York: Knopf), p.93.

21 Ibid., p.94.

22 Ibid.

23 Ibid., p.91.

24 *Vogue*, June 1980, p.238.

25 Halston's embrace of the maxim less is more, attributed to Mies van der Rohe's, in the early 1970s, and the widespread description of him as a minimalist, forces the question of what sort of influence the visual arts had on each other in this era. The first and seminal, anthology on minimal art was published by Gregory Battcock in 1968. A review of the Avery Index to Architectural Periodicals finds no references to minimalism in architecture in the sixties or seventies and demonstrates that the discourse on this subject was generated in the 1990s in the face of boutique architecture and figures like John Pawson.

26 www.ultrasuede.com.

27 This ability and great willingness to fit his work into the emerging corporate world that distinguished Halston's success and precipitated his professional downfall. His company entered into numerous licensing agreements for a variety of products at different price points. He sold his company to the conglomerate Norton Simon Inc. in 1973. Norton Simon welcomed and appreciated the prestige of Halston Enterprises, but in a series of leveraged buyouts, takeovers, and mergers – fully prescient of the rapacious 90's – Norton Simon was acquired by Esmark, which in 1984 became a division of Beatrice Foods. In the end, Halston lost his company and the right to use his name. After becoming one of the most successful figures in his business, he was unable to work under his own name.

28 For a discussion of the idea of the platform in architecture see the essay by Jørn Utzon, "Platforms and Plateaus: Ideas of A Danish Architect," *Zodiac*, 1962, v. 10, p.112–140.

29 Peter Carlsen, "A Minimalist's Paradigm," *Interiors*, October 1975, p.123.

30 For more on carpeting see Robert W. Kirk, *The Carpet Industry: Present Status and Future Prospects* (Philadelphia: University of Pennsylvania Press, 1970); *George Robinson, Carpets and Other Textile Floorcoverings* (Textile Book Service, 1972); and *William A. Reynolds, Innovation in the United States Carpet Industry 1947–1963* (Van Nostrand, 1968).

31 See George Wagner, "Looking Back Towards the Free University, Berlin," *Berlin Free University*, (London: Architectural Association, 1999), p.14–23.

32 Michael Fried, "Art and Objecthood" in *Minimal Art*, Battcock, ed. (New York: E. P. Dutton, 1968), p.127. The idea of situation is informed by Michael Fried's "Art and Objecthood," and is here used to describe the building's position in the landscape. It might also be a key to other work that attempts to express, some of that unwritten relationship between minimal art and architecture in the years the former was being produced.

33 Erickson also used seating platforms at Simon Fraser University and the Museum of Anthropology at the University of British Columbia, as did Skidmore Owings and Merrill at Louis Jefferson Long Library at Wells College. If Eliel Saarinen was the Michelangelo of the carpet, the Michelangelo of wall-to-wall had to be Verner Panton. See *Verner Panton: The Collected Works* (Vitra Design Museum, 2001).

34 Donald Judd, "Specific Objects," *Art in Theory 1900–1990*, p.813.

This paper was supported by The Graham Foundation and the MacDowell Colony. Anne Wagner and Jennifer Dee offered insight and helpful criticism. Dallas Hong and Sandra Eng were invaluable Research Assistants.

MICHAEL STANTON

The Good, the Bad and the Ugly: Urbanism and Intention

*Moreover, since architecture enters directly into everyday life
(for example, through its extra-artistic functionality), it creates
a permanent bond that provides a firm critical base from which
to pass judgment upon many 'good intentions.'*
GIORGIO GRASSI [1]

SIENA

Two cities face each other across an Italian room. One radiates tidiness, order, and abundance. The other is disheveled and chaotic. One basks in the strong light of the room's north wall. The other is always in shadow. In 1338–40 Ambrogio Lorenzetti painted the frescoes of *The Allegory of the Effects of Good and Bad Government in the City and Country* in the Sala dei Nove in the Palazzo Pubblico in Siena. Despite the title, the image is primarily urban. The countryside falls away into the distance from the foreground of the city. This is predictable. From ancient times, the city stood for culture, was an intricate metonym for something even more intricate. The metanymic relation twists back on itself as the citizen and collective reflexively represent and are represented by the urban.

In Lorenzetti's work, the city, more or less Siena itself, is narrative. Given that it is painted, it is visually opaque. We cannot see around its corners or penetrate its bedrooms. It is socially transparent, however, for we do see its political message. Hovering above it are virtues and sins. One can presume that Siena had the potential of both cities, that she was divided by the painter for didactic purposes: certainly to oppose republic to despotism, but also to oppose to all that civic virtue a nearly equal dose of civic vice. The bad city tantalizes. As Giotto had demonstrated at the Scrovegni Chapel in Padova, thirty years before the Siena frescoes: presenting the contrast between vices and virtues is a provocation. Who really studies the pious images of righteous action on the right wall in Padova when the left offers such sublime and perverse acts? The postcards in the museum store only show the deadly sins. In Siena, urban form represents value as much as those who are depicted as being in it or the myriad spirits that preside over it. In the good city, citizens mingle, teachers instruct attentive students, and a hanged malcontent dangles discreetly from the scaffold held by Securitas. The buildings are painted gay colors. Workers construct a new edifice from a platform cantilevered from its facade.

The holes of the next layer down are still evident. All is equally sensible and detailed. The Tuscan hill upon which the painted city rests rises to the striped cathedral. The landscape stretches rich and calm to the horizon. Peasants bring in the riches of the land, and the nobility go into the country to hunt, but only where the fields have already been harvested. In the bad city, the same buildings are crumbling and stones fall into the street. An androgynous Timor (fear) replaces the feminine Securitas over the city gate. The land is ravaged and smoking. The city is crime-ridden and in fear of the oppression that lies across from the republican harmony on the other wall. To the right in the painting sits Tyranny himself, a snaggle-toothed devil attended by fearsome and mutant lackeys. At their feet is a bound and weeping Justice.

In the fourteenth century, when good and bad could in fact be spoken of without qualification, when a city was furthermore seen as having a direct equivalence to these terms, and these terms as having absolute value, then comparison could

seem precise. Now when such oppositions have faded to gray we may find that the city painted by modern politics and Post-Modern imagery cannot so clearly sit across from its other, that the space of the Sala dei Nove has been crossed, and the blurring and disruptions of these two urbanisms have become the field of discourse. But it should also be remembered that both painted cities were Siena, that one had become two for descriptive purposes. The apparent dialectic presented was just that, insisting finally on a synthesis that was the actual complex Tuscan place.

Today two real cities sit across from each other, across the divide that separates the Near East from Europe, that separates the Social Darwinism of the former Third World from the Social Contract of the former First. These two cities sit as well across that topographic divide that separates the cultures of the Mediterranean from those that edge the northern seas that touch Europe. One city is dark and wet in a flat, constructed landscape. Dry and too bright, the other city dangles precariously from the mountains into the sea and scrambles resolutely up those mountains in its attempt to consolidate a nation into one metropolis. One appears to be the product of state control and incessant planning. The other seems to be the almost automatic product of capitalism in full rut. Both were radically damaged by war. One began repair a half a century ago, a renewal that continues but that is now a history itself. Largely unreconstructed, the other has remained for ten years like a patient open on the operating table waiting for the biopsy news that never arrives. Rotterdam and Beirut are indeed a study in difference on the surface almost as precise and antithetical as Lorenzetti's two Sienas.

So why bother to compare two cities reconstructed almost a half-century apart and whose political/economic realities appear opposite? Even the wars and damage were different. Rotterdam was devastated in one night by another nation. Beirut eroded over fifteen years of civil war aug-

mented by intervention from across Lebanon's borders. Furthermore, comparison itself, and especially that which relies on the dialectic, is suspect now: definitely out-of-intellectual-fashion. Nonetheless it is interesting, in this case, to exercise such an antiquated practice because of the fluttering reciprocities that emerge when the two opposed cities are viewed with a slightly finer focus. As with Lorenzetti's frescoes, the various Sienas merge with the viewer into one blurred vision that approximates the intricacy and difference that actual cities project and that neither good nor bad can singly describe.

Rotterdam and Beirut are the primary links to the sea for two little nations: new nations in the modern sense but of ancient and shrewd traders. They exist under the feet of larger but clumsier societies.[2] Each city is now part of an urban sprawl much larger than its original self. A nearly unbroken linear fabric connects Amsterdam to Rotterdam through Haarlem, Leiden, den Haag, Delft, and other smaller cities. Beirut now extends more than thirty miles along the precipitous coast, uniting a string of municipalities — from Damour in the south to Jbeil (the ancient Byblos) in the north. Erasure is a leitmotif in both places. As exhausted a theme as it may be, none other suffices. The center of Rotterdam was destroyed in 1940, and the void produced has been a laboratory for urban experiment presided over by a host of well-intentioned social planners and form makers. The amount of brilliance bought to bear — from Bakema to Koolhaas — is overwhelming, but the product is problematic. Civil war chewed on Beirut. Small arms fire melted the buildings. Shells punched great holes in them. Sophisticated Israeli bombing caused them to collapse in concrete cascades. And many remain so damaged ten years after the cessation of hostility. But mostly the destruction in Beirut, at the scale of the void left by one night of blitzkrieg in Rotterdam, came from the real-estate activities that immediately followed the end of fighting. As in London in the 1940s and

1950s, war was an excuse for much more radical demolition. In Beirut, the property of a quarter-million owners was commandeered and replaced with devaluing shares in Solidere, a corporation run by the nation's new Prime Minister.[3] This deal is nothing in its scale next to the demolition campaign that ensued before and after Rafil Hariri's ascension to the nation's most powerful political post. The city center was gutted. Remnants of historical building were eradicated, with the exception of the diverse religious institutions that could not be touched,[4] in an area that had defined the limits of the small city before the remarkable expansion of the twentieth century.

Beirut in the 1990s was Rotterdam in the 1940s: a tabula rasa produced by bombs and ambition. Despite the generational difference, the similar situation of erasure and reconstruction has, and is, defining these two places in an exceptional manner. Surely Berlin or other German cities — Dresden, Köln — were equally mangled by war, or farther afield Stalin(Volga)grad or Hiroshima, or Sarajevo more recently. But there is a difference. In Beirut and Rotterdam, in very different political/economic environments, the decision has not been to rebuild or fill in, but to transform. The devastation has forced the hand of civic agencies and private interests. The wheels can be seen turning, and the connection of their rotation to the proposals and built projects that refill the vast voids made by war and desire is evident. More than most war-damaged places, these two cities have used war to remake themselves and the motivations and methods are obvious — and the problems that continue to plague all intentions make themselves plain.

THE GOOD

The almost total eradication of the center of Rotterdam in 1940 was seen as an opportunity to effect Modernism of the sort the country had patented in the period after 1910. It hardly needs to be said that the Netherlands has a special place

in the history of the Modern. This small state has had an inordinately large role in development and innovation in Western art, reaching a peak during the last century. Enthusiasm has yet to wane and is largely free of the doubt and compromise that have crawled like a mold through the body of Modernist belief in other quarters, leaving a vulnerable and appropriated field where more persuasive formats for cultural development and resistance, have yet to emerge. The Netherlands still debates the value of Modernist formats while recognizing their essential fallibility. Who more than Rem Koolhaas both embraces and debunks them simultaneously — and by so doing functions as a consummate post-structuralist? While so much has been lost in the currently troubled discourse and commodified practice elsewhere, Holland hangs on to the critical transformation of a culture established nearly one hundred years ago. For example, it is still often accepted there that architecture can make a better society. Forms are seen as specific political devices. Thus there is a datum, a degree zero of cultural engagement, in the work of Koolhaas, and of Arets, van Berkel, Claus, and Kaan et. al., that allows their work to respond metamorphically, rather than desperately, to the dictates of contemporary culture. It is a case of continuous redefinition, a much more credible critical position in fact than that of reinvention, given that the latter inevitably falls prey to the historical mistakes that it ignores in its quest for novelty.

In the period of recovery after World War II, Rotterdam was a laboratory for continuing formal and spatial experimentation, as well as revamped infrastructure and reworked city pattern. Inevitably, a simultaneous reassessment of social systems and class configurations accompanied the tacit assumption that architecture and urbanism could have a vital role in reforming these phenomena. Radical redevelopment was already being planned in 1941 to become the Inner City Reconstruction Scheme in 1946, a year after the German occupation ended. The commitment appears to have lacked doubt. "The authorities did not flinch from demolishing any remaining buildings which stood in the way of new development."[5] Certain cardinal structures were set in the fabric, among them several large projects by Oud and Dudok,[6] Modernist icons themselves. But most significantly, around these new monuments and the restored City Hall and Post Office, the Lijnbaan network of pedestrian shopping streets and residential slabs was begun in 1951. To make slabs, individual lots have to be consolidated, even eradicated. The tra-

ditional economic structure implied by the marketing of urban parcels is challenged. Almost all slab construction is a sign of government intervention. Thus, in Beirut for instance, blocky buildings are the standard of private construction, maximum extrusions of individual real estate allotments. Rotterdam's slabs by Maaskant rise, not on top of but next to or behind, low shops by Van der Broek and Bakema. Each group of housing blocks forms a green square just off the busy shopping promenade, a revolutionary concept fifty years. The insertion of green spaces and housing in the downtown was also seen as innovative, and given that this is the Netherlands, social mixing in the housing was encouraged. It all sounds ideal, a brochure for happy modern life.

In fact the shopping district, while remaining successful as a pedestrian mall fifty years later, is quite ugly. But, in the last century, the sublime has clearly defeated the beautiful in the art world and, to a lesser extent, in design. This is nowhere more evident than in the latest architecture in Holland, where the ugly has become of serious value: for example in the work of Neutelings-Riedijk or MVRDV. There is a valuable quotidian character to the shopping streets of Bakema and Van der Broek. They withstand, even support, tawdry excesses of advertising, neon, and vulgar promotion. The Lijnbaan is coarse and very popular, in both the European and American senses.[7] It has that sordidness that also makes Berlin, Copenhagen, Barcelona, even Paris and Rome, something other than precious. And the housing remains extremely effective. So what is wrong here or is this the perfect world promised by our Modernist ancestors? First, the ensemble relies on extensive governmental maintenance of the generous public spaces to keep the fine line drawn between domestic and commercial. Public space becomes universal. Another problem is subsequent development after this initial, delicate insertion. Mountains of commercial space hover over the downtown now with the grace, scale, and density of Denver or Houston. Throughout the fabric, weird experiments in various phases of Post-Modernism are scattered like shabby harlequins. Behind these physical problems sit methodological ones: the formula of developer/government collaboration; the competition system and lists compiled by the authorities of eligible architects for given jobs; the abrupt shifts in urban strategy brought on by the excesses of febrile genius that address the poor city, half-dead from all the attention; the failure to integrate all this intention and the actual mess.

Paradox confounds the clarity of urban discourse. Rotterdam embodies the contradiction inherent in the varied and often opposed attempts to counter the tendencies of capitalism as they present themselves physically. Its urbanism forms a layer of reaction complicit with that it is reacting against. Social mixing, very nineteenth century in its character, is related to an egalitarian politics that relies on retail activity and commercial development for its energy while on some basic level rejecting those as primary social motivations. After all, developers finally implement all this benevolence. They work closely with the authorities, accept the lists of approved architects, etc. – but their motive is profit. The very point of its leftist good intentions turns back on itself as the downtown becomes a shopping and entertainment emporium. This basic contradiction, that socialism appears to encourage materialism, may account for the vitality of a city that is neither beautiful, ancient nor trendy, in the way that Amsterdam is. There is a reciprocity between use and form that makes absolute value impossible when discussing cities. Rotterdam's vitality stems finally from the exuberance of its market culture, confounding, and enriching the good intentions of its concept.

THE BAD

Now turn to the south wall. The buildings remain pockmarked or collapsed from the shooting and bombing. The spectacular landscape beyond Beirut is ravaged more by indiscriminate speculation since the beginning of hostilities in 1975 than by war. The infrastructure is in a state of delicate crisis. Traffic snarls the streets. Wires dangle promiscuously in ad hoc wartime arrangements. It is not as if Lebanon has not initiated urban programs or attempted to define the maniacal growth of its capital since 1990. As in that other clever little nation Holland, talent is abundant in Lebanon. The discourse on the city is continuous, and ambitious proposals appear regularly, and fade, to be replaced by others: the fate of Planning everywhere. In Beirut there is a powerful history of such initiatives and a legacy of really superior Modern architecture from the era of independence: 1943 to 1975. Especially during the Shihabist[8] period, the nation brought to bear a Dutch degree of genius in an attempt to order the physical progress of culture. Strategizing was constant. Activity included the involvement of Michel Ecochard and Henri Eddeh, and even the participation of Constantinos Doxiades and the application of ekistics to the chaotic urban growth underway in the young and enthusiastic nation. The country too is exotic. That manicured foil of town does not pertain in a place where there is astounding landscape for sure but where the nurtured, pastoral, implications of country are alien.[10] The good intentions embedded in these notions could not be implemented at the municipal level as they were in Holland. In a culture that is not civil[11] in the social-democratic sense, it is not surprising that the intense speculation on the application of the Modern as a public phenomenon – producing new infrastructure, new quarters, a new society – finally resulted in exceptionally high quality building financed largely from the private sector. After fifteen years of fighting and, more destructively, fifteen years of unregulated construction, any signs of "good intentions" in Beirut are faint. It is hard to discern the repercussions of all the pre-war planning now.

The overriding difference between these two cities is obviously chronological. Fifty years after, Rotterdam is mostly done. Development continues along the city's edges, in implants in the center or in places where program is changing radically from industrial to more domestic or commercial functions, like the former docks of Kop Van Zuid. In Beirut, despite the extensive amount of repair, demolition, and new construction throughout the extended city, reconstruction often seems not to have begun. The city has expanded exponentially since 1975 thanks to the influx of refugees from other zones of hostility and also to the natural demographic shifts brought on by the urbanization of a country so small that the entire nation can be seen as the region, if not the metropolitan area, of its capital. The war destroyed means of production and tribal loyalties that kept people rooted in villages and smaller cities, many of which are now consumed in Beirut's sprawl. As mentioned, more construction occurred than destruction, but this was often on the periphery or beyond, while the existing city suffered from the innumerable battles that erupted between every military and para-military entity. Most of what had been Beirut before the war is the site of maximum devastation and, of course, maximum economic potential. And in the center of this large, fractured yet vital, urban organism is the most radical condition, the

Above
Destroyed buildings in central Beirut. Photographs by Michael Stanton.

Opposite
The Allegory of Bad Government. Ambrogio Lorenzetti, 1338–46. Sala Dei Nove, Palazzo Publico, Siena. © La Scala/Art Resource.

absent downtown. As the Russian Ossip Zadkine called his 1946 sculpture executed for Rotterdam, Beirut is a "city without a heart." Only the most extreme Stalinist urban programs – where state ownership allowed total erasure – produced comparable voids at the center of cities. But in Beirut extravagant speculation – developer and government one and the same – are responsible, an arrangement without precedent in the rest of the capitalist world. As happens with extremes, polar political/economic strategies come full circle to produce similar formal results.

Too much has already been written about this extraordinary void. As Saul Bellow said of Henry James, we may have "chewed more than we bit off." Its particular interest is how private interests and what passes for government interact to produce the urban. It would be comforting to find Rotterdam to be an example of "good" relations – egalitarian, fair, socially responsible – between capital and the collective as represented by the social-democratic regime, and likewise to find Beirut as its opposite, a study in self-interest, exploitation, tyranny, weak government in complicity with wealth. But such easy readings do not hold beyond a superficial view of the places or a superficial understanding of the societies that these two cities represent. In Beirut, somehow, despite the apparent enigma of such a close complicity of development and the state, despite a profound Social-Darwinism determining most decisions, despite the shadow of Syria that falls over all events, things do get done. Infrastructure is repaired or replaced and plans for renewing the city spew out with an almost Dutch regularity. True, much of this revitalization has come from the same source. In a paradigm of power relations in socialist and high-capitalist cultures, all the anonymous public officials and private developers who collaborate to produce Rotterdam are congealed into one astoundingly rich and powerful figure in Beirut, but the effect is not so different.

Assuredly Rotterdam is in a lot better shape than Beirut. And this is not just because the Dutch have had a half-century to repair the damage. All the Dutch "good intentions" did produce results, many of them beneficial. But the gestures of Mr. Hariri have likewise reformed the city, not just by eviscerating it but also in the provision of new roads, monumental new facilities, and myriad less evident public structures. In both cases nonetheless, the basic disorder of the place overpowers any organization. As Milizia wrote two centuries ago: "He who does not know how to vary our pleasure will never give us pleasure. [The city] should

in fact be a varied picture of infinite unexpected episodes … a great order in the details, confusion, uproar and tumult in the whole … Order must reign, but in a kind of confusion … and from a multitude of regular parts the whole must give a certain idea of irregularity and chaos, which is so fitting to great cities."[12] This statement emanates, as Tafuri points out, from the Enlightenment and particularly from Laugier. It stands against the attempts at control and order that characterized the following 150 years of urban initiatives.[13] Viewing the city as a pleasure device, understanding its basic "tumult" and infinite, precise details (as opposed to the inverse strategy of post-Enlightenment urbanism) did not in urban thinking until Post-Modernity and the emergence of "the analogous city," "the culture of congestion," and their kin.

The disarray is very different than the nearby cities of Amsterdam on one hand or Damascus on the other: both ancient and picturesque, one suffering from an effervescent superfluity of open-mindedness, the other from a overbearing ballast of control. Rotterdam is a riot of conflicting ideologies embedded in disparate city fabric: from the global/corporate grandeur of the Weena corridor, to the comic hipness of Adriaan Geuze's reformation of the Schouwburgplein, to the consumerism of the Bursplein integrating Marcel Breuer and Bakema, to the new hyper-scale of the massive structures at the Kop Van Zuid. Beirut is a turmoil of diverse urban material produced by pure speculation, a powerful form of ideology itself. The development of the Verdun corridor in West Beirut, of the Dunes and Concorde complexes in particular, rival, at least in their exuberance, the shopping zones of Rotterdam. But more vital even are the traffic circulation cores and attendant ad hoc working-class retail commotion of Cola Square or Dora in Borj Hammoud or the social mixing of Hamra, none of which was particularly planned and where shopping is only an aspect at best. The downtown hosts temporary events like a monster-truck rally next to the most active of functioning mosques, reaching a peak during Ramadan of revving motors and electronically enhanced calls-to-prayer battling for audio-space.

The two cities are produced by a similar friction between capital and authority even if "intentions" are quite different. The apparent self-interest of Hariri and his kind and the apparent interest-in-the-common-good of the Dutch planners have produced a similar pitch of urban pandemonium. On the other hand, the teeming pedestrian streets of central Rotterdam have to be

compared to the nearly empty streets of the meticulously renovated center of Beirut. In this homogenous wonderland far from the vital Third-World scruffiness of the rest of the metropolis, people are eerily absent during the day and move like tourists at night. Class can partially explain the problem since the place is clearly meant for haute-bourgeois use and they prefer to drive. The New Urbanist rhetoric of pedestrianism and streetscape falls on deaf ears, as it seems to in most places. And rents are prohibitive. The city of the flâneur is still vital in places like Rotterdam or, for that matter, Milan or Barcelona and not so in Beirut despite the global illusion that Mediterranean culture lingers in a twilight of social mixing: of piazzas and their kin. The different politics of the places has direct effect on the physical fabric. But there also may be a very simple, almost aesthetic, explanation as well. The Lijnbaan is common in its mercantilism and not refined in its architecture. It reflects the teeming commercial centers of cities that have not been reconstructed wholesale. Beirut's downtown is, due to single ownership and a supremely bourgeois notion of urban quality, evolving to be uniformly precious, over-restored – like a rhinestone encrusted, beige poodle clipped too perfectly: no vulgar signage, no street vendors. The flâneur is not welcome, let alone the underclass.

THE UGLY

Beirut's subtext of monopoly and state control dilutes the city's apparent free-market anarchy, providing a crucial counterpoint to the inevitable urban entropy that is the endgame of speculation. Nevertheless, the frenetic expansion of the metropolis in the form of new residential and mercantile fabric essentially without civic space or adequate infrastructure certainly maximizes revenue but obviously will arrive at intolerable conditions. The relief promised, the open space and facilities projected for the new city center, may be as illusory as have been other proposed amenities, but they also tend to emerge in random and spontaneous locations. The undeveloped landfill of the huge Joseph Khoury development in Dbaiye, a few miles north of the city-center, is filled on weekends with activity. The streets are edged with parked cars. The corniche is humming. People stroll window-shopping. Yet there are no buildings. This ten-million-square-foot landfill stretches more than a mile along the coast. Begun by Ricardo Bofill with the local office of Pierre Khoury, this project was completed by the even more bland Dar al Handasah as a grid of streets and lots with a Bofill marina at its center. Streets, even trees and lights, frame deep holes

awaiting construction. The yachts and Mercedes of the anticipated upper-middle-class population that will fill this new city are yet to arrive. The empty excavated lots are sites for football practice or bicycle-riding. The infrastructure is heavily used by the nearby population of overcrowded residents packed into existence-minimum tower blocks. Presumably, once the new buildings are constructed and occupied, these people will be discouraged from visiting.

To some extent both cities are victims of their respective eras, are indicative of shifting global urban enthusiasms coincident with their reconstruction. Rotterdam's grimmest moments come from the heavy-handed utopianism of a Late-Modernism that was guiding the development process after World War II. It should also be said that the city's finest fabric (the housing squares and pedestrian streets) also came from these intentions, but often evolved despite them in unexpected and hybrid configurations far more successful than the stern planners could have imagined. Beirut was similarly affected at the same time, but without the realization possible in a social-democracy, and now has to attempt to rebuild in the pastel shadow of Post-Modernism and of

the ersatz nostalgia of "contextualist" approaches that accompanied Post-Modern revivals of historicist pastiche and invented reference. "New Urbanist" rhetoric guides reconstruction. In fact, if the development of pre-war Beirut responded to many of the same planning enthusiasms as that of post-war Rotterdam, then post-war Beirut is not so much different in its desires and contradictions as is post-unification Berlin and many other cities world-wide.

Unlike much urbanization in the Middle East, [the Beirut Central District] has so far managed to avoid the 'rush to modernize and impress,' and is recognized as perhaps the most important undertaking in urban regeneration in the world today.
Angus Gavin[14]

Solidere is trying in the decade after the end of the Cold War[15] to retroactively install a nineteenth-century urbanism that probably never existed and is certainly anachronistic in the twenty-first. Allusions to "tradition" pepper their writings as they erase almost all structures more than one hundred years old. In his descriptions of the new codes for building in the center, Angus Gavin's referents are Haussmann or Regency England. "Town-

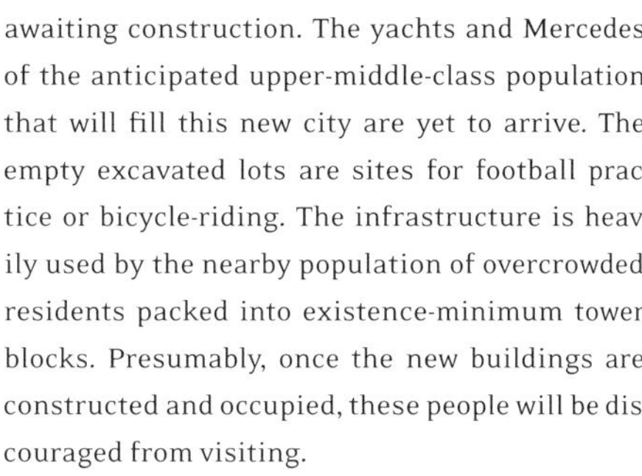

Above, middle, below
Soldiere redevelopment in central Beirut. Photograph by Michael Stanton.

Redevelopment in central Beirut. Photograph by Michael Stanton.

The world's largest construction site: A demolished section of central Beirut. Photograph by Michael Stanton.

scape" is again invoked. Even more incongruous than its use in pre-war Lebanese planning initiatives, this exotic term is now used in reference to the development of the downtown of a city of more than two million. Gavin's Picturesque admiration of "views" and "a more Anglo-Saxon search for context and cultural continuity that seemed more appropriate" calls forth a Pastoral that fits the attitude of the entire project. Even "the Orientalist painters of the last century" offer inspiration. Seen in this Raj-tinted light, the restoration of mostly French colonial architecture with a dash of the Ottoman is not accidental. "Tradition" here is nothing less than the Romantic invention of history itself to suit current politics. Any such call can only be assumed to be for speculative purposes. As always, real estate is well served by the production of identity. The erasure of history through the annihilation of the urban fabric in

which it is embedded offers a chance to rewrite that history: amnesia as urban strategy. In psychotherapy shock-treatment obliterates traumatic memory, allowing the recreation of personality in a more docile mode. Its urban counterpart subdues cultural flux, permitting a redefinition of cultural values.

Regionalism and nationalism are different cuts of the same ideological suit of which identity is also a variation. The Dutch appear to have little concern for their sense of themselves. It is there for sure, open to new vectors: immigrant contributions and globalized imagery for instance. There are windmills and wooden shoes, but they mostly appear as props in Jackie Chan movies or on tourist brochures. It is just as likely that the new architecture of Rotterdam will be featured even in these popular venues. Post-unification German planners, on the other hand, while not attaching

Gothic details or half-timber to their skyscrapers as is happening in Lebanon with "Arab" or "French" touches, are adopting antiquated urban formats in a parallel attempt to produce a sense of history for a culture with a problematic recent past. The planners of modern Berlin or Beirut are generating an ersatz production of what is essentially a global romanticization of a nineteenth century city probably only historically realized in the images of Caillebotte or the musings of de Maupassant: a city of arcades and boulevardian culture. This is now the universal image of identity, passing for cultural congruity, itself a difficult concept and one that may have no exact architectural or urban equivalent. In the cases mentioned above, a New Urbanist generic is intent on exploiting a market that is almost exclusively bourgeois. New Urbanism, another closed meta-narrative like the Modernism it sets up as a foil, attempts to manifest the same utopian intentions, if for antithetical purposes: a move politically from left to right. The basic and flawed notion that good urban/architectural language makes good community persists. In wealthy countries of the European Union these policies are merely elitist. In Beirut, in a realm of pure business, that is racked with poverty, they constitute discrimination.

There is a third wall in the Sala dei Nove. On it is represented the good commune – a parallel scene to the devil and his minions on the adjacent south wall. A patriarchal figure embodies republicanism. Faith, Hope, and Charity float over his head. He sits surrounded by lounging virtues, one of whom ominously holds a severed head in her lap. This painting officiates between the good and bad cities to its sides and recalls that other modern republic that clutches, even in its corrupt present, to its image of ideal virtue. Reciprocal influence now flows back across the Atlantic, carried by media and economy. The American city is a player in this story, setting up a resonance between the other two. This influence on modern urban development is not a new story. The title of this essay[16] acknowledges both the "spaghetti Western" nature of American urbanism and its role as global spoiler.

In Rotterdam and Beirut, the dissimilarities of the political motivations that underwrite the urbanism of good, and bad, intentions become less distinct when form is realized. Their development is highly dependent on the model of the American city, both obviously in the look of the places, the skyscrapers and traffic arteries either built or projected, but also in the very notion, endemic to American development, that a plan (either graphic or administrative) can generate the urban and, by extension, culture itself. In the United States that figure is obviously the grid, but the concept that the physical fabric of society will rise like corn from this contrived landscape, controlling and liberating, has now saturated, if not produced, Urban Planning itself and the way we make, or remake, cities. As in Lorenzetti's frescoes, power sits, contained in and containing at the same time, all that apparent chaos and heterogeneity that is the city. It is this fact that allows Rotterdam and Beirut to be different and the same simultaneously. This incongruity embodies the exciting fact of the modern, as Karl Marx said "pregnant with its contrary."[17]

NOTES

1 Giorgio Grassi, "Avant-Garde and Continuity," *Oppositions* 21 (Summer 1980), p.398.

2 Germany in one case and Syria in the other, in regions of more powerful entities, the uncomfortable camaraderie of the EU giants and the stentorian discord of a sectarian Middle East.

3 As I wrote elsewhere: "It was as if the United States government gave Manhattan to Donald Trump, he leveled it but for a few monuments and then was made President, thus making easier the implementation of development strategies and giving new meaning to conflict-of-interest. More than a thousand buildings disappeared. The war continues in the building process, both in the demolition of the heterogeneous downtown and in the ideological assault that is its rebuilding." Rewritten after publication of "On Realism and the Observer" in *ARCHIS* 9 (September 2000).

4 Religious structures and property are legally protected by *waqf* arrangements, but more importantly by the enduring power of religion as the first political fact, masking economy and class. In this nation with Druze, Sunni and Shiite Muslim, Greek and Armenian Orthodox, Maronite, Greek and Roman Catholic (to name just the major religions that form modern politics in this place where there is no separation of church and state), there are many such properties including, in the downtown, a synagogue and a Protestant church, forming "identity" fragments in the void of demolition.

5 Paul Groenendijk and Piet Vollaard, *Guide to Modern Architecture in Rotterdam* (Rotterdam: 010, 1996), p.8.

6 The Kantoorgebouw by Oud and the De Nederlanden by Dudok begun under the Germans.

7 Both "of the people/proletariat" (popolare, populaire) and "liked by people."

8 Fuad Shihab was president from 1958 to 1964, with vestiges of his influence surviving until 1970. His tenure marked the high point of government initiatives for social reform and planning.

9 The Directorate-General for Town Planning along with the Higher Council for Town and Country Design were prolific. Neither town nor country, in the Anglo-American sense, exist semantically in the Mediterranean. Although Arabic does have a word, *baldèh*, that may be interpreted as town, the term, implying not just scale but lawns and balloons, is something alien.

10 Equally foreign was all the fine modern architecture that was realized during the period before the civil war. The imposition of external formats is not necessarily an urban sin.

11 I owe this concept to Robert Saliba who, in conversation, described Lebanese culture as "not civil." By that he meant having no sense of the public, of the dependency of culture on the collective and the manifestation of this relation in both public space and social programs.

12 Francesco Milizia, *Principi di architettura civile* (Bassano 1813), vol. II, p.26–28 as quoted in Manfredo Tafuri, *Architecture and Utopia* (Cambridge: MIT, 1976), p.20–21.

13 From the American gridiron, to the allées of Haussmann, to the Siedlungs of Modernism, to colonial impositions like the French restructuring of Beirut, to the origins of "City Planning;" the post-Enlightenment engaged in an exercise that can be compared to what Foucault characterized as "repression."

14 Angus Gavin, from "Heart of Beirut: Making the Master Plan for the Renewal of the Central District," *Projecting Beirut*, Rowe and Sarkis eds. (Munich, London, New York: Prestel, 1998), p.217. Gavin is described therein as "urban planning advisor to the chairman of Solidere."

15 It is not a coincidence that the Cold War and the Lebanese Civil War ended simultaneously.

16 *The Good, the Bad and the Ugly*, Dir. Sergio Leone, 1966. In that film title "ugly" carries the fluttering fascination that good and bad will never have. Eli Wallach, the film's ambiguous odd man out, forms a third to Clint Eastwood and Lee Van Cleef. It is the direction that the "ugly" Wallach will shoot in the last showdown that determines the scene's exquisite tension.

17 "In our day everything is pregnant with its contrary … All our invention and progress seem to result in endowing material forces with intellectual life, and stultifying human life into material force." Karl Marx, "Speech at the Anniversary of The People's Paper," *The Marx-Engels Reader* (Norton: New York, 1978), p.578.

Opposite
The Allegory of Good Government. Ambrogio Lorenzetti, 1338–46, Sala Dei Nove, Palazzo Publico, Siena.
© La Scala/Art Resource.

HASHIM SARKIS

Constants in Motion

Le Corbusier's "Rule of Movement" at the Carpenter Center [1]

GIEDION'S APOLOGIA

Writing in 1964 about the newly completed Carpenter Center for the Visual Arts at Harvard University, Sigfried Giedion criticized the design for the "hollow spaces around the workshop pilotis." The criticism was wrapped in the suggestion that Le Corbusier must have "somehow felt the incompleteness of the programme" as he was working on its design. Even though, according to Giedion, "the most striking innovation of the building is its programme," meaning the idea of educating non-artists in the visual arts, "Corbusier would certainly have been able to incorporate a spacious — and sadly needed — lecture hall into the massive building." [2] He also laments the inadequacy of the site for the building. Giedion had played his part in convincing Le Corbusier to accept the commission to design the Carpenter Center, and he had also experienced the building firsthand a year ear-

lier while lecturing at Harvard, but he seemed to have been slightly disappointed by the end result.

Other critics have addressed these aspects of the building even less apologetically. Two years after Giedion, historian Henry Russell Hitchcock expressed a stronger disagreement with the site selection and the awkward relationship between the building and its immediate surroundings. He complained that Le Corbusier, the urbanist, had shown too much elasticity, and his client too little, when it came to choosing an adequate site to which the building could relate.[3]

These comments about the Carpenter Center's siting and programming are significant because they accurately detect the omission of two qualities that have traditionally been considered essential to any building conceived around the promenade architecturale. Le Corbusier had intended that the Carpenter Center be a lesson

in his architecture. For that, he had mobilized the whole repertoire of pilotis, brise-soleils, ondulatoires, free plan, free forms, and, most ostensibly, the ramp.[4] His veteran advocates would have expected that such a building would effect the most elaborate and scenographic promenade. Regrettably, the building did not live up to their expectations.

However, neither in the *Oeuvre Complète* nor in *Le Corbusier at Work*, a thorough documentation of the design process of the Carpenter Center, does Le Corbusier seem to show dissatisfaction with either the site or the program. In the *Oeuvre Complète* the tightness of the site is described as a challenge. As documented in *Le Corbusier at Work*, many decisions made by the architect deliberately enhance the attitude towards the site and the emptiness of the building. Although Giedion's observations are precise, his assessment is based on previous built manifestations of the

promenade and on provocative but vague descriptions by Le Corbusier. As this essay hopes to show, because of its peculiar relationship with context and content, the Carpenter Center offers a different angle on the promenade architecturale. While it does connect views of the interior and the exterior of the building, the promenade here depends on the architectural heightening of visual constants, attributes of a space that remains fixed as the viewer moves. It also depends on transforming these constants in order to deceive the viewer. The focus will be primarily on the Carpenter Center, but the essay aims to elaborate on this new angle in the work of Le Corbusier in general by questioning a commonly held interpretation of the perception of architecture in motion.

HOLLOW SPACE AROUND PILOTIS

Gideon elaborates on the dilemma of the Carpen-

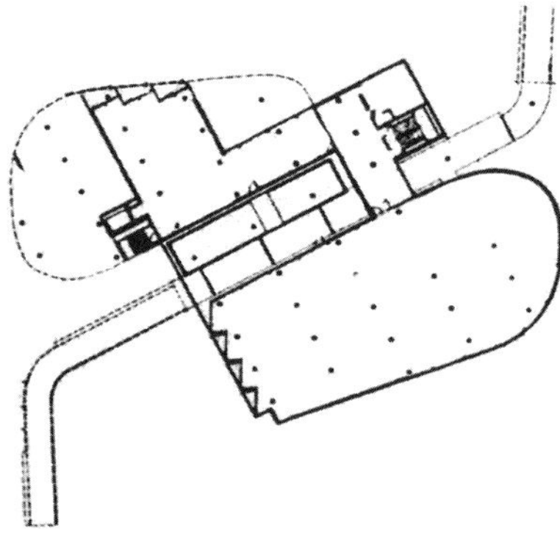

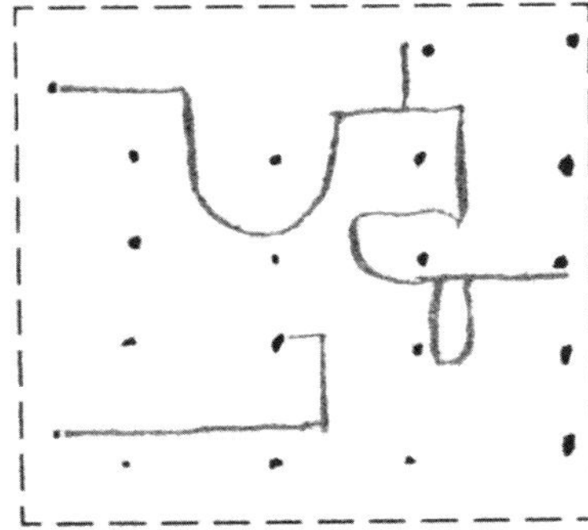

Top to bottom
Plans of Carpenter Center
Villa Savoye
Photoshop by Elysse Newman.

Opposite
Column of the Carpenter Center and the tree beyond.

ter Center's programming, arguing that "such an institute, unlike an institute of chemistry or physics, cannot establish a routine plan. For this reason, as a detailed plan was drawn up, Le Corbusier was only asked to create as flexible a space as possible, even at the risk that the interior might look like a warehouse."[5] Indeed the interior of the building does look a bit like a warehouse, even when it is made out of the same components as other free plan buildings by Le Corbusier: the column grid, the rectangular shapes, and the free forms. However, when compared with other free plans such as the four canonical manifestations that Le Corbusier had described in his famous sketch in *Précisions*, this building deploys them in a very different manner. The free-standing partitions, which had always been set up against the free plan's grid of columns and within a rectangular boundary are here expelled from between the columns and pushed out to the edge, to replace the rectangular boundary. From the outside, however, the neighboring buildings, the Fogg Art Museum and the Harvard Faculty Club, are solicited as the container of the Carpenter. Suggestions, that were rejected by Le Corbusier, of the building being too big for the site, confirm the importance of the tension achieved between the building's forms and the abutting buildings. Importantly, from the first time he *drew* the plan on the actual site, Le Corbusier *had asked* that the existing trees be accurately located on it. The columns, against which the main entrance is located, are aligned with a tree on the Faculty Club lot, suggesting continuity between the field of columns and the trees. Furthermore, the column grid extends beyond the paved area of the entrance and into the same terrace, as if the Carpenter extends all the way to the Faculty Club façade.

Not only has the outside container been removed, the floors have as well. The domino slabs that usually frame and confine the free forms in the interior between floors and ceilings are also removed. The free forms are exposed to the outside and they acquire an urban scale. Here again the building creates a surrogate to what has been removed. The slabs are graphically inscribed into the concrete of the curved forms. On the Prescott Street façade the slabs are also revealed as the horizontal members of the brise-soleils get clipped to allow for the passage of the ramp. By setting up the column/tree field, by pushing the free shapes against the abutting buildings, and with the full scale exposure of the free forms, Le Corbusier carries out the intention of demonstrating his architectural principles, but in this case turned inside out in order to display them didactically on the exterior. Contrary to the assessments of Giedion and Hitchcock, the building seems very urban in its outlook.

However, as a result of this investment in the public display of the promenade, the inside does seem to be hollowed out, and as Giedion says, turned into a warehouse-like space. When the partitions have been pushed out, we are left with nothing inside the plans. Hitchcock returned to the drawings that Le Corbusier had chosen for the *Oeuvre Complète* to argue that Le Corbusier's intentions were not the same as what was finally built.[6] But in the *Oeuvre Complète*, the most obvious aspect of the plans selected by Le Corbusier is how empty they really are. Furthermore, Le Corbusier chose not to include the full basement plan. He selected a sequence of five stark plans – the only major inaccuracy in them being not so much the unfulfilled relationship with the context, or the emptiness of the interiors, but the inclusion of a ramp that was never built and that connects the third floor gallery space to the fourth.

When looking from the inside out, the building does seem to ignore its surroundings. There are many decisions in the interior layout indicating that Giedion's criticisms of the inattentiveness to the site and the emptiness of the plans are related. However, the building is not so much inattentive to the context as it is blind towards it. For one, the shear wall that holds up the ramp of the Carpenter Center blocks the view through the large and open lobby window. And at the moment when the viewer is on axis with the window and the lobby, this wall cuts off the visual connection to the outside. The mullion-less window, through its correspondence with this direct view, seems at once to demonstrate and deny everything that has been said about the free façade and the window in relationship with the free plan. On the one hand, the view is there available, and the inside and the outside extend into each other. But when one is on axis, looking outside frontally, the wall crawls by and cuts off the view. The lobby does not get closed off or confined, and even from this window, the view tends to open up to the sides of the shear wall when one approaches the window. The main stair facing Quincy Street provides another example of willful blindness. This is a volume that could afford excellent views of the campus and of Cambridge, situated as it is on a diagonal with the Lamont yard. However, the façade of the staircase is filled in with glass blocks that only allow the light to come in but not the privileged view. One more confirmation can be found in the way the trees and shrubs are repeatedly drawn in plan in order to block the window walls from direct viewing to the outside even between the two sides of the building.

These blinders act locally to prevent the view from penetrating deep into the workshop and studio spaces. But Le Corbusier deploys this blindness at a more general level in the way that the diagonal brise-soleils disallow a direct view to the exterior, particularly in the workshops and stu-

dios. An emphatic remark in a sketch by Le Corbusier on the spatial proximity of the brise-soleils to the columns, may help explain this. Between the column and the brise-soleils, a small space is defined for viewing outside, but at that point, we are almost outside the room. From the middle of the plan, the view is reduced to meaningless background, and in many instances, the proximity to the neighboring buildings acts as a foil as well. When a direct view to the outside becomes possible, either the building's own walls or the walls of neighboring buildings block the view. Only after having moved across the room, traversed the last row of columns, and reached the delineated space in front of the windows, on the edge of the free plan, does one get to an uncropped view of outside features, and then usually only by looking sideways.

The conventional attitude towards the presence of the exterior view in the free plan seems to apply only to the periphery of the plan, to the zone defined by the separation between the columns and the exterior wall. A familiar illustration of the five points indicates a similar distinction in relation to the degree of lighting as a result of the fenêtre en longueur. Conventionally, architectural historians have emphasized the space between the grid of columns and the façade that displays the properties of transition between the free plan and the free façade. This space has been explained as a rhetorical structural cantilever to exaggerate the separation between the column and the wall.

It is this movement from the confined and free space to the open but contained view that characterizes the free plan in the lobby of the Carpenter Center and in its empty spaces, the main studios and workshops. When one is within the emptiness of the plan, it is necessary not to overwhelm the plan with the exterior views. The building has to be continuous, open, but unto itself.

We cannot fully explain these observations with the conventional wisdom about the free plan and the promenade architecturale that insists on the openness of both façade and plan in order to have direct connection between inside and outside but which also insists on variations in views and their disconnection. In the Carpenter Center, views are systematically and gradually transformed by the viewer's movement. It is, finally, a different kind of movement from the one associated with the conventional interpretation of the promenade

THE RULE OF MOVEMENT

Le Corbusier's promenade builds upon a long tradition of thought regarding movement in modern architecture. Conceptions of movement in architectural design are generally based on the simple fact that buildings are perceived by people in motion and on the difficult challenge that architects should respond to this fact when designing build-

ings.[7] Inquiries into this subject have informed modern architecture at least since the Picturesque, particularly in the design theories of Humphry Repton, Auguste Choisy, August Schmarzow, Adolf Loos, and Le Corbusier and through an extended interaction between architects, modern artists, and Gestalt psychologists in the 1920s and 1930s. Each of these theories has advanced specific compositional strategies, such as undulation, seriality, and juxtaposition. Engaging the moving subject in the definition of the form of a building generally implies that the architect, or the building, is aware of the presence of the occupant and reciprocally, that the viewer becomes aware of the way that his/her viewing habits are formed by the surrounding space.

Within each theory, when the subject moves, s/he acquires certain social attributes. For example, ambulation in the Picturesque asserts individual freedom. For modern life to be appreciated to its fullest, the Futurists and Le Corbusier had to observe the city from a fast car or plane. With Kevin Lynch in urban renewal America, daily commuting on the highway implies social mobility. More recently different kinds of formal agitation such as formlessness, folding, and computational materialism have been justified as enhanced experiences of the information age.

Within each theory, the kinetic relationship between the viewer and the building could be located on a spectrum between two poles. On the one end, the building is understood as a sequence of static images that are connected by a moving viewer (e.g., Loos and Le Corbusier), and on the other, the buildings' surfaces are warped and stretched in order to simulate or represent motion for a static viewer (e.g. from Borromoni to Ben van Berkel). Either we move and connect between still images of the building or the building feigns movement. Interpretations of the promenade architecturale have moved between those two poles. Projects of Le Corbusier's like the Philips Pavilions and formal motifs like the curved wall, the spiral staircase, and the diagonal ramp have been taken to insinuate motion in a pictorial sense or from a static position. But most interpretations of the promenade in the free plan have been closer to the former, less representational, pole.

The promenade is the experiential corollary of the free plan. The most basic definition of the free plan is the idea that the building's vertical partitions are disengaged from its structural elements and freely employed to respond to inhabitation. The inhabitation and articulation of the free plan is guided by circulation, by movement, not only inside the plan itself but between one floor and others, and importantly, between the plan and the exterior now that their relationship has been freed from the constraints of the facade.

The accepted interpretation of movement in the free plan is guided by Le Corbusier's own writings about the "promenade" inspired in part, as a notion, by the more introspective promenades of Jean-Jacques Rousseau. In his book *Talks with Students*, written in 1942 during the Second World War and addressed to the Beaux Arts students,

Left to right
Sequence of 5 images, 4 showing relationship between ramp shear wall and window of the Carpenter Center along Quincy Street, and a 5th, showing the view of the wall from the interior.

and then published again with renewed commitment to its content in 1957, Le Corbusier describes the promenade in the following manner:

An architecture must be walked through and traversed. It is by no means that entirely graphic illusion certain schools of thought like us to believe in, organized around some abstract point that pretends to be a man, a chimerical man with the eye of a fly and vision simultaneously circular. Such a man simply does not exist, and in consequence of this misconception, the classical era baited the trap for the total destruction of architecture. Instead, our man has two eyes set in the front of his head, and he stands six feet above the ground and looks ahead. These biological facts are enough to damn the whole batch of plans that have the wheel revolving around a fictitious pivot. Thus, equipped with his own two eyes and looking straight ahead, our man walks about and changes positions, applies himself to his pursuits, moving in the midst of a succession of architectural realities. He re-experiences the intense feeling that has come from that sequence of movements. This is so true that architecture can be judged dead or living by the degree to which the rule of movement has been disregarded or brilliantly exploited.[8]

This description has been central to the interpretation of the promenade architecturale among historians and critics. More recent interpreters of Le Corbusier's work have tried to focus on understanding precisely what this "rule of movement" is. It has been discussed by Bruno Reichlin, Beatriz Colomina, and Yves-Alain Bois who have relied on a range of theories, from the Picturesque, to space-time theories, to the interpretation of visuality by Jacques Lacan and to the advent of cinema

and its impact on Le Corbusier's architecture. Even though they may differ on the cultural interpretations of the rule, they do concur that it entails unraveling the building to the moving subject in bits or as still frames that unfold one after the other, whether in smooth transitions or in surprising breaks, created by the free-standing interior partitions and the intermingling of interior spaces with outside views. Recently, Beatriz Colomina has provided the following interpretation:

Modern eyes move. Vision in Le Corbusier's architecture is always tied to movement: "You follow an itinerary," a promenade architecturale. The point of view of modern architecture is never fixed, as in baroque architecture, or as in the model of vision of the camera obscura, but always in motion, as in film or in the city. Crowds, shoppers in a department store, railroad travelers, and the inhabitants of Le Corbusier's houses have in common with movie viewers that they cannot fix (arrest) the image. Like the movie viewer that Benjamin describes they inhabit a space that is neither an inside nor an outside, public nor private. It is a space that is not made out of walls but of images.[9]

The spaces of Le Corbusier's houses are less about enclosure than the entanglement of inside and outside, less about a traditional interior than about following an itinerary (no matter how many times redrawn, no matter how linear) the enclosure resulting from the collage of fleeting images assembled as the reader moves through too much material, too many images, too many stimuli.[10]

This interpretation combines different conceptions about the view, as fleeting image, as photograph, and as moving picture, but in all cases, the building is conceived as an orchestration of

views. When one moves, these views, which are predominantly turned to the outside, are connected together in the mind of the viewer. In his own writings, Le Corbusier does refer to this unraveling, but not solely to that.

An even more basic assumption underlies these interpretations of movement in Le Corbusier. It is that visual perception, as a mental process, entails the interpretation of two-dimensional stimuli as they register on the retina. After undergoing a perceptual process that takes the two-dimensional image from the retina to the brain, we can finally infer the third dimension back out of the visual cues. As the viewer changes position in relation to the object being viewed, the brain connects the sequence of two-dimensional images as a rolling film does and interprets them. Perceptual theorists have employed the media of photography and cinema as metaphors to explicate the different levels of seeing. As our mechanical and electronic equipment becomes more complicated so, it would seem, are our models for vision.[11]

This digression into perceptual psychology is significant for historical reasons. In his canonical *Space, Time, and Architecture*, Giedion himself had proposed that changes in modes of perception are effected by changes in technology and the introduction of new media. Technological changes therefore affect both the production and the reception of architecture. He identifies Futurism and Cubism as two attempts at representing the space-time fusion.[12] Following along his well known elucidations of the relationship between technology and perception, modern architects and artists in the twenties and thirties turned to Gestalt psychology in order to shape or confirm their positions about composition and perception of form.

Reciprocally, Gestalt theorists looked extensively at abstract visual art in order to study figure and ground, their relational effects and the whole/part interactions between them.[13] Gestalt theories have primarily concentrated on two-dimensional illustrations and borrowed visual theory in relation to painting. It would seem that the discussions of motion in architecture are indebted to this pictorial aspect of perception as well. Le Corbusier does appear to rely on a similar interpretation of perception in motion. Colin Rowe and Robert Slutzky have exhaustively analyzed this aspect of his work, but it is not the only way his work relates to the idea of movement.[14]

Le Corbusier's early writings on painting and architecture with Amedée Ozenfant attempted to ground the purist theories of painting and of architecture in scientific evidence from such perceptual psychologists as Hermann von Helmholtz and Charles Henry.[15] Their journal, *L'Esprit Nouveau*, published several papers by Charles Henry, director of the Laboratory of Physiological Sensations at the Sorbonne. Henry sought to identify scientific justifications for aesthetic preferences. He developed the "aesthetic protractor," an instrument that produced "rhythmic angles" based on simple number proportions that were supposed to yield more satisfactory, therefore aesthetic, sensations in the observer.[16] Both Henry and his artist-readers like Le Corbusier were aware of the cultural factors involved in the definition of aesthetic preferences, but they placed their inquisitions at a level that they believed preceded the establishment of cultural signification, at what they understood to be a universal base. Le Corbusier and Ozenfant often cautioned their readers that the main quest was not for an absolute (even if the rhetoric often slipped in that direction).[17] These "constants" emerge out of chaos in order to establish "classifications founded on the appearances of nature." This underlies the difficult pursuit of constants (not absolutes) and the apparent (not the actual).

This pursuit would guide Le Corbusier in many aspects of his work, whether through the development of the tracées regulatoires, the modulor, in the polychromie, or in defending purist shapes. In each of these aspects of design, whether it was the compositional organization of the façade, the measurements of spaces, gradations of color, or the determination of free forms, Le Corbusier identified rules derived from what he believed remained constant for all users. Neither the rule of movement nor the constants associated with it were ever explicitly spelled out. They have to be derived from passing references and from buildings like the Carpenter Center, where he seemed to employ this rule.

Among his other pursuits of constants, a possible connection to the rule of movement can be found in his theory of color. This may be a rather oblique way of interpreting the idea of movement, but the Polychromie Architecturale does embody, in a less implicit manner, his views of perception and the interpretation of constants across subjects. Interestingly, it is also a place where Le Corbusier moved away from the compositional and painterly attributes of color and focused on its psychological impact in everyday encounters with a moving subject. According to Arthur Ruegg, Le Corbusier derived his approach from physiological as well as psychological effects of colors which could fully unfold in the white space. Vice versa, he also took its legitimization from the laws of perception and association that are presumed to be constant, from the unchangeable "mécanisme de l'emotion."[18] His color concept in this respect differs from that of the Dutch de Stijl movement or from German post-expressionism.[19]

Helmholtz, Henry, and other psychologists whom Le Corbusier read argued that color exhibited certain psychological and physiological effects that were constant among different viewers. Blue, for example, made forms recede whereas brown stabilized them. Since Pessac, Le Corbusier had been experimenting with this employment of colors. However, Ruegg reminds us that Le Corbusier skipped the scientifically-determined color schemes, such as the classified color circle of Ostwald, and connected directly to the daily experiences of people with colors deployed polychromatically around them. It was not the intrinsic qualities of materials that he was after. Instead he wanted to understand their effects and the constants that they displayed in the chaos of daily life. Moreover, while he discussed color as a factor that affected the composition of architecture to a static viewer (it recedes from one position at one point in time), it is the free plan that removed the boundaries between rooms and allowed for the different colors to interact independently of the forms that they covered. The free plan makes such ideas as the "Rose Room," obsolete. It therefore encourages using colors polychromatically, against each other. The *Polychromie Architecturale*, Le Corbusier's systematic approach to the deployment of colors, was established in the 1930s for a paint company. It was then loosened up in the 1950s so that decisions could be based more on observing the effect of colors on viewers. According to Ruegg, this happened after the creation of a new collection of colors in 1959, around the same time as the Carpenter was being designed.

We can also go back to Gestalt psychology to find a rule of movement that is similar to the one Le Corbusier may have been trying to articulate. A second generation of Gestalt psychologists released the viewer from the confines of the fixed laboratory chair and from the limited results that they would get in making the viewer look at pictures simulating motion. Ultimately, they proposed that perception of motion did not occur by connecting different static images and comparing them, but rather by identifying what was fixed and what changed with movement. Some threads of such an alternative to the pictorial model of movement could be traced back to early Gestalt theorists, but the development of a comprehensive theory of vision based on this model took place after the Second World War. James Gibson, an American perceptual psychologist who had spent some time researching how pilots orient themselves in the scarce environment of the sky, came to realize that neither the restricted environment of the lab nor the pictorial approach to perception suffice to explain how we see in everyday life.[20] He shifted the emphasis away from the retinal image as the effective stimulus for vision, away from the image, towards the totality of the environment, what he called an "optic array."[21] According to Gibson, when we move within this array, we make sense of the world by way of relating our movement to what he called "invariant patterns in the environment," certain constant properties, as opposed to variant patterns, or those that move as we move. Invariants are properties or patterns that remain constant when the observer, the environment, or both change their position. Recent elaborations on Gibson's idea discern two types of invariants: transformational invariants are patterns of change that can reveal what is happening to an object. For example, when an object moves away from the viewer at a regular speed, its apparent area (the size of the angle apprehended at the eye) diminishes in a predictable manner. The decrease of the area is proportional to the square of the distance. Whenever this relationship is present it must mean that the distance between the viewer and the object is changing in a regular manner. Gibson and his followers placed a strong emphasis on the role that textures of surfaces play in the orientation and guidance of the viewer in a space. Structural invariants, the second kind, are a higher order of patterns that remain constant despite changes in simulation. For example, the horizon ratio, the relationship between the height of the object and its apparent distance from the horizon remains constant, allowing the viewer to locate the object's real position as either of them moves.

Gibson's ideas quickly caught the attention of artists and architects. He published some of his research in visual arts journals and was frequently featured in the George Braziller series on art edited by Gyorgy Kepes. He was also frequently quoted by the likes of Rudolf Arnheim (who lectured in and about the Carpenter Center). Nelson Goodman, a philosopher and interlocutor of Gibson, would insist that we should pay close attention to how artists construct their own worlds in order to under-

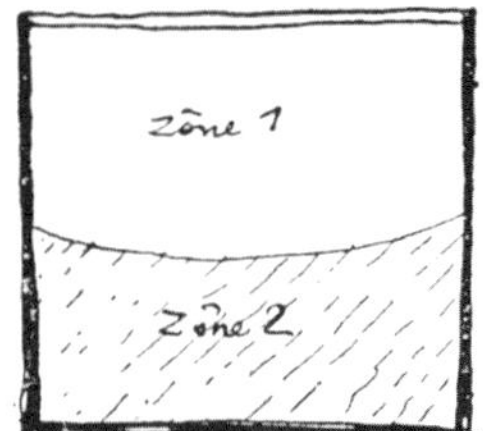

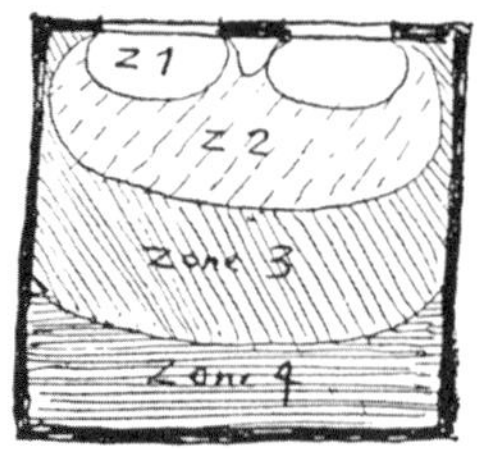

Top
View of studio space Harvard Grad-
uate School of Design, Loeb Library,
Visual Collections.

Above, left to right
Zones of light in room.

View of studio. Photograph
by Hashim Sarkis.

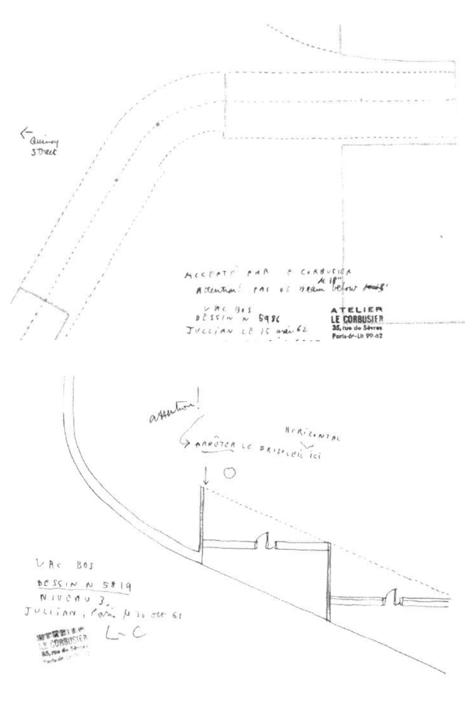

Left
Ramp of Le Corbusier's Villa Savoye, photograph by
Hashim Sarkis.

Top to bottom:
Detail Plan of Carpenter Center ramp Harvard Graduate School of Design, Loeb Library, Sert Collection.

Plan of brise soleil
Harvard Graduate School of Design, Loeb Library,
Sert Collection.

Zoned plan of studio space, photoshop on plan of
level 3, south side of Carpenter Center. *Le Corbusier
at Work*, edited by Eduard Sekler and William Curtis,
(Cambridge, MA: Harvard University Press, 1974),
figure 153, p.154.

stand better how the perceptual world works.[22]

In brief, this "direct" approach to perception, what is also referred to as the "ecological approach," shifts the emphasis away from pictures and towards invariants, constants. It elevates the role of such attributes as ratios, textures, and spaces between objects because of their ability to guide the moving subject. Importantly, as Gibson observed, the reliance on these invariant attributes increases in a rarefied, empty environment.

CONSTANTS IN ACTION

In an empty building, pictorial compositional strategies would be impossible to employ. The Carpenter Center's spaces rely on a series of invariants in order to delineate the spaces. Accounts of the building design agree on the importance Le Corbusier gave in this project to materials, textures, colors, and surface treatments. It was necessary for him to capture a rough and continuous texture for the ceiling and to maintain a regularity to the floor patterns in the studio spaces, as if for the eye to measure against them. Whenever he employs a smooth surface, with the exception of the columns, a gradated texture is used in order to introduce certain references in this surrogate environment.

A strong emphasis is also placed on bringing the horizon line into every space, be it in the form of a retaining wall that runs behind the pilotis on the street level entrance or in the form of a shelf that is placed almost at eye level to tie the curvature of the room and its brise-soleils together. The curvature of the studio walls is exaggerated by the ondulatoires so that even in the absence of direct light, they appear curved.

In all, however, it is not so much the specific material qualities of things but their relational qualities that seem to affect our perception in motion. Textures are not understood as intrinsic qualities but are to be experienced in relation to each other.

In keeping with the criticisms presented against it, the Carpenter Center seems to separate almost graphically, the "pictorial" model of the promenade from another, "direct" one. This is perhaps the aspect of the building that Le Corbusier was most dissatisfied with, and it shows most clearly in the way that he republished the plans of the building by including the interior ramp going from the third to the fourth level. This ramp would have acted as a continuation of the exterior ramp and established a continuity between the two models.

However, the constants do not always operate as cues, as guiding lights in the emptiness of the studios. Le Corbusier also uses these attributes of his building to deliberately confuse movement or to feign certain counter effects. We are constantly presented with modularized paneling systems imprinted in the concrete against irregular patterns in the floor. Shiny surfaces are juxtaposed against rough ones. The ondulatoires not only emphasize the curvature, but given their irregular spacing, they also confuse its apparent curvature, particularly as one moves along the wall. It is as if by playing out these attributes of the architecture against each other, he is reminding the occupants of the visual arts center not to fully trust their eyes. Giedion insisted in his discussion of the Visual Arts programme that the psychology of vision was much more important than the optics, particularly in the electronic age that he was heralding.

THE PURIFICATION
OF ARCHITECTURE BY THE VOID

Much is yet to be said about emptiness in architecture, a phenomenon once described by Le Corbusier as the "purification of architecture by the void."[23] It would be impossible to elaborate on all aspects of the rule of movement in Le Corbusier's architecture by studying only one building. Even if, as Stan Allen astutely observes, the Carpenter Center is a place where Le Corbusier's concepts are condensed, we would still need to follow the way in which the rule was employed more diachronically.[24] Still, this alternative proposes that if the free plan had been initiated by releasing the interior space from the constraints of structure, this freedom could only be fully gained if those aspects of architecture, formerly understood as secondary and isolated qualities of form, are elevated into constants that operate according to the rules of movement.

The effect produced by the emptiness of the Carpenter Center and the challenges presented to its inhabitation recall some of the techniques of eighteenth and nineteenth century Picturesque composition, particularly in the work of Humphry Repton. Repton's designs forced the viewer to change position in the landscape in order to be able to determine the actual measurement of objects. If an object is viewed from one position, the deliberate distortions of ground, reflections, and tampered sizes of comparative objects all contribute to giving the viewer a false measurement of the object being contemplated. In Repton's Picturesque it is the difference between the apparent and the real that prompts the viewer to move. The viewer searches for true measurement. Importantly, the viewer is still moving from one static position to another, relying on one composed picture after another but trusting none in itself. Like the surveyor of land, the stroller triangulates before being able to fix the object of his contemplation in place and true dimension and against the deceptions of the landscape designer.[25]

Le Corbusier maintains the games of measurement but departs from fixed points and compositions. Perhaps here we can detect a more funda-

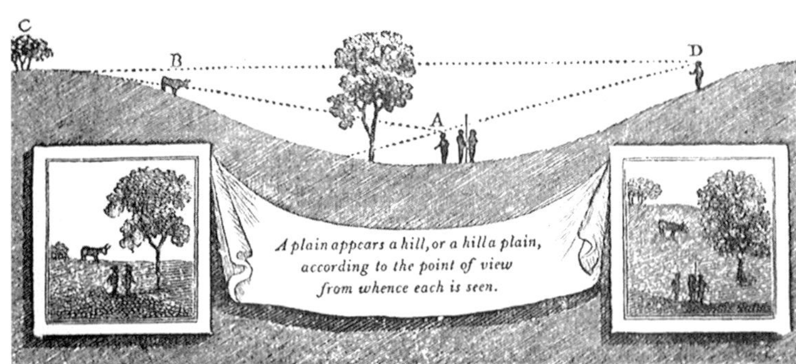

Triangulation in the picturesque, Humphry Repton, *The Art of Landscape Gardening*, Boston and New York: Houghton Mifflin Company, 1907) Figure 10, p.87

mental cinematic influence on his architecture but one that does not rely on "stills" or the "freeze-frame" approach maintained by the abovementioned cinematic interpretations of his work. In the "American Prologue" to *Précisions*, Le Corbusier challenges any Hollywood director to capture what he describes as a cinematic moment:

in an ordinary small restaurant, two or three customers are having coffee and talking. The table is still covered with glasses, with bottles, with plates, with the bottle of oil, the saltshaker, pepper mill, napkins, napkin ring, etc. Look at the inevitable order that relates these objects to each other; they have all been used, they have been grasped in the hand of one or the other of the diners; the distances that separate between them are the measure of life.

He goes on to criticize the Hollywood cinematic approach by saying, "There isn't a false point, a hiatus, a deceit . . . no false harmonies, fakes, dodges."[26] It is through these mechanisms of filmmaking that we can think of the work of Le Corbusier as cinematic, not because of the guided viewing along the ramp that connects between different static views nor for the ribbon windows which frame the panning view as if it were a film, but because of the manipulation of constants. The emptier the space is, the more active the constants.

Commenting on certain associations between film and Le Corbusier's architecture, Arnaud François proposes that Le Corbusier relied precisely on this quality of emptiness to introduce a different cinematic vision into architecture. Beyond the cinematic understanding of an architecture that cannot be perceived fully from one point of view (a non-perspectival architecture), François proposes that "the more the elements are situated on planes that are distant from one another, the more the tension between them increases. The orchestration of concordant and discordant objects is the source of this spacing. Cinematographic perspective is a medium for expressing tensions between beings and objects rather than a unified and spatial a priori."[27] François reminds us that Michaelangelo Antonioni had very skillfully exploited this quality of emptiness in his films.

It is as if the representational model of movement takes place on the exterior and another form of engaging movement is reserved for the inside of the Carpenter Center. Here, we are confronted with an architecture that does not even allow for the conventional understanding of the cinematic

in architecture to take place, for when you enter a studio space you experience it all at once. There is no sequence of views. Eventually, however, you start seeing in a different way. The drawings that traveled from Paris to Boston drawn by Guillermo Jullian de la Fuentes, an apprentice fascinated by the films of Michaelangelo Antonioni and his representation of spatial emptiness, render the textures of the surfaces very expressionistically as if they were the main attribute of the space and as if they contained a code to the architects on site as important as the shapes and their dimensions.[28] This recalls the way the lonely figures move in empty spaces of Antonioni's "Red Desert" and the way the crisp outlines of their colored coats rub against the rust of industry and the rough textures of weathered walls.

Ultimately, the rule of movement does not only govern circulation, figurative forms, and ramps. It operates in the free plan beyond the guided path of the ramp and the confined frame of the ribbon window. It extends to the articulation of the building's surfaces and planes. These two approaches to vision in motion, even in the Carpenter Center, need not be mutually exclusive. Seemingly opposed ideas about how we conceive of architecture, whether as an image or as an array, as full or as empty, could be reconciled or at least held in tension with each other, even in the same spaces.[29] This possibility is heightened in the Carpenter Center given the ostensible ramp, the peculiar relationship with the context, and the emptiness.

It is the pursuit of the latter, less obvious, approach that has driven this inquiry. Whether in the Carpenter Center or elsewhere in Le Corbusier's and other architectures, this approach of describing and designing the relationship between the building and the viewer emphasizes different attributes of architecture than have previously been discussed when it came to vision in motion. While re-invoking concerns about materials, formal composition, and construction, this approach makes it possible to address movement without having to agitate the forms or the path, without being figural, and without being narrative. In this approach, attention shifts from the object to the background, the field. (After all, the field may very well be emptied of objects.) For example, the materials of construction are selected and composed in a relational manner, based on how they behave in motion, not as properties of the objects of observation but as background. The compo-

sitional logic does not merely aim to enhance movement, to heighten the sense of motion. By manipulating the constants, or the invariants, the architect is also able to feign different speeds and different perceptions of depth and size than the actual ones. Architecture is not simply an object that fills the visual field. In its deceptive emptiness, it simultaneously plays the role of a surrogate visual field and its foil. The building provides a sense of diminution in depth, a surrogate horizon, and patterns and textures to measure against, but it also interrupts their function as invariants. Even the delimitation of the space, the field of vision, changes in motion. Spaces are enclosed in a suggested, incomplete manner and the gradients of enclosure change with movement. Yet in such a rarified environment, it is not the architecture that is eventful. It does not captivate the viewer's attention with its own forms and apparent transformations but pushes back and allows the activities in the space, that are nevertheless guided by the architecture, to become the events. Through this approach, it is possible to think of an architecture that anticipates events rather than creates them.

NOTES

1 This essay grew out of a lecture from "Constructing Vision," a course that I teach at the Harvard Graduate School of Design. I am indebted to the insights of the students in this course and also to discussions with Eduard Sekler, Francesco Passanti, Guillermo Jullian de la Fuente, Preston Scott Cohen, and George Baird. I am also very grateful to Lauren Kogod for her careful and insightful comments on this paper and for her cinematic vision.

2 Sigfried Giedion, "Das Carpenter Center for Visual Arts der Harvard-Universität in Cambridge (MA)," *Bauen +Wohnen*, Vol. 18, #8, (Zurich, August 1964), p.331–334

3 See Henry Russell Hitchcock, "Le Corbusier and the United States," *Zodiac* 16, 1966.

4 Eduard F. Sekler and William Curtis, *Le Corbusier at Work, The Genesis of the Carpenter Center for Visual Arts* (Cambridge: Harvard University Press, 1978), p.57.

5 Sigfried Giedion, "New Ventures in University Building (Le Corbusier, Sert)," *Zodiac* 16 (1967), p.31.

6 See Henry Russell Hitchcock, "Le Corbusier and the United States."

7 Similar discussions occur in the questions of distribution of uses around the notion of circulation or in the work of Bill Hillier on how space is used. The definition of movement in relation to design here has to do with the manipulation of form that responds to the changing perceptual framework when one is in motion.

8 Le Corbusier, *Talks with Students From the Schools of Architecture* (New York: The Orion Press, 1961), p.44–45.

9 Beatriz Colomina, *Publicity and Privacy, Modern Architecture as Mass Media* (Cambridge: MIT Press, 1994), p.5–6.

10 Ibid., p.11.

11 David Marr wrote his book *Vision* in 1979 in which he presents a computational approach to visual perception. According to this approach, initially, a primary sketch is formed from what is called a zero-crossing of an image. Zero crossings are sudden changes in contour, shadow and are mostly related to shape rather than to color or medium changes. The primary sketch consists mainly of very faint impressions that remain very subject based. What is called a 2-dimensional sketch is then intensified from this information. Even though it is still vague and also subject-based, the 2-D sketch begins to suggest a three dimensional form, which becomes better sculpted in a following stage, the 3-D model stage. In this last stage, the visual process breaks the image down into simple geometrical solids and then recognizes the object by identifying the composition of these solids. Marr's interpretation of the perceptual process forms the culmination of years of studying vision as an indirect process which is achieved more by inference from an image, the retinal image. Sometimes physiological evidence is inferred: the number of nerves that control the eye's movement from the brain are more numerous than those that send stimuli to the brain. At other times, simple experiments and complex mathematical calculations are used. In all, the idea is that when we move, we see by way of transforming the retinal image, it is a still image presented to us in sequence but transformed into a form of knowledge. Today this model prevails over any other form of interpretation of vision and viewing.

   A computational approach, unlike a psychological or physiological approach, does not aim to describe the visual process directly but to model it, simulate it for other purposes, but inadvertently, it helps explain how the visual-mental process actually works. The pictorial (or freeze frame) interpretation of movement in the free plan confirms Marr's model. See David Marr, *Vision, A Computational Investigation into the Human Representation and Processing of Visual Information* (New York: W.H. Freeman and Company, 1982).

12 Sigfried Giedion, *Space, Time and Architecture, The Growth of a New Tradition* (Cambridge: Harvard Univesrity Press, 1976), p.443–448.

13 For a discussion of the relationship between psychology and art and architecture, see Mark Jarzombek, *The Psychologizing of Modernity* (Cambridge: Cambridge University Press, 2000).

14 Colin Rowe and Robert Slutzky, "Transparency: Literal and Phenomenal," in *The Mathematics of the Ideal Villa* (Cambridge: The MIT Press, 1976), p.159–183.

15 Ozenfant and Jeanneret, *La Peinture Moderne* (Paris:G. Cres, Collection de "L'Esprit nouveau," 1925), p.165.

16 Charles Henry, "La Lumière, La Couleur, La Forme," *Suite* 4 (1), *L'Esprit Nouveau*, #9, p.1068–1079.

17 See Arthur Ruegg, "Le Corbusier's Polychromie Architecturale," in *Polychromie Architecturale*, (Basel: Birkhauser, 1999).

18 Ibid.

19 It is important to note that David Marr, while trying to model movement, initially used Gibson's invariants but concluded that they required as complex a process of interpretation as that of his images and were not always easy to detect.

21 James J. Gibson, *An Ecological Approach to Visual Perception* (Hillsdale, NJ: Lawrence Erlbaum Associates, Publishers, 1986).

22 Reciprocally, Nelson Goodman, who was one of the main interlocutors of Gibson. See for instance, *Ways of Worldmaking* (Indianapolis: Hackett Publishing Company, 1978).

23 See Arthur Ruegg, op. cit.

24 Stan Allen, "Le Corbusier and Modernist Movement, The Carpenter Center for Visual Arts, Cambridge, MA," *Practice: Architecture, Technique and Representation* (Amsterdam: G+B Arts International, 2000), p.121.

25 Humphry Repton, *The Art of Landscape Gardening* (Boston and New York: Houghton Mifflin Company, 1907).

26 Le Corbusier, *Précisions*, (Cambridge: MIT Press, 1999), p.9.

27 See Arnaud François, "La Cinématographie de l'oeuvre de le Corbusier," *Cinémathèque* 9 (Spring 1996), p.39–55, p.50, my translation from original French text.

28 I am grateful to Guillermo Jullian de la Fuente for pointing me in the direction of Antonioni but also for helping me make the connection between the theories of color and the theories of motion.

29 Michael Baxandall has already illustrated how these two models could be used to effectively describe Enlightenment paintings. See Michael Baxandall, *Shadows and Enlightenment* (New Haven: Yale University Press, 1996).

Belonging: Towards a Theory of Identification with Place

NEIL LEACH

Architecture is often linked to questions of cultural identity. For what sense would discourses such as critical regionalism or gender and space make unless they assumed some connection between identity and architectural space?[1] And yet architectural theorists have seldom broached the question of how people actually identify with their environment. Instead they have been preoccupied almost exclusively with questions of form, as though cultural identity is somehow constituted by form alone. It is clear, however, that if theorists are to link architecture to cultural identity they must extend their analyses beyond any mere discourse of form to engage with subjective processes of identification. This has long been acknowleged by cultural theorists, who have developed a sophisticated understanding of the mechanisms by which culture operates. For them culture is constituted not by a system of objects alone, but by a discourse that imbues these objects with meaning.

Cultural identity, therefore, emerges as a complex, rhizomatic field of operations that engages with – but is not defined by – cultural artifacts such as architecture.

It is perhaps by following the notion of the nation as "narration" – of identity as a kind of discourse – put forward by cultural theorist Homi Bhabha that we can grasp the importance of understanding form as being inscribed within a cultural discourse. The nation, for Bhabha, is enacted as a "cultural elaboration." To perceive the nation in this way in narrative terms is to highlight the discursive and contested nature of identities: "To study the nation through its narrative address does not merely draw attention to its language and rhetoric; it also attempts to alter the conceptual object itself. If the problematic 'closure' of textuality questions the 'totalization' of national culture, then its positive value lies in displaying the wide dissemination through which we construct the field of meanings and symbols associated with national life."[2]

Of course, it would be wrong to reduce the nation to mere narration, as though form were totally unimportant. Rather we have to recognise the nation as being defined within a dialectical tension. It is a tension, for Bhabha, between the object and its accompanying narrative: "signifying the people as an a priori historical presence, a pedagogical object; and the people constructed in the performance of narrative, its enunciatory present marked in the repetition and pulsation of the national sign."[3] If, then, the nation is a kind of narration, it is never an abstract narration, but a contextualized narration inscribed around certain objects. And it is within this field of objects that have become the focus of narrative attention that we must locate architecture, as a language of forms not only embedded within various cultural discourses, but also given meaning by those discourses.

This brings us close to Pierre Bourdieu's concept of habitus, as a non-conscious system of dispositions that derive from the subject's economic, cultural, and symbolic capital. Habitus, for Bourdieu is a dynamic field of behavior, of position-taking, when individuals inherit the parameters of a given situation and modify them into a new situation. As Derek Robbins explains: "The habitus of every individual inscribes the inherited parameters of modification, of adjustment from situation to position which provides the legacy of a new situation."[4] This approach supposes an interaction between social behavior and a given objectified condition. It is here that we may locate the position of architecture in Bourdieu's discourse.

Architecture, in Bourdieu's terms, can be understood as a type of "objectivated cultural capital." Its value lies dormant and in permanent potential. It has to be reactivated by social practices that will, as it were, revive it. In this respect,

Shimon Attie, *Linienstrasse 137: Slide projection of police raid on former Jewish residents, 1920*, Berlin, 1992.

architecture belongs to the same category as other cultural objects:

Although objects – such as books or pictures – can be said to be the repositories of objectivated cultural capital, they have no value unless they are activated strategically in the present by those seeking to modify their incorporated cultural capital. All those objects on which cultural value has ever been bestowed lie perpetually dormant waiting to be revived, waiting for their old value to be used to establish new value in a new market situation.[5]

In other words, what Bourdieu highlights is the need for praxis to unlock the meaning of an object. This comes close to the Wittgensteinian model wherein linguistic meaning is defined by use. Just as words can be understood by the manner in which they are used, so buildings can be grasped by the manner in which they are perceived – by the narratives of use in which they are inscribed.

This opens up a crucial problem within an architectural discourse that has traditionally been premised almost solely on questions of form. It is as though narratives of use stand largely outside architectural concerns. As a result, there is no accepted framework for examining how people make sense of place and identify with it. Without this, the relation of architecture to cultural identity can hardly be addressed. In order for architecture to be understood in terms of cultural identity, some kind of identification with architecture must have taken place. But how does this identification occur?

This article attempts to address this question by sketching out a schematic framework for a tentative theory of identification with place by bringing together three discrete theoretical models. Starting with a theory of how we territorialize and make sense of place through a process of narrativization, it goes on to investigate how a sense of belonging to that place is achieved through performativities, before finally suggesting how eventual identification with a particular place is forged through a series of mirrorings.

NARRATIVISATIONS

In *The Practice of Everyday Life*, Michel de Certeau has developed a theory of territorialization through spatial tactics. Through habitual processes of movement, by covering and recovering the same paths and routes, we come to familiarize ourselves with a territory, and thereby find meaning in that territory.[6]

De Certeau draws the distinction between "place" (lieu) and "space" (espace). Somewhat confusingly, he inverts their usual relationship so that space becomes a contextualization of place. For him, space is place made meaningful – awakened by practices that contextualize it:

Space occurs as the effect produced by the operations that orient it, situate it, temporalize it, and make it function in a polyvalent unity of conflictual programs or contractual proximities. In this view, in relation to place, space is like the word when it is spoken, that is, when it is caught in a proximity of an actualization, transformed into a term dependent upon many different conventions, situated as an act of a present (or of a time), and modified by the transformations caused by successive contexts . . . space is a practiced place. Thus the street geometrically defined by urban planning is transformed into a space by walkers.[7]

The problem of space is, for de Certeau, ultimately a problem of representation. With Maurice Merleau-Ponty he draws the distinction between geometrical space and anthropological space, famously observing the impossibility of grasping the concept of space as a map, with his description of New York as seen from the top of the World Trade Center. De Certeau is close to Fredric Jameson's concern for cognitive mapping in his quest for various tactics that overcome this problem.[8] Hence he formulates a "rhetoric of space" that amounts to an individualized process of spatial demarcation, based on a linguistic model of narrativity. "The opacity of the body," de Certeau notes, "in movement, gesticulating, walking, taking its pleasure, is what indefinitely organizes a here in relation to an abroad, a 'familiarity' in relation to a 'foreignness'. A spatial story is in its minimal degree a spoken language, that is, a linguistic system that distributes places insofar as it is articulated by an 'enunciatory focalization', by an act of practicing it."[9] The city turns into a theatre of actions, narratives of space, pedestrian speech-acts: "It is a process of appropriation of the topological system on the part of the pedestrian (just as the speaker appropriates and takes on the language); it is a spatial acting out of a place (just as the speech-act is an acoustic acting out of language)."[10] It is about tours and not maps. If any map is achieved, it is not some abstract map, but an individualized "cognitive map" to use Jameson's term. In other words it is born of a strategic engagement with the city, and does not reside in the city itself as a collection of buildings.

"To walk," notes de Certeau, "is to lack a place. It is the indefinite process of being absent and in search of a proper."[11] As Ian Buchanon observes, this suggests the reliance of de Certeau on Lacan.[12] For it is the traumatic mirror-stage – and the seemingly paradoxical attempt to overcome that alienation through repetition, as demonstrated in Freud's example of the child playing the fort-da game – that establishes Lacan's primordial place in de Certeau's work. Space must be theorized by means of the mirror-stage, and spatial practices are none other than repetitive gestures aimed at overcoming the alienation of all conceptual, abstract space. As de Certeau comments: "In the initiatory game, just as in the 'joyful activity' of the child who, standing before a mirror, sees itself as one (it is she or he, seen as a whole) but another (that, an image with which the child identifies itself), what counts is the process of this 'spatial captation' that inscribes the passage toward the other as the law of being and the law of place. To practice space is thus to repeat the joyful and silent experience of childhood; it is, in a place, to be other and to move toward the other."[13] What de Certeau articulates, then, is a model for how we make sense of space through walking practices, and repeat those practices as a way of overcoming alienation.

By basing his model of spatial appropriation on linguistics, de Certeau emphasizes the narrative aspect to spatial stories. Spatial tactics offer ways of making connections, and finding meaning in otherwise abstract places. But de Certeau says little about the actual identification with those spaces, being more concerned as a theorist with otherness than with assimilation.[14] If, then, we wish to extend de Certeau's theory for making sense of place into one which establishes a mode of identification, we must also consider how these spatial tactics help to forge a sense of identity.

BELONGING

Here we should turn to the work of Judith Butler, who has elaborated a vision of identity that is based on the notion of "performativity." Butler is a theorist of lesbian politics, and her concerns are to formulate a notion of identity that is not constrained by traditional heterosexual models and to offer a radical critique of essentializing modes of thinking. According to Butler, our actions and behavior constitute our identity, and not our biological bodies. Gender, she argues, is not an ontological condition, but it is performatively produced. It is "a construction that conceals its genesis, the tacit collective agreement to perform, produce and sustain discrete and polar genders as culturalfictions is obscured by the credibility of those productions."[15] By extension — without wishing to collapse sexuality, class, race and ethnicity into the same category — all forms of identity can be interpreted as dependent upon performative constructs.[16]

We may rearticulate our identities and reinvent ourselves through our performativities. Here it is important to note that identity is the effect of performance, and not vice versa. Performativity achieves its aims not through a singular performance — for performativity can never be reduced to performance — but through the accumulative iteration of certain practices. For performativity is grounded in a form of citationality — of invocation and replication. As Judith Butler explains: 'Performativity is thus not a singular 'act', for it is always a reiteration of a norm or set of norms, and to the extent that it acquires an act-like status in

the present, it conceals and dissimulates the conventions of which it is a repetition."[17]

This has obvious ramifications for a theory of identification with architecture. Butler's incisive comments on gender identity being defined not in biological terms, but in performative terms as an identity that is "acted out" can be profitably transposed to the realm of identification with place. This makes possibile, of a discourse of performativity and 'belonging' as Vikki Bell has shown.[18] "The repetition," she notes, "sometimes ritualistic repetition, of these normalized codes makes material the belongings they purport to simply describe."[19] It suggests a way in which communities might colonize various territories through the literal performances—the actions, ritualistic behavior and so on — that are acted out within a given architectural stage, and through those performances achieve a certain attachment to place.

Central to this latter notion is the idea that just as communities are imagined communities, so the spaces of communities — the territories that they have claimed as their own — are also imagined. "Imagining a community," as Anne-Marie Fortier observes, "is both that which is created as a common history, experience or culture of a group — a group's belongings — and about how the imagined community is attached to places — the location of culture."[20] Fortier has examined how through ritualized repetition of symbolic acts, often conducted within an overtly religious context, these imagined communities can "make material the belongings they purport to describe."[21] Crucially these acts are performed within specific architectural spaces.

What then happens through these stylized spatial practices is that spaces are demarcated by certain groups by a kind of spatial appropriation. Through the repetition of those rituals, these spaces are re-membered, with participants reinscribing themselves into the space, evoking corporeal memories of previous enactments. The rituals are naturalized through these corporeal memory acts, and the spaces in which they are enacted become spaces of belonging:

Belongings refer to both 'possessions' and appartenance. That is, practices of group identity are about manufacturing cultural and historical belongings which mark out terrains of commonality that delineate the politics and social dynamics of 'fitting in.'[22]

The concept of 'belonging' as a product of performativity enables us to go beyond the limitations of simple narrative. It privileges the idea not of reading the environment, as though its meaning were simply there and waiting to be deciphered, but rather of giving meaning to the environment by collective or individual behaviour. Belonging

to place can therefore be understood as an aspect of territorialization, and out of that belonging a sense of identity might be forged. The attraction of Fortier's application of performativity to place is that it resists more static notions of dwelling emanating from Heideggerian discourse that seem so ill at ease with a society of movement and travel. What Fortier proposes is not some discourse of fixed 'roots', but rather a more transitory and fluid discourse of territorializationin the Deleuzian sense, which provides a complex and ever renegotiable model of spatial "belongings." Fortier's model is essentially a rhizomic one of nomadic territorializations and deterritorializations. For territorialization belongs to the same logic as deterritorialization. The very provisionality of territorializations colludes with the ephemerality of any sense of belonging. Just as territorializations are always shifting, identifications remain fleeting and transitory, while leaving behind traces of their passage. As Bell comments: "The rhizome has been an important analogy here, conveying as it does an image of movement that can come to temporary rest in new places while maintaining ongoing connections elsewhere."[23]

Butler's discourse extends Pierre Bourdieu's debate about habitus. She adds the possibility of political agency, and of subverting received norms. Through its repetitive citational nature, that performativity has the power to question and subvert that which it cites. For mimicry, as Homi Bhabha has illustrated, is invested with the potential to destabilize and undermine, as in the case of political satire. Performativity, in this sense, is not some uncritical and ultimately nihilistic acceptance of the given, but rather a mode of operation charged with a certain political efficacy. Moreover, whereas Bourdieu stresses the production of the subject through culture, for Butler, social structures have themselves been performed. Hence performativity offers an obvious mode of challenging those structures. In an age colonized by "fictional worlds" (as Marc Augé has described our present era), Butler locates performativity at the heart of our cultural identity today.[24]

Yet if we are to understand belonging as a product of performativity, we must still construct an argument to explain exactly how this comes into operation. The argument above merely assumes that a sense of belonging will emerge as a consequence of progressive territorialization, without fully accounting for this process of identification.

IDENTIFICATION

Here it is useful to consider psychoanalytic theory, which has long been preoccupied with these questions.[25] For while both de Certeau and Butler engage psychoanalysis, they do not follow its full ramifications through in their work. According to psychoanalytic theory, identification is always specular. It is always a question of recognizing — or mis-recognizing — the self in the other. There has been little discussion of this within architectural theory, but within the context of film theory, Christian Metz has outlined a series of mirrorings that occur within the cinema that constitute the basis of identification.[26] These mirrorings depend upon the nature of vision itself. Vision operates with a double-movement, being both projective and introjective. As one casts one's eye projectively, one receives and absorbs introjectively what has been illuminated. Consciousness therefore serves, for Metz's terminology, as a "recording surface":

There are two cones in the auditorium: one ending on the screen and starting both in the projection box and in the spectator's vision insofar as it is projective, and one starting from the screen and 'deposited' in the spectator's perception insofar as it is introjective (on the retina, a second screen). When I say that 'I see' the film, I mean thereby a unique mixture of two contrary currents: the film is what I receive, and it is also what I release. . . Releasing it, I am the projector, receiving it, I am the screen; in both these figures together, I am the camera, which points and yet records.[27]

What happens, then, in the process of viewing is a series of mirror-effects. "Am I not myself looking at myself looking at the film?" asks Metz.[28] As a result, the spectator is both absent from the screen as perceived, but so too present there 'as perceiver.'"At every moment," Metz notes, "I am in the film by my look's caress.[29]" Multiple series of specular identifications take place in viewing a film, identifications that are connected with the mirror as the original site of primary identification.

For identification to take place with a spe-

cific architectural space, we should look for an equivalent process of mirrorings. This process would depend on the introjection of the external world into the self, and the projection of the self on to the external world, so that there is an equivalence — the one reflects the other — and identification may take place.

The sense of introjection, of the absorption of the external world described by Metz, is echoed within an architectural context in the work of Benjamin, who presents the mind as a kind of camera obscura, a photosensitive plate onto which certain interiors are etched in moments of illumination. But this occurs only at certain moments, when a particularly memorable event serves as a kind of flash bulb, flaring up like magnesium powder to imprint that interior on the mind:

Anyone can observe that the duration for which we are exposed to impressions has no bearing on their fate in memory. Nothing prevents us keeping rooms in which we have spent twenty-four hours or less clearly in our memory, and forgetting others in which we have passed months. It is not, therefore, due to insufficient exposure if no image appears on the plate of remembrance. More frequent, perhaps, are the cases when the half-light of habit denies the plate the necessary light for years, until one day from an alien source it flashes as if from burning magnesium powder, and now a snapshot transfixes the room's image on the plate. Nor is this very mysterious, since such moments of sudden illumination are at the same time moments when we are beside ourselves, and while our waking, habitual, everyday self is involved actively or passively in what is happening, our deeper self rests in another place and is touched by the shock, as is the little heap of magnesium powder by the flame of the match.[30]

We should perhaps extend Benjamin's suggestive model of the camera to that of the camcorder, for spatial experiences are seldom static. The photograph gives way to the video movie as the primary

model for understanding how memories of spatial experiences are etched on to the mind.

The second part of Metz's "double-movement of vision" is projective. This remains a crucial aspect of the process of identification that involves a two-fold mechanism of grafting symbolic meaning onto an object and then reading oneself into that object, and seeing one's values reflected in it. The environment must therefore serve as a kind of screen onto which we project our own meaning, and into which we would read ourselves. As was observed by Robert Vischer in the context of empathy theory, we need to project something of ourselves onto the other in order to recognize — or mis-recognize — ourselves in the other:

At this point, however, our feeling rises up and takes the intellect at its word: yes, we miss red-blooded life, and precisely because we miss it, we imagine the dead form as living. We have seen how the perception of a pleasing form evokes a pleasurable sensation and how such an image symbolically relates to the idea of our own bodies — or conversely, how the imagination seeks to experience itself through the image. We thus have the wonderful ability to project and incorporate our own physical form into an objective form, in much the same way as wild fowlers gain access to their quarry by concealing themselves in a blind. What can that form be other than the form of a content identical with itself? It is therefore our own personality that we project into it.[31]

This projection of personality or intentionality onto an object is one that is overlooked by much mainstream architectural commentary. The investment of meaning not only explains the creative potential of seeing oneself in the other in moments of identification, but it also explains the problematic foundation of any discourse of authenticity that "projects" authenticity onto an object.[32] In the hermeneutic moment one tends to read that projection as though it were a property of the object. And yet in reality, intentionality, authenticity, and all kinds of content are merely projections. Buildings, according to Fredric Jameson, do not have any inherent meaning. They are essentially inert, and are merely invested with meaning.[33]

Walter Benjamin, however, adds a crucial gloss to these processes of introjection and projection:

Buildings are appropriated in a twofold manner: by use and by perception — or rather, by touch and sight. Such appropriation cannot be understood in terms of the attentive concentration of a tourist before a famous building. On the tactile side there is no counterpart to contemplation on the optical side. Tactile appropriation is accomplished not so much by attention as by habit. As regards architecture, habit determines to a large extent even optical reception. The latter, too, occurs much less through rapt attention than by noticing the object in incidental fashion. This mode of appropriation, developed with reference to architecture, in certain circumstances acquires canonical value. The tasks which face the human apparatus of perception at the turning points of history cannot be solved by optical means, that is, by contemplation, alone. They are mastered gradually by habit, under the guidance of tactile appropriation.[34]

In Benjamin's terms, buildings are appropriated. They are introjected — absorbed within the psyche not just through vision, but also through touch. We may extend this to include the full register of senses. Moreover, for Benjamin, these appropriations are reinforced by habit. Here memory plays a crucial role. Over a period of time, the sensory impulses leave their mark, traces of their reception. These traces are themselves not forgotten, but constitute a type of archive of memorized sensory experiences. Indeed, life itself can be seen to be conditioned by these impulses; they constitute our background horizon of experience. In this sense, identification is as an ontological condition consolidated through memory. We could therefore reflect upon the model of the oneiric house offered up by Gaston Bachelard in *The Poetics of Space*.[35] It is precisely the odor of drying raisins — parallelling Lefebvre's equally evocative description of the sound of singing echoing through the cloisters — that points to the Proustian way in which the oneiric house is a type of introjection of previous experiences.[36]

Identification with a particular place may therefore be perceived as a mirroring between the subject and the environment over time. Here we might understand the subject, in Metz's terms, can be both screen and projector, for in moments of identification we see ourselves in objects with which we have become familiar. At the same time, we have introjected them into ourselves. That registering of impulses leads to one type of reflection — the recognition of the other in the self. Mean-

while the projection of the self onto the external world leads to a second type of reflection — the recognition of the self in the other. In either case, a type of mirroring results leading to a fusing between self and other. Here we can recognize a second order of mirrorings, for mirrorings occur not only in the engagement between the self and the environment, but also between that engagement and memories of previous engagements. An originary experience is repeated in all similar experiences. And that process of repetition reinforces of the original moment of identification. In this sense habit — as a ritualistic replication of certain experiences — consolidates the process of identification.

The seemingly static model of identification forged through a reflection — as though in a mirror — appears at first sight to contrast markedly with the more dynamic notion of identity based on performativity. And yet, if we perceive the former as being grounded in intentionality, we should recognize the active dimension to the gaze itself. For performativity is not merely a question of physical performance. It extends also to modes of perception, such as the gaze. Butler has already addressed how the gaze should be seen as the site of performativity in the context of race:

I do think that there is a performativity to the gaze that is not simply the transposition of a textual model onto a visual one; that when we see Rodney King, when we see that video we are also reading and we are also constituting, and that the reading is a certain conjuring and a certain construction. How do we describe that? It seems to me that that is a modality of performativity, that it is radicalization, that the kind of visual reading practice that goes into the viewing of the video is part of what I would understand as the performativity of what it is 'to race something' or to be 'raced' by it. So I suppose that I'm interested in the modalities of performativity that take it out of its purely textualist context.[37]

This can be extended to the gaze as the potential site of an identification with place, since any act of viewing may be charged with a conscious moment of politicized reading. Visual attachments might therefore be read as containing an active, performative moment. What applies to the gaze may equally apply to the other senses. What we find, then, is that identification based on a process of mirroring is but a variation on the active identification with place embodied in ritualistic patterns of behavior. Through the repetitive performativities of these various modes of perception, a mirroring can be enacted and a sense of identification with place can be developed and reinforced through habit.

CONCLUSION

Identity, Freud once remarked, is like a graveyard of lost loves and former identifications. Among these identifications, we could include architectural ones. Through a complex process of making sense of place, developing a feeling of belonging, and eventually identifying with that place, an identity may be forged against an architectural backdrop. As individuals identify with an environment, so their identity comes to be constituted through that environment. This relates not only to individual identity, but also to group identities.

Architecture therefore offers a potential mechanism for inscribing the self into the environment. It may facilitate a form of identification, and help engender a sense of belonging. From this point of view, architecture plays a potentially important social role. The significant factor, however — beyond the nature of our architectural environment — is our engagement with that environment. Identification is a product of the consciousness by which we relate to our surroundings, and not a property of the surroundings themselves. Nor does matter — in Butler's terms — exist outside of discourse. As Mariam Fraser observes, following Butler: "Matter does not 'exist' in and of itself, outside or beyond discourse, but is rather repeatedly produced through performativity, which "brings into being or enacts that which it names."[38] This approach brings us close to Bhabha's and Bourdieu's observations on the ways in which culture operates. It allows us to understand architecture as a system of objects situated within a cultural discourse, deriving its meaning from that discourse.

All this helps us to reassess the relationship between architecture and cultural identity. The message is clear: we should focus not only on architectural forms themselves — for we would be wrong to dismiss these forms as irrelevant — but also on the narrative and performative discourses that give them their meaning.[39] With time the specific features of architectural forms tend to lose their prominence, and slip into becoming part of an unnoticed and marginal background landscape. If identity is a performative construct — if it is acted out like some kind of film script — then architecture can be understood as a kind of film set. But it is as a film set that it derives meaning from the activities that have taken place there. Memories of associated activities haunt architecture like a ghost.

NOTES

1 The implication that critical regionalism may contribute in some way to cultural identity is made, at least, in one of the chapter titles, "Critical Regionalism: Modern Architecture and Cultural Identity," used by Kenneth Frampton in his seminal study, *Modern Architecture: A Critical Study* (London: Thames and Hudson, 1992). But it appears that Frampton himself has explored this connection just once, briefly: "Among the preconditions for the emergence of a critical regional expression is not only sufficient prosperity but also a strong desire for realising an identity. One of the mainsprings of regionalist culture is an anticentrist sentiment – an aspiration for some kind of cultural, economic and political independence." Frampton, "Prospects for a Critical Regionalism," *Perspecta* 20, 1983.

2 Homi Bhabha, "Introduction" in Bhabha ed., *Nation and Narration* (London: Routledge, 1990), p.3.

3 Homi Bhabha, "DissemiNation," ibid., p.298–299.

4 Derek Robbins, *Bourdieu and Culture* (London: Sage, 2000), p.30.

5 Ibid., p.35.

6 Michel de Certeau, *The Practice of Everyday Life*, trans. Stephen Rendell (Berkeley: University of California Press, 1984).

7 Ibid., p.117.

8 Jameson analyzes the homogenizing placelessness of late capitalism through the confusing spatial layout of the vast atrium of the Bonaventure Hotel in Los Angeles. He goes on to study the process of what he terms cognitive mapping as a means of inscribing oneself in the environment, and overcoming this placelessness. In his view, capitalist society co-opts everything into signs, images and commodities, so that the world threatens to become depthless. But aesthetics also promises a way out of this condition. While it contributes to the aestheticization of the world, it promises to counter that tendency by offering a mechanism of identification. Jameson's arguments suggest that we need today a viable aesthetic practice that reinserts the individual within society. Aesthetics may serve as a form of cognitive mapping. We therefore might recognize the primary social role that architecture may play.

9 De Certeau, op cit., p.130.

10 Ibid., p.97–8.

11 Ibid., p.103. "Proper" here appears to be referring not to "propriety" but to a sense of "appropriation"

12 Ian Buchanon, *Michel de Certeau* (London: Sage, 2000), p.108–120.

13 De Certeau, op cit., p.109–110. "Captation" might equally be translated "appropriation."

14 See, for example, his book on otherness: Michel de Certeau, *Heterologies: Discourse on the Other*, trans. Brian Massumi, (Manchester: Manchester University Press, 1986).

15 Judith Butler, *Gender Trouble* (London: Routledge, 1990), p.140, as quoted in Vikki Bell ed., *Performativity and Belonging* (London: Sage, 1999), p.3.

16 Bell discusses the possibility of understanding Jewishness in this light in Vikki Bell ed., *Performativity and Belonging*. See also Sneja Gunew, "Performing Australian Ethnicity: 'Helen Demidenko,'" in W. Ommundsen and H. Rowley eds., *From a Distance: Australian Writers and Cultural Displacement* (Geelong: Deakin University Press, 1996), p.159–171.

17 Judith Butler, *Bodies that Matter* (London: Routledge, 1993), p.12.

18 Vikki Bell ed., *Performativity and Belonging*.

19 Ibid., p.3.

20 Anne-Marie Fortier, "Re-membering Places and the Performance of Belonging(s)," in Vikki Bell ed., *Performativity and Belonging* (London: Sage, 1999), p.42.

21 Ibid., p.3.

22 Ibid., p.42.

23 Ibid., p.9.

24 Marc Augé, *A War of Dreams*, trans. Liz Heron (London: Pluto, 1999).

25 For Butler's engagement with psychoanalysis, see especially Butler, *The Psychic Life of Power: Theories of Subjection* (Stanford: Stanford University Press, 1997).

26 Christian Metz, *Psychoanalysis and the Cinema*, trans. Celia Britton, Annwyl Williams, Ben Brewster and Alfred Guzzetti (London: Macmillan, 1982), p.48

27 Ibid., p.51.

28 Ibid., p.52.

29 Ibid., p.54.

30 Walter Benjamin, *One-Way Street* (London: Verso, 1979), p.342–3.

31 Robert Vischer, *Empathy, Form and Space*, p.104.

32 If we are to look for a model of the way in which content might be understood as a kind of 'projection' we could consider the work of the Polish-Canadian public artist, Krzysztof Wodiczko, who literally projects politically loaded images onto buildings as a commentary on the politics of use of that building. In 1985, Wodiczko projected the image of a swastika onto the pediment of South Africa House in Trafalgar Square, London. This act was intended as a political protest against the trade negotiations then underway between the apartheid government of South Africa and the British government under prime minister, Margaret Thatcher. The projection of the swastika onto the building highlights the condition of buildings which have been blemished with the stain of evil. His projection of content-laden images on monuments and buildings echoes the process by which human beings project their own readings onto them. On the work of Krzysztof Wodiczko, see 'Public Projections' and 'A Conversation with Krzysztof Wodiczko', *October*, 38, p.3–52.

33 "I have come to think that no work of art or culture can set out to be political once and for all, no matter how ostentatiously it labels itself as such, for there can never be any guarantee that it will be used the way it demands. A great political art (Brecht) can be taken as a pure and apolitical art; art that seems to want to be merely aesthetic and decorative can be rewritten as political with energetic interpretation. The political rewriting or appropriation, then, the political use, must be allegorical; you have to know that this is what it is supposed to be or mean – in itself it is inert." Jameson in Neil Leach ed., *Rethinking Architecture*, p.258–59.

34 Walter Benjamin, *Illuminations*, ed. Hannah Arendt, trans. Harry Zohn (New York: Schocken Books, 1969), p.233

35 The notion of oneiric space is also central to de Certeau's concept of space. As he observes: "From this point of view, after having compared pedestrian processes to linguistic formations, we can bring them back down in the direction of oneiric figuration, or at least discover on that other side what, in spatial practice, is inseparable from the dreamed place." de Certeau, p.103.

36 Gaston Bachelard *The Poetics of Space*, trans. Maria Jolas (Boston: Beacon Press, 1994), p.13; Henri Lefebvre, *The Production of Space*, trans. Donald Nicholson-Smith (Oxford: Blackwell Publishers, Ltd., 1991), p.225.

37 Judith Butler (interviewed by Vikki Bell), "On Speech, Race and Melancholia," in Bell ed., *Performativity and Belonging* (London: Sage, 1999), p.169.

38 Mariam Fraser, "Classing Queer," ibid., p.111.

39 Thus regionalism, for example, should be more properly understood in narrative terms as a discourse of regionalism.

Contributors

STANFORD ANDERSON

was born in Minnesota in 1934. He was educated in architecture at the universities of Minnesota and California, and holds a PhD in history of art from Columbia University. He is Professor of History and Architecture and Head of the Department of Architecture at the Massachusetts Institute of Technology. He was a resident Fellow of the Institute for Architecture and Urban Studies in New York, 1970-72. He was director of MIT's PhD program in History, Theory and Criticism of Architecture, Art and Urban Form from its founding in 1974 to 1991 and in 1995-96. He is a registered architect. Anderson's research and writing concern architectural theory, early modern architecture in northern Europe, American architecture and urbanism, and epistemology and historiography. He has published in numerous journals; his *Peter Behrens: A New Architecture for the Twentieth Century* was published by The MIT Press in 2000.

BERNARD CACHE

began as a senior consultant in image telecommunications and digital television where he conducted strategic studies for companies like Philips, Canal Plus, France Telecom and France Television. He has written articles on communication, economics and policy in newspapers like *Libération* and *Médiapouvoirs* and taught social sciences at ESSEC and information economics at IFP.

His writing on architecture includes *Earth Moves* (MIT 1995) and *Terre meuble* (HYX, 1997). He has lectured in Rotterdam (1994), Oslo (1995), Amsterdam, Paris, Geelong, Melbourne, Adelaide, New-York, Yale, Los Angeles, Columbus (1997).

As an architect, he developed the Objectile software with MISSLER. In 1996, he founded the company Objectile, together with Patrick Beaucé and Jean-Louis Jammot. Since September 1998, Bernard Cache has been Associate Professor at the Faculty of Architecture, Landscape and Design (AL&D) at University of Toronto

HUBERT DAMISCH

is on the faculty of the Ecole des Hautes Etudes en Sciences Sociales in Paris. Both art historian and philosopher, he is the author of *Théorie du Nuage* and *Fenêtre Jaune Cadmium* as well as *The Origin of Perspective and Skyline: The Narcissistic City*.

DIANE Y. GHIRARDO

is Professor of the History and Theory of Architecture in Los Angeles, California. She received her M.A. and PhD from Stanford University, was a Fulbright Fellow in Rome in 1976 and 2001, and a Fellow of the American Academy in Rome in 1987-88. In 1994, she was president of the Association of Collegiate Schools of Architecture, and was editor of *Journal of Architectural Education*. She has published articles in numerous journals and magazines, including *Journal of the Society of Architectural Historians*, *Art Bulletin*, *Journal of Contemporary History*, *Lotus*, *Cite*, *Harvard Design Magazine*, *Perspecta* and *Casabella*. She has published four books: *Building New Communities: New Deal America and Fascist Italy* (1989); *Out of Site: A Social Criticism of Architecture* (1991); *Mark Mack* (1994); *Architecture After Modernism* (1996), which received the Phi Kappa Phi award for excellence in 1997. In 1999, she was selected ACSA Distinguished Professor for outstanding Creative Achievement. She is currently working on a book about women and spaces in Renaissance Italy.

ELIZABETH GROSZ

teaches feminist theory in the Department of Women's Studies at Rutgers University. She is the author most recently of *Architecture from the Outside: Essays on Virtual and Real Space* (MIT Press, 2001) and has published widely in the areas of contemporary French philosophy, feminist theory and architectural theory.

ANN HAMILTON

was born in Lima, Ohio, in 1956. She received a BFA in textile design from the University of Kansas in 1979 and an MFA in Sculpture from the Yale University School of Art in 1985. Known for her large-scale ephemeral installations, Ann's work has been widely exhibited in America and abroad, including The Museum of Modern Art in New York; The Art Institute of Chicago; the Musée Art Contemporain Lyon, in France; the Musée d'Art Contemporain De Montreal in Canada; and the Akira Ikeda Gallery in Taura, Japan. Among her many awards and honors, she received a MacArthur Fellowship in 1993 and was chosen to represent the United States at the 48th Venice Biennale in 1999. In 2001, she joined the Department of Art faculty at The Ohio State University.

K. MICHAEL HAYS

is the Eliot Noyes Professor of Architectural Theory at the Graduate School of Design, Harvard University, and Director of the Advanced Studies Programs. In 2000 he was appointed the first Adjunct Curator of Architecture at the Whitney Museum for American Art. He founded and, until last year edited *Assemblage*, a critical journal of architecture and design culture that helped develop architectural theory as a scholarly discourse.

Hays received the Master of Architecture in Advanced Studies and the Doctor of Philosophy degrees in History, Theory and Criticism from the Massachusetts Institute of Technology. He received the Bachelor of Architecture from Georgia Institute of Technology.

Hays has written extensively on twentieth-century architecture, focussing on ideological issues in the history of the avant-garde and on current debates in architecture and critical theory. His books include *Modern Architecture and the Posthumanist Subject* (1992) and the recent *Architecture Theory since 1968*, both published by the MIT Press. He is currently working on a history of architectural discourse from 1968 to 1983.

LAUREN KOGOD

Lauren Kogod teaches architectural history and theory at the School of Architecture at Yale University. She is a PhD candidate at Harvard University and practices architecture with David Smiley in New York.

NEIL LEACH

teaches at the Architectural Association in London and the University of Bath, where he is Professor of Architectural Theory. He has also taught at the University of Nottingham and Columbia University, New York. He is the author of *The Anaesthetics of Architecture* (MIT, 1999) and *Millennium Culture* (Ellipsis, 1999); editor of *Rethinking Architecture* (Routledge, 1997) *Architecture and Revolution* (Routledge, 1999), *The Hieroglyphics of Space* (Routledge, 2001) and *E-Futures* (Wiley, forthcoming); and co-translator (with Joseph Rykwert and Robert Tavernor) of *L.B. Alberti, On the Art of Building in Ten Books* (MIT, 1988).

HASHIM SARKIS

is a practicing architect in Lebanon. His work includes a housing complex in Tyre, schools in North Lebanon and designs for public spaces in Beirut and Tripoli. Sarkis is Associate Professor of Architecture at the Harvard Graduate School of Design. In the past, Sarkis was a lecturer in MIT's Department of Architecture and a research associate in MIT's Department of Urban Studies and Planning. He has also taught at RISD, Yale University and the American University of Beirut. Sarkis is the author of several articles on design theory, on American architecture and urban design, and on Beirut. He is executive editor of CASE, a publication series of case studies in architecture and urbanism, and editor of *Le Corbusier's Venice Hospital and the Mat Building Revival* (Munich: Prestel, 2002) in that series. He is author of *Circa 1958, Lebanon in the Plans and Photographs of Constantinos Doxiadis*, (Beirut: Dar an-Nahar, 2002) co-editor with Peter G. Rowe of *Projecting Beirut* (Munich: Prestel, 1998), and occasional contributor to *An-Nahar* newspaper in Beirut. He received his BArch and BFA from the Rhode Island School of Design, his MArch from the GSD, and his PhD in architecture from Harvard University.

ROBERT SOMOL

teaches design and theory in the Department of Architecture and Urban Design at UCLA. His office, PXS, just completed off-use, a residence and studio in Los Angeles.

MICHAEL STANTON

was educated at Antioch College and Harvard University and received his Masters in Architecture at Princeton University. He has worked in the offices of Agrest and Gandelsonas in New York and Hartman/Cox in Washington, DC and independently since 1985. His design work has won an ACSA Design Award, the Young Architect's Award from the Architectural League of New York, the Biennial Steedman Prize and been selected for Progressive Architecture awards plus several competitions. He was a Fellow in Architecture at the American Academy in Rome in 1990-91 and the first Aga Kahn Traveling Fellow in 1980. He has published many articles in journals including *Archis* and *Modulus* and has contributed chapters in the University of Minnesota Press books *The Discipline of Architecture* on knowledge and *White Papers/ Black Marks* on the African-American city. He has taught at The Institute for Architecture and Urban Studies, RISD, Catholic University, The University of Miami and, for much of the last decade, at Tulane University in New Orleans. He was a Guestprofessor at the Royal Danish Academy in Copenhagen. He is currently Associate Professor and Chair of the Department of Architecture and Design at the American University of Beirut.

ANTHONY VIDLER

is Acting Dean of the Irwin S. Chanin School of Architecture at The Cooper Union in New York City. He was the Chair of the Department of Art History at UCLA and has taught at Princeton University where he chaired the Ph.D. Program and directed the European Cultural Studies program. From 1996-1998 he served as Dean of the College of Architecture, Art and Planning at Cornell University. Mr. Vidler is the author of *Claude-Nicolas Ledoux: Architecture and Social Reform at the end of the Ancient Regime, The Writing of the Walls, Architectural Theory in the Late Enlightenment*. He is also the author of *The Architecture of the Uncanny and Warped Space*.

GEORGE WAGNER

is a Professor in the School of Architecture at the University of British Columbia in Vancouver. His writing has been included in the books *Architecture and Feminism* (Berlin Free University), and *Stan Douglas*. He has edited monographs on Stanley Saitowitz, Thom Mayne, and Barkow Leibinger, and published essays in *Harvard Design Magazine, Harvard Architecture Review, Journal of the Society of Architecture Historians, Center* and *Bauwelt*.

SARAH WHITING

is an assistant professor in the Department of Architecture at the Harvard Graduate School of Design and is also a design principal of WW in Cambridge, MA.

CHRISTOPHER WOOD

teaches Renaissance art at Yale and is the editor of *The Vienna School Reader: Politics and Art Historical Method in the 1930s* (ZONE Books, 2000). Professor Wood has been teaching at Yale since 1992. He has received Harvard's Jacob Wendell Scholarship and Sheldon Fellowship, a Deutscher Akademischer Austauschdienst Fellowship, and a Morse Junior Faculty Fellowship from Yale. Professor Wood has been a guest scholar at the Institut für Europäische Kunstgeschichte in Augsburg (1994), and a Junior Fellow of the Harvard Society of Fellows.